Buddhism with an Attitude

Buddhism with an Attitude

The Tibetan Seven-Point Mind-Training

by
B. Alan Wallace

edited by
Lynn Quirolo

Snow Lion Publications
Ithaca, New York
Boulder, Colorado

Snow Lion Publications
P O Box 6483
Ithaca, NY 14851 USA
607-273-8519
www.snowlionpub.com

Printed in Canada on acid-free, recycled paper.

ISBN 1-55939-200-0

The Library of Congress catalogued the previous edition
of this book as follows:

Wallace, B. Alan.
    Buddhism with an attitude: the Tibetan seven-point
mind-training / by B. Alan Wallace; edited by Lynn
Quirolo.
        p. cm.
    ISBN 1-55939-159-6 (alk. paper)
    1. Spiritual life–Bka'-gdams-pa (Sect) 2. Bodhicitta
(Buddhism) 3. Dge-lugs-pa (Sect)–Doctrines. I. Quirolo,
Lynn. II. Ye-śes-rdo-rje, mChad-kha-ba. Theg pa chen po'i
gdams ngag blo sbyong don bdun ma rtsa ba. III. Title.
BQ7670.6 W35 2001
294.3'444—dc21   2001000622

Table of Contents

Preface

All of us have attitudes. Some of them accord with reality and serve us well throughout the course of our lives. Others are out of alignment with reality, and they cause us unnecessary problems. Tibetan Buddhist practice isn't just sitting in silent meditation; it's developing fresh attitudes that align our minds with reality. Attitudes need adjusting, just like a spinal column that has been knocked out of alignment. Among the many types of practices in Tibetan Buddhism, in this book I will explain a type of mental training Tibetans call *lojong*, which is designed to shift our attitudes so that our minds become pure wellsprings of joy instead of murky pools of problems, anxieties, fleeting pleasures, frustrations, hopes, and fears. The Tibetan word *lojong* is made up of two parts: *lo* means attitude, mind, intelligence, and perspective; and *jong* means to train, purify, remedy, and clear away. So the word *lojong* could literally be translated as *attitudinal training*, but I'll stick with the more common translation of *mind-training*.

Over the past millennium, Tibetan lamas have devised many lojongs, but the most widely taught and practiced of all lojongs in the Tibetan language was one based on the teachings of an Indian Buddhist sage named Atisha (982-1054), whose life spanned the end of the first millennium of the common era and the beginning of the second. Atisha brought to Tibet an oral tradition of lojong teachings that was based on instructions that had been passed down to him through the lineage of the Indian Buddhist teachers Maitriyogin, Dharmarakshita, and Serlingpa. This oral tradition may represent the earliest such practice that was explicitly called a lojong, and it is probably the most widely practiced in the whole of Tibetan Buddhism. This training was initially given only as an oral instruction for those students who were deemed sufficiently intelligent and highly enough motivated to make good use of it. Only about a century after Atisha's death was this secret training written down and made more widely available in monasteries and hermitages, Tibet's unique kinds of attitudinal correction facility. This delay probably accounts for the minor variations in the different versions of the text we have today.

For centuries we in the West have wondered whether intelligent life exists elsewhere in the universe. If there are highly advanced, intelligent beings out there, what might they have to teach us? What have they learned that we have not? Along similar lines we can ask: is there intelligent life on our planet outside of our Euro-American civilization? Of course that sounds like a dumb question, but it's still worth asking, since there still persists an attitude in our society that we know more about everything than any previous generation and more than any other, "less developed" society today. It takes quite an ethnocentric leap of faith to swallow that, but many people seem to manage it. Indian civilization a thousand years ago, during the time of Atisha, had evolved with very little influence from European civilization; and Tibetan civilization, tracing back more than two millennia, was hardly influenced by the West until the mid-twentieth century. Ironically, Tibetans' first major encounter with Western thought occurred due to the invasion of their homeland by the Chinese Communists in 1949, who forced upon them the economic doctrine of Marxism and scientific materialism.

Have Indian and Tibetan civilizations made any great discoveries of their own that we have not, and might they have anything to teach us? I will be tackling these questions throughout this book, drawing on a thousand-year-old set of aphorisms that embody much of the wisdom of ancient India and Tibet. If these aphorisms strike a chord of wisdom for us living today, whose lives span the end of the second millennium and the beginning of the third, that wisdom will be something that is not uniquely Eastern or Western, and not ancient or modern. It will be a type of wisdom that cuts across such cultural divides and eras, something universal that speaks deeply to and from the hearts and minds of humanity.

Over the past millennium, Tibetan Buddhism has maintained its vitality from generation to generation by teachers passing on oral commentaries to traditional "root texts" such as the Seven-Point Mind-Training. Root texts preserve the depth and wisdom of the teachings, and the oral commentaries link these texts with the experiences and views of practitioners of each generation. In the explanation of the text I offer here, I draw upon the earliest Tibetan commentary I have been able to find, composed by Sechil Buwa, who was a direct disciple of Chekawa Yeshe Dorje (1101-1175), who first wrote down this mind-training. Chekawa Yeshe Dorje had received the transmission of this teaching from Sharawa, and the lineage before him goes back to Langri Thangpa, Potowa, Dromtonpa, and Atisha. I also draw on a very recent commentary entitled *Enlightened Courage: An Explanation of Atisha's Seven Point Mind Training* by the late Dilgo Khyentse Rinpoche, one of the greatest Tibetan meditation masters of the twentieth century.

The teacher from whom I received the oral commentary on this training was a learned, humble, and compassionate Tibetan named Kungo Barshi. I was living in Dharamsala,

India, at the time, in 1973, and there were many erudite lamas from whom I could have sought this instruction. But I was particularly drawn to Kungo Barshi for various reasons. At that time, he was the chief instructor in Tibetan medicine at the Tibetan Astro-Medical Institute, and he was renowned for his mastery of many of the fields of traditional Tibetan knowledge. But he was not only an outstanding scholar. As a member of the nobility in Tibet, he had owned several estates and devoted himself to the life of a gentleman scholar, while his wife largely took over the practical affairs of running their estates. But when the Chinese Communists invaded Tibet and especially targeted the aristocracy for imprisonment and torture, he, his wife, and one of his sons fled to India. Others of his children remained behind, only to be killed by the Chinese, and the son who fled with him into exile also met a tragic end. Adversity mounted upon adversity in Kungo Barshi's life, and yet when he was passing on this teaching to me, he told me, "Personally, I have found the Chinese invasion of Tibet to be a blessing. In Tibet before this cataclysm, I took much for granted, and my spiritual practice was casual. Now that I have been forced into exile and have lost so much, my dedication to practice has grown enormously, and I have found greater contentment than ever before." Rarely have I met anyone whose presence exuded such serenity, quiet good cheer, and wisdom as he did. He was for me a living embodiment of the efficacy of this mind-training, and his inspiration has been with me ever since.

As I pass on my own commentary to this text, I address many practical and theoretical issues that uniquely face us in the modern world. This book is based on a series of public lectures I gave in Santa Barbara, California, during the years 1997-1998. Tapes of those lectures were transcribed and edited by my old and dear friend Lynn Quirolo, to whom I owe a deep debt of gratitude; then I made final revisions to the edited transcripts. I have tried at all times to be faithful to the original teachings I received, while making them thoroughly contemporary to people living in a world so different from that of traditional Tibet. If even a fraction of the wisdom and inspiration of Atisha, Sechil Buwa, Kungo Barshi, and Dilgo Khyentse Rinpoche is conveyed to the readers of this book, our efforts will have born good fruit.

B. Alan Wallace
Santa Barbara, California
Summer, 2000

The First Point:
The Preliminaries

First, train in the preliminaries.

The goal of Dharma practice is to realize a state of genuine well-being that flows from a wellspring of awareness that is pure and unobscured. The ancient Greeks called such a state *eudaimonia*, a truth-given joy. The ancient Indians called it *mahasukha*, great bliss that arises not from pleasurable stimuli, but from the nature of one's own pure awareness itself. This is not simply a happy feeling; it is a state of being that underlies and suffuses all emotional states, that embraces all the joys and sorrows that come our way. It is a way of engaging with life without confusion. The ancient Greeks knew about it. The Indians and Tibetans know about it. Funny that we don't have a word for it in modern English. Maybe it has something to do with the fact that we know a lot more about mental disease than we do about mental health.

Years ago I asked the Director of the National Institute of Mental Health how the medical profession defined mental health. He replied that they didn't have any widely agreed upon definition, *for they didn't have enough data!* They have plenty of data on mental disorders, though, and according to conservative estimates, one in five persons, at least in the United States, will have a serious, diagnosable, and treatable mental disorder some time during their lifetime.[1]

Even for those of us who are not presently suffering from a diagnosable mental disease, it's high time to ask: what's so great about being normal? When we're normal, we're still subject to a wide range of mental problems, with their resultant distress. Let's now ask the provocative question: how mentally healthy could we possibly we be? Is there a limit? How in touch with reality would we have to be to achieve supreme mental health? A path that has stood the test of centuries is the practice of Dharma. And what is Dharma? One meaning of "Dharma" is simply truth, specifically those truths that, when realized, lead to a state of genuine, lasting happiness that is not contingent upon pleasurable stimuli. In terms of our overall well-being, Dharma includes important truths concerning diet, exercise, and medication, as well as spiritual practice. Indeed, the theories and practices of traditional Tibetan medicine are commonly viewed by its practitioners as integral elements of Dharma.[2]

In the Tibetan Buddhist context, there are several criteria for discriminating between what is and is not Dharma. One criterion for Dharma is whether or not a theory or practice leads to spiritual awakening. From a traditional viewpoint, another criterion for Dharma is anything that aids spiritual awakening in this life or *beyond this life*. Using this criterion, there are ways of conduct and ways of viewing reality that are beneficial beyond the context of this present life. There is a third very pragmatic criterion for determining what can be considered Dharma that doesn't depend on belief in enlightenment or reincarnation. This criterion of practicing Dharma is engaging with all events in ways that are realistic and conducive to one's own and others' well-being. When things go well, are there ways to experience deeper joy and satisfaction? When things go wrong, is there anything we can do that would still enhance our overall well-being? Ways of bringing forth a sense of fulfillment and meaning during the inevitable ups and downs of life are also considered Dharma.

These three criteria define Dharma but are not exclusive to Buddhism. Dharma can be found in non-Buddhist paths and even outside of religious practice altogether. The test of whether a practice or theory is Dharma is whether it results in benefit throughout the inevitable vicissitudes of life.

On the one hand, we may feel Dharma practice seems difficult, time-consuming, and filled with problems. From another perspective, if what we really want is to practice Dharma, we get immediate gratification. Dharma can be practiced anytime: on happy occasions or when we are sick. Just as soon as we want to practice, we can. But if Dharma is practiced only as a means to an end, such as to get more money or have people like us, then we are in a situation of delayed gratification.

What does it mean to "practice Dharma"? It is not one technique, not just meditation. You can develop a repertoire of Dharma practices for every occasion. When you start to understand the richness and diversity of Dharma practice, you will see that even if you are stressed out, tired, or depressed, you can still practice. Even when you are dying, you can practice Dharma. You can become a skillful chef of Dharma using its rich and varied recipes to make any situation into a source of fulfillment and happiness. When what you really want is to practice Dharma, you find more and more ability to do so in a wider variety of situations. Dharma is like medicine; it is designed to help stop the habitual behaviors and attitudes that impede the capacity of the mind to heal itself. The more you practice Dharma, the more Dharma unveils your natural inborn happiness.

The Seven-Point Mind-Training is the essence of Dharma, a concise array of methods to achieve genuine happiness no matter what our circumstances. In its fullest dimension, the Mind-Training is also a complete path to enlightenment. The seven points begin, "First, train in the preliminaries," and lay the foundation for effective Dharma. You don't have to be spiritual or intellectual to practice Dharma effectively. What's needed is to saturate the mind with two challenges: a thorough evaluation of ordinary life and a thorough evaluation of human potential.

This First Point, a single line of a text of only about four pages, represents a vast Tibetan Buddhist teaching. In the metaphor of spiritual practice as a journey, the practitioner must find a qualified guide, a reliable vehicle, an accurate map, and the best methods. The "preliminaries" serve as a compass, keeping efforts directed toward the ultimate goal. The preliminaries address unexamined assumptions not easily identified and even more difficult to root out. There-fore, at the beginning of Dharma practice and periodically afterward, returning to the preliminaries keeps spiritual practice well-tuned and prevents wasting time in detours.

"Preliminary" isn't a code word for "skip this and get to the important stuff." The important stuff starts here. This is it, no warm-up. When I went to Dharamsala, India, in 1971 to study meditation, I received teachings from the Tibetan lama Geshe Ngawang Dhargyey. He spent weeks discuss-ing the preliminaries and I kept wondering when he was going to get around to meditation. Slowly it dawned on me that he was teaching *discursive* meditation. Meditation is not only settling your mind and finding stillness, it is also bringing shape and meaning to conceptual thought by refining the way we view the world. It is the quality of practice of the preliminaries that determines over the long run whether what we are practicing is genuine Dharma or a dharma look-alike. The preliminaries are discursive meditations, situated at the very beginning of the Mind-Training to save time.

All of my Tibetan teachers have emphasized the preliminaries, but none more so than Gyatrul Rinpoche. He was raised and trained in Tibet and has taught Dharma in the West for twenty-five years. He sees his long-term students struggling with the same old stuff and asks us, "Why do I teach you all the advanced practices of Dzogchen and Mahamudra when you are still in kindergarten? Go back and learn your ABC's." He is referring to the preliminaries, especially relevant for Westerners who tend to put a lot of muscle into spiritual practice and later, sometimes years later, wonder why there is so little result. The preliminaries are Dharma insurance to prevent spiritual practice from just being new packaging for old habits.

The preliminaries are four traditional discursive meditations called "the four thoughts that turn the mind." These meditations turn our minds toward our highest aspirations and progressively reorder priorities. Discursive meditation is thinking deeply about a chosen subject and can be done in spare moments during the day. No special posture is required. Discursive meditation is a very practical way of integrating Dharma practice into everyday life.

The Rare and Precious Human Life of Leisure and Opportunity

The first of the four thoughts that turn the mind is: "the precious and rare human life of leisure and opportunity." Each of the terms in this phrase—precious, rare, leisure, and opportunity—is a mnemonic to bring to mind instantaneously and deeply specific teachings and experience.

In the line "precious human life of leisure and opportunity," leisure means time. Some people live in situations in

which there is no leisure, in which every breath is committed to finding food, keeping warm, or dodging bomb shells.
If you live in an area of pestilence, famine or war, you have
no leisure. Leisure means having time to breathe the present,
and it makes it possible to drench the heart and mind in
Dharma. Leisure is an empty vessel that can be filled with
the nectar of Dharma.

Leisure is one of the greatest benefits of civilization.
Without civilization, life is absorbed with growing, killing
or protecting the next meal. With civilization, we can ar-
range time off, vacations, weekends, a lunch break. We can
decide how to use leisure. This first discursive meditation
increases appreciation for free time. Unfortunately, in our
culture leisure time is often devoted to catching up, getting
ahead or battery recharging for a return to work. We have
this weird phrase that leisure time is "time to kill." We need
to work and we need to sleep, but the critical point here is
that leisure should not just be a way to revitalize after a
hard day at work. Using leisure time beneficially within a
workaholic ethic requires shifting our priorities. This means
gradually having work support spiritual practice and en-
suring that spiritual practice does not just become a tool
for improving work performance.

Opportunity is the second quality of this precious human
life. Tibetans have a list of ten kinds of opportunities that
focus on the ability, desire, open-mindedness, and faith to
engage in spiritual practice. Opportunity also includes finding the appropriate circumstances for practice, including a
spiritual tradition that is compatible with your own aspiration and temperament. The benefits of Dharma arise from
leisure and opportunity, the fortuitous combination of ability and circumstances. The coming together of these factors,
at any time in any human life, is "rare." These factors are
"precious" because they are what is necessary to obtain the

jewel of life, genuine happiness, and spiritual awakening, the results of successful spiritual practice.

Spiritual practice is not a shortcut to the American Dream nor is it an embellishment to a comfortable life. Dharma addresses the root causes of suffering and requires that we take a hard look at the preconceptions that maintain our worldview and perpetuate our problems. As much as success seems to be the source of the good things in life, happiness included, success isn't the goal of spiritual practice. Our ideas about success are themselves based on preconceptions and are also part of a self-perpetuating cycle preventing us from achieving the genuine success and happiness that we seek.

The Buddhist tradition addresses preconceptions about success head-on with an eight-term differential diagnosis called "the eight mundane concerns," eight orientations toward the pursuit of happiness based on unexamined assumptions. Fixation on these concerns subverts our best efforts, leading either to counterfeit success or true frustration.

The eight mundane concerns consist of four pairs of priorities: the pursuit of material acquisitions and the avoidance of their loss; the pursuit of stimulus-driven pleasure and the avoidance of discomfort; the pursuit of praise and the avoidance of blame; and the pursuit of good reputation and the avoidance of bad reputation. These eight concerns commonly sum up our motivation for the pursuit of happiness, and this is exactly the problem. The eight mundane concerns, not wrong in themselves, underlie our motivation, and it is motivation more than any other single factor that determines the outcome of spiritual practice.

There is nothing bad about having material acquisitions— a car, a house; and, conversely, poverty is not necessarily a virtue. There is nothing wrong with enjoying a sunset, a good book, pleasant conversation, or beautiful music. It is not a bad thing to be praised. Being loved and respected by others is not bad either. On the other hand, it is not bad to be rejected by others if you are leading a wholesome and meaningful life. Many accomplished Dharma practitioners are content and happy living in total poverty. Reputation may go up and down, but it is possible for contentment to remain constant. The true source of happiness does not lie in mastery of the eight mundane concerns. Rich, poor, praised, blamed, stimulated, bored, respected, reviled— none of these mundane concerns are in themselves sources of happiness. Nor do they prevent happiness.

The problem is that when we focus on mundane concerns as a means to happiness, life becomes a crap shoot. There are no guarantees. If you aspire to material wealth, you may not get it, but if you do, there is no guarantee you will be happy. If you aspire to pleasure, once a stimulus is over, so is satisfaction. There is no lasting happiness in scurrying after praise. People who are respected and famous tend to have the same personal problems as everyone else. The fatal shortcoming of the eight mundane concerns is that they are counterfeit Dharma, misguided ways of seeking happiness, and by habitually mistaking mundane concerns for genuine Dharma, our efforts to achieve genuine happiness are continually undermined.

The First Point of the Mind-Training is to train in the preliminaries in order to be able to differentiate between genuine and counterfeit Dharma. If you bank on achieving genuine happiness and fulfillment by finding the perfect mate, getting a great car, having a big house, the best insurance, a fine reputation, the top job—if these are your focus, wish also for luck in life's lottery. The objective of the First Point is to save time. Don't wait until you are eighty years old to realize the shortcomings of the eight mundane concerns; examine your priorities now. There is no need to reject these mundane concerns altogether. What is necessary is to shift your primary investment elsewhere, to genuine Dharma. Once priorities shift, the mundane concerns serve as supports for Dharma practice. Learning to distinguish between the many types of pseudo-success, the many facsimiles of happiness, and genuine happiness saves time and grief in the long run. The goal of genuine Dharma is to achieve genuine happiness.

We have covered two words, leisure and opportunity, in the first of four preliminary discursive meditations, "precious human life of leisure and opportunity." Leisure and opportunity mean having the time, motivation, and circumstances to engage in spiritual practice. "Preciousness" refers to our human potential to eliminate the sources of suffering within our own being, to transform the mind so that, no matter what the circumstances, we need never suffer from mental afflictions again. How? By identifying and progressively eradicating the full spectrum of the afflictions that are the source of suffering. Buddhism takes a radical view on suffering, presenting the hypothesis that it can be eliminated altogether. Suffering is eradicated not by finding psychological anesthetics or disengaging from the world, but by working from within to transform the mind itself. The way to eliminate suffering is to transform the mind. The Seven-Point Mind-Training is a flash card owner's manual on how to transform the mind using the raw material of life.

The word "precious" in the first of the four thoughts that turn the mind serves to point out that this human life is not as it first appears; it is a precious and unique opportunity. A human life of leisure and opportunity is "precious" because it is an opportunity to eradicate suffering and achieve genuine happiness. As we witness other people's suffering and experience our own, freedom from personal suffering and having compassion for others appear to be mutually exclusive. Compassion for others' suffering seems to increase our own suffering, making detachment seem like the only reasonable route to one's own individual happiness. But is this really so?

In 1992, I went with a group of neuroscientists to the Himalayas to study the effects of meditation. One of our topics of investigation was compassion. We asked an old Tibetan monk, a teacher of many of the other yogis who lived in the mountains, about the relationship between suffering and compassion. It is said in the Buddhist tradition that a *bodhisattva,* a person who is continuously motivated to help sentient beings achieve spiritual awakening, looks upon all sentient beings as a mother looks upon her child. When a child is hurt, the mother feels compassion and suffers. Since the goal of Dharma is to alleviate suffering, the neuroscientists and I asked the yogi about the relationship between suffering and compassion.

The old monk explained the relation of compassion and suffering: "Empathetic suffering comes *before* compassion." The first stage of compassion is empathy. With empathy, there is suffering. But the suffering you feel by empathizing then becomes fuel for the fire of compassion. Empathy combined with what Tibetans call *sem-shuk,* or "power of the heart," kindles compassion. The power of compassion is beyond personal suffering and focuses on solutions, what can be done. The old yogi explained to the neuroscientists that when compassion arises, suffering is transcended and one attends to how to be of service. Suffering is the fuel of compassion, not its result.

The cumulative wisdom of centuries of Dharma practitioners states that with this precious human life of leisure and opportunity we have a fathomless capacity for compassion.

This same wisdom tradition tells us we have a fathomless capacity for wisdom and power. The human potential for contemplative wisdom, compassion, and power, known to Buddhist, Hindu, Taoist, Christian, Jewish, and Muslim contemplatives, remains virtually unexplored in the modern West. We have a dismissive term for the potential of the mind— "placebo." Western culture associates the power of the mind with the power of a sugar pill. During the past four hundred years, while delighting in its growing scientific prowess, the West has neglected the exploration and development of the innate human potential for wisdom and compassion.

In the early 1970s, a friend of mine complained to the Dalai Lama about how difficult it is to become enlightened in such a "degenerate time" as ours. This has been a familiar refrain throughout the history of Buddhism, with just about every generation referring to its own era as a degenerate time. But the Dalai Lama's response cut him short. He told him that the only reason so few people attain enlightenment these days is that they are not practicing with the same diligence as the great adepts of the past. If people were to practice today with the same dedication as such great contemplatives as the Tibetan yogi Milarepa, they would achieve the same results, regardless of how degenerate their times are.

A key element in realizing the potential of our precious human life of leisure and opportunity is faith. Faith is also a prerequisite for a successful career. If you don't have faith in your chosen field, physics for example, it will be difficult to complete a Ph.D. As in many endeavors, in science it is necessary to take many things, such as research outside your specialty, on well-grounded faith. Well-grounded faith in our potential for wisdom, compassion, and power is an important part of what Buddhists mean by "opportunity."

Another type of faith, blind faith that has no basis in reality, is useless at best.

The preciousness of life is having time and circumstances to fulfill what Tsongkhapa, a great fifteenth-century Tibetan Buddhist contemplative, called our "eternal longing." This is a very significant statement because the Buddhist meaning of "eternal" includes all previous lifetimes, a very long time. The Seven-Point Mind-Training advises us to recognize right at the beginning our opportunity and potential. Also, be effective; don't get sidetracked. In this life, you have a precious opportunity to fulfill your eternal longing to find genuine happiness.

Leisure and opportunity are precious and *rare.* The Buddhist meaning of "rare" is based on Buddhist cosmology, which in some respects is similar to modern astronomy concerning the size and age of the cosmos. Western astronomers speak of solar systems, galaxies, galaxy clusters, and galaxy super-clusters. Western astronomers attempt to pinpoint the date of the Big Bang, one estimate being thirteen billion years ago. Buddhist cosmology agrees in principle with the theory of the universe oscillating between cycles of Big Bang/development/Big Crunch, another Big Bang/development/Big Crunch, but it places the history of our present universe at considerably longer than thirteen billion years.

The Buddhist meaning of "rare" is embedded in the Buddhist cosmological worldview. Within the vast, oscillating billion-fold world systems inhabited by sentient beings, Buddhists speak of six different modes of sentient life, each with a different range of experience. Some beings have incredible misery, some incredible bliss. Human beings have the widest spectrum of experience extending from misery to bliss. Hell and heaven, it is all here, giving "rare" a special meaning.

Within this cycle of existence, rebirth after rebirth, extending back through immeasurable time in an infinite cycle of universes, there are rare occasions when we rise to a human rebirth of leisure and opportunity. The Buddha used a metaphor to exemplify the rarity of a precious human life of leisure and opportunity: Imagine a tortoise swimming submerged in a vast ocean and resurfacing only once every one hundred years. The times of human rebirth are similar to the infrequent times the tortoise comes up for air. Now imagine an ox's yoke floating on the same ocean. Consider the tortoise's chances of poking his head through the yoke when he comes up for air every hundred years. This is the meaning of "rarity" in "rare and precious human life of leisure and opportunity." The object of discursive meditation on the rare opportunity of a precious human life of leisure and opportunity is to motivate us to use our rare opportunity wisely.

There is another layer of meaning here which addresses basic assumptions about our life. Just as Buddhist cosmology describes the outer world as infinite in space and time, Buddhists also describe human potential, the inner world, as infinite. Lama Yeshe, a fine Tibetan Buddhist teacher who passed away some years ago, used to tell this parable to his Western students: "You are like beggars living in a shack, ignoring your poverty. Meanwhile, just under the dirt floor, there is a treasure of immeasurable value. You just need to scrape off the dust and you will find it."

The treasure is really within your own mind and heart. Teachers, traditions, techniques, all have the single purpose of helping unveil that which is already within you. If you think otherwise, if you believe happiness is "out there" in a religious tradition or "with your teacher" or "in the spiritual community," you are missing the point. Dharma consists of methods to unveil what is already within you.

The preliminaries require us to examine our basic assumptions about the nature of life and its potential. This examination shifts the focus of attention and shakes loose preconceptions. Buddhists aren't alone in realizing the crucial importance of focus and attention in the quest for well-being and psychological balance. William James, the eminent American psychologist, said at the end of the scientifically over-confident nineteenth century, "our *belief and attention are the same fact. For the moment, what we attend to is reality...*"[3] When you begin to attend to facets of reality uncovered by discursive meditation, when you notice, for example, that your opportunity for realizing your innate human potential is very rare and precious, the practice of Dharma begins to flow naturally from your heart. Tibetan lamas emphasize the importance of this life by advising their students, "If you have a precious human life of leisure and opportunity, use it well. If you don't have one, get one."

Death and Impermanence

The second of the four thoughts that turn the mind is discursive meditation on death and impermanence. The first thought is about the preciousness of having a human body, and the second thought is about that body being on loan. The purpose of pondering death and impermanence is to invert the pernicious tendency of the human mind to view things as being more stable than they are. Young people don't take getting old seriously; healthy people don't take illness seriously. The mind has a deep-rooted tendency to interpret whatever is happening in the moment as "this is it." We even grasp onto emotions as enduring even though all experience indicates otherwise. We tend to hold a personal worldview in which death and illness are for other people. You will die, but not me, at least not for a long,

long time. Our unexamined sense of immortality teams up with the eight mundane concerns to shape a working hypothesis that death is so far in the future that it is functionally irrelevant. The intention of the second of the four discursive meditations, impermanence, is to counteract this unexamined assumption about our personal immortality. The Buddha taught that everything that is conditioned is impermanent. Even on a subtle level, everything is in flux all the time. All that ascends to a high position will fall to a lower position, all that comes together comes apart, all that is gained will be lost, and all that is created will be destroyed. These are universal truths. Any situation dependent upon conditions will pass. This includes relationships, possessions, and our own bodies.

When we overlook our own impermanence, there is a natural tendency to grasp onto the good things that come along. We grasp onto nice people, family, nice material stuff as we try to create a comfortable environment. Then we hold on for dear life. This is called attachment, and once we are set in this pattern of holding on, only one of two things can happen—either the object of attachment will disappear or we will disappear. There is no third possibility. No matter how skilled we are at attachment, a life dominated by grasping is still ruled by the law of impermanence.

What is the nature of these phenomena that we care so much about? What are these feelings and mental states that propel us through life? The pursuit of happiness and avoidance of suffering is the central axis of our lives, and the feelings and behaviors these pursuits generate have a huge impact on our lives. Yet the source of the problem remains elusive. Why? Because we identify with our feelings. We know how we feel by identifying with feelings. The alternative to identification is observation, attending to mental phenomena rather than grasping onto them.

Mindfulness of feelings is a key to understanding subtle impermanence. The practice of observing feelings starts with very sharp attention. What is the nature of feelings? What is involved in the arising of a pleasurable feeling? When the stimulus is withdrawn, what happens to the feeling? Closely observing the feelings that you take so seriously, that guide your decisions, will radically alter the course of your life, because feelings are ephemeral, or, as the Buddhists say, "subtly impermanent."

Experiment with observing joy or sorrow, feelings that arise every day. When one or the other of these feelings arises, attend to it and see if you can observe whether the mind that experiences the feeling has the same feeling as what it is observing. Is there a correspondence between the feeling tone of the observing awareness and the feeling that is being inspected? Can a mind in a state of equanimity observe misery or joy? This exercise leads to insight into the nature of subtle impermanence.

Meditation on the nature of gross and subtle impermanence is also strongly emphasized in the Buddhist tradition. Going even deeper into the nature of impermanence, Tibetans meditate on death. There is a reasonable objection to meditation on death. Since we are alive now, why not attend to being alive and save meditating on death for when we are dying? After all, when your time comes to die, you don't want to be nostalgic about life.

The reason for meditating on death is not to spoil happiness, but to find it. Human beings tend to get into a lot mischief, and the religions of the world have taken on the responsibility of reforming humans for the better (with mixed results!). Since much of our habitual behavior is not good, we have to be persuaded to improve our behavior. Fear is a very effective method of persuasion. Religious authorities have traditionally attempted to persuade people to be good not only by fear of death but also by fear of the unknown and fear of the very unknown, the afterlife. Religious doctrines on death are purposefully scary.

The Buddha taught that the purpose of his teaching on death was not just to scare people into being good but to prepare for death in this lifetime. The teachings were not designed specifically to be frightening, but if there is already fear of death, better to acknowledge that fear, engage with it and move through it so that when death actually arrives, there is no fear.

By attending to the preciousness and rarity of our lives, we recognize that life is passing right now. We will never have this day again. This enormous opportunity passes quickly and then comes to a complete stop. When your body is finished, your precious human life is finished. Attending to the preciousness and impermanence of life provides incentive. If there is something worthwhile doing here, do it.

There is still more in these first two of the preliminary meditations. Consider again the eight mundane concerns— the acquisition of material belongings and the prevention of material loss, the desire for pleasure and the avoidance of discomfort, praise and blame, and the deeper concerns for good and bad reputation. The mind becomes disgruntled. Buddhists get compound interest on disgruntlement. Buddhists get irritated about being irritated and this gets out of hand. It is helpful to have a generally relaxed attitude and be passionate about one thing—spiritual practice.

Meditation on death helps extricate you from small preoccupations, the little stuff that gnaws away at your limitless potential. Meditation on death is a wake-up call. Its purpose is not to frighten you with what the boogie man will do to you after you are dead, but to get you to look at the opportunities you have right now, realize they are for a limited time only, and take advantage of them. Additionally, make sure what you are practicing is really Dharma and not one of the mundane concerns, which, in the face of death, lose their allure altogether.

Buddhist meditation on death has three parts. The first is meditating on the inevitability of our own death. We can say we already know that. Easy. But are we attending to it? If we are not attending to it, we are not factoring it into our decisions. If we are not taking the inevitability of death seriously, then we don't really believe it.

However carefully we live, there will come a time when death arrives. Death will step forward. It will happen. It happened to Buddha and Jesus and it happens to presidents and kings. Rich or poor, sooner or later you will die and your death will be yours alone. Inevitability is the first of the three parts of the meditation on death.

When I was twenty-three, I was living in India and became very ill with hepatitis. In addition to hepatitis, I was suffering from malnutrition, intestinal parasites, and a cat crawled into my sleeping bag and gave me lice. Each day of this illness was like tumbling down the stairs of life, and I was dying. There were a couple of nights when I figured I had a 50% chance of living through to morning. I was so close to death that the monks in my monastery began doing a death ritual for me. Dr. Yeshi Dhonden, the Dalai Lama's personal physician at that time, saved my life. My health turned around. I began climbing back up the stairs and knew I was not going to die. What really struck me as I lay on my bed dying was that everything else was just going on more or less normally. If I died, my fellow monks would feel sorry for me and perhaps miss me for a little while, but classes in the monastery would be held the next day. My parents would grieve for a long time. But it would all go on. I came out of that experience with a very clear sense that my life was not so much saved as my death was postponed. Death had just been shoved back. This is true for all of us.

The first part of the meditation on death is to become more and more aware of its inevitability. Whatever we identify with, all of it will come to a total halt. In death you lose everything. Your relationships are over, somebody gets all your stuff, and somebody else has to deal with your body.

The second part of the meditation on death is that it can arrive any time. Death is unpredictable. It doesn't make an appointment. Tibetans have a list of times when death can arrive—in the womb, at birth, in infancy, childhood, youth, adolescence, young adulthood, middle age, old age—any time is perfect for dying. You can die in good health or bad, rich or poor, educated or not. A big one for Westerners is that you can die whether or not your projects are finished. Death can happen any time. What is the basis for confidence that death can come at any time but not for me? Wishful thinking, nothing else. The second part of the meditation on impermanence is realizing death's unpredictability.

The third part of the meditation on death is attending to what is of value in the face of death. Death is part of life, not life's antithesis. With an awareness of death, what is the value of life? This question is the basis upon which Dharma is defined. With an awareness of your own mortality, Dharma is that which is of highest value. What is of value—a mind of clarity, a heart of compassion, a sense of wisdom, equanimity, patience and forbearance, serving other people? Meditation on death is the most direct way to check and refine values.

The great Tibetan yogi and poet Milarepa is an inspiration as an example of the power of the Dharma to transform our lives. As a young man, Milarepa killed thirty-five people in an act of revenge. Afterward, deep remorse and the desire to die without regret motivated him to immerse himself in Dharma for the rest of his life. Tibetans regard Milarepa as an example of the power of Dharma to transform anyone, no matter what his past behavior, into an enlightened being in a single lifetime.

The central question about death, raised in all religious traditions, is, Who is it that dies? Jesus speaks of having to "die" to gain everlasting life. Similarly, the Buddha said he had attained the "deathless state," also called the "unborn state." Who is it that is "deathless"? References to a "deathless state" and "everlasting life" in the world's religious traditions bring into question materialistic assumptions taken for granted in the West. Are we inevitably death's victims? Spiritual traditions point to a deeper reality in which the afterlife is malleable. Who is it that dies? Insofar as I identify with this body, then I am going to die. If I identify with my intelligence, my education, talents and accomplishments, desires, imagination, projects, achievements, thoughts, memories, I am going to die. All mental events contingent upon the human nervous system will cease when the nervous system dies. The mind and its intelligence, contingent upon the brain, will die when the brain dies.

What is not contingent upon the body may not die. What Buddha referred to as "deathless" is pure awareness—spacious, vivid, attentive without grasping or identification—awareness free from identification with the body, and which observes sensations arise and pass, observes mental events and feelings, observes all phenomena arising and passing into space like clouds dissolving into the sky. If I am not identified with body, memories, desires or feelings, who dies?

I will give you a brief account of the Tibetan description of the dying process and then some evidence to support it.

I was able to confirm the first stage of dying from my own experience when I had hepatitis at age twenty-three. Before this, I thought the perfect death would be to die peacefully during sleep. When I started dying in my sleep, I woke up. It wasn't peaceful. I was awake and entered the first stage of dying as described by Tibetans. The Tibetan Buddhist description of the death process is experiential. Senses gradually shut down and feeling of the body shifts. The first thing that happens is a tremendous sense of heaviness. There is a leaden quality to the body as you lose control and can't move. This first stage is called "the collapse of the earth element," the element of solidity. As the death sequence continues, the moisture of the body seems to dry up. This is the collapse of the water element. Heat dissipates from the body and you feel cold. This is the collapse of the fire element. Your senses shut down one by one—sight, taste, smell, hearing—and in the deeper stages the tactile sense also stops—you lose the sense of having a body at all. The air element has collapsed when the breath stops. But this is not death yet. In the Tibetan description of death, the power of the elements is lost one by one, first earth, then water, fire, and lastly, air. Death comes *after* the breath has stopped.

Death continues in the progressive withdrawal of life from the physical down into the mental. Gradually, the various mental operations shut down and dissolve into a state of simplicity. Memory, the power of recognition, imagination, and emotions all dissolve. The Tibetan Buddhist account of the death process reports that first you will see a red sheen, then a whitish appearance, then a total blackout. Many people believe the final phase of death is a total obliteration. The Tibetan account is that after a brief phase of obliteration, you emerge into the "clear light of death." The clear light of death is a state in which consciousness has dissolved into its primordial state, a state that is no longer human and is independent of a functioning brain. We don't know whether there is any kind of measurable brain activity during the clear light of death, but this is something that might be researched within the next few years.

When I went to Dharamsala with the neuroscientists in 1992, we were presented with some stunning evidence supporting the Tibetan account of the dying process. His Holiness the Dalai Lama encouraged us to visit a Tibetan contemplative who had died six days before we arrived. The yogi's name was Ratö Rinpoche, and he had been born in Tibet, only in the later part of his life escaping to India as a refugee from the Chinese Communist invasion. All of his bodily functions stopped six days before we arrived. In the Tibetan view, Ratö Rinpoche had entered into the non-conceptual state of the clear light of death; that is, his awareness had withdrawn into its primordial state. For six days his body did not deteriorate.

The clear light of death is described as "boundless space," "luminosity," "utter limpidity," and "innate bliss." This primordial state is totally transpersonal and yet it is the very essence of our being. During death, everyone enters into the clear light of death, but only a few recognize it. Failing this recognition, after death most people feel disoriented and seek to be incarnated again from force of habit. For most people, the clear light of death is a brief, unrecognized state. Ratö Rinpoche recognized the clear light of death and sustained it. In the October heat of 65-70 degrees, six days after clinical death, without breath, his cheeks were rosy and there was warmth around his heart. His Holiness was aware we had high-tech equipment with us and wanted to find out what could be measured in the brain of Ratö Rinpoche during the clear light of death. According to everything the neuroscientists knew, a dead body should be decomposing six days after death, and they were a bit intimidated by this phenomenon completely outside their experience. When we saw Rinpoche on the seventh day, his body remained untouched on the bed where he had died, his face still had a bit of pink to it but the warmth at his heart had vanished. We missed the yogi's sustained clear light of death by just a few hours.

In the Buddhist contemplative tradition, if one experiences the ground state of all other forms of awareness prior to death, then there is a good chance of being able to ascertain this "deathless state" during the dying process. This is the final opportunity presented to us in this life for transformation. Experiencing while in good health the nature of primordial awareness, which later manifests as the clear light of death, is one of the main goals of Tibetan Buddhist meditation.

There are a lot of obstacles in meditation—knees ache, the back hurts, somebody makes a noise, duties and projects beckon, always something. The one meditation session in which all obstacles vanish is the dying process. There is no pain because your body has shut down and you won't hear noises because the senses have stopped. The great problem of meditation, distraction, is solved when you die because your brain won't support a scattered mind any more. The Tibetan Buddhist tradition claims that it is possible to sustain the clear light of death and emerge from it with the clarity and freedom to choose conditions of rebirth.

While death is inevitable and unpredictable, it is also malleable. In the Tibetan Buddhist tradition, death is considered the most marvelous opportunity life presents for meditation. You have a choice whether to be prepared for the opportunity presented at death or to freak out at death, clinging desperately to all the people and things we have to leave behind.

It is ever so easy to fall into uncritical complacency with regard to death, based on the belief that death is just the cessation of life and therefore nothing to worry about. I have often heard the claim that religious people cling to beliefs in the immortality of the soul or the continuity of individual consciousness after death because they simply cannot cope with the reality of personal annihilation at death. I find this hypothesis dubious at best. Which is more daunting: to consider the Buddhist hypothesis that each of us will experience the ethical consequences of our behavior in future lifetimes, or to believe that death will simply terminate our experience forever, with no more problems and no more worries? I think in many cases people cling to the speculative notion of personal extinction at death as an absolute fact because they are intimidated by the thought that they might depart this life and consciously enter a vast unknown. Now that's scary!

While many people are committed to the belief that death brings the total cessation of personal existence, many others claim to be agnostic, quite honestly admitting that they don't know what happens at death and therefore have no views on the matter at all. At first glance, this seems quite a reasonable and intelligent position to take, for, after all, who among us really *does* know what happens at death? On the other hand, if we examine our *working hypotheses* regarding the significance of death, I think we will all find that we do indeed hold onto beliefs in this regard, whether or not we regard ourselves as agnostic. In our day-to-day lives, do we yearn for any kind of favorable experience or hope to avoid any misfortune after death? If so, do these concerns actually influence the way we lead our lives and the kinds of choices we make from day to day? Do we have any plans, hopes, or fears that are not confined to this life alone? If the answer to all these questions is no, then we are basing our lives upon the assumption that we will experience nothing after death. Even if we say we do believe in the continuity of consciousness after death, if all our desires and concerns are confined within this lifetime, we are still using the working hypothesis that we will experience nothing after death. This assumption is as much a belief as the assertion of the continuity of individual consciousness after death. Adherents of both positions are "believers."

The basis of the Buddhist assertion of the conservation of consciousness is the experience of the Buddha himself, corroborated by countless Buddhist contemplatives after him. The insights from such direct experience were then formalized within the context of a coherent, rational account of the nature and causes of consciousness. Many Buddhist and other contemplatives have claimed to *know* that consciousness continues on after death, and many have given clear instructions on how to discover this truth for oneself.[4] Many cognitive scientists, on the other hand, also claim to *know* that consciousness ceases at death. What is the basis of their assertion? Modern science has no means of objectively detecting the presence or absence of consciousness in anything—human, animal, plant, or mineral. It has no widely accepted definition of consciousness, nor have cognitive scientists discovered either the necessary or sufficient causes that lead to the emergence of consciousness. They are discovering more and more brain correlates to specific states of consciousness, but they have yet to discover what it is about the brain that enables it to produce or even have an influence on conscious states. In short, as the materialist philosopher of mind Daniel Dennett acknowledges, "With consciousness...we are still in a terrible muddle. Consciousness stands alone today as a topic that often leaves even the most sophisticated thinkers tongue-tied and confused."[5] In the absence of clear scientific evidence, it seems that the basis of the materialist view of consciousness is simply a metaphysical predilection, or an article of faith in the primacy of matter.

With science providing so little actual knowledge about the nature and origins of consciousness, what grounds do we have for the belief in eternal, mindless death? As soothing as this notion may be, it seems to be little more than sheer conjecture at this point. Moreover, it simply ignores the experiences of countless contemplatives throughout the world who have achieved deep states of meditative concentration and claim to have seen for themselves the existence of their own past lives. Buddhist contemplatives do not regard themselves in "terrible muddle" with regard to consciousness. Perhaps that's because they are part of a rigorous heritage that has taken the experiential investigation of consciousness very seriously for over two millennia, whereas modern science largely overlooked consciousness until the last decade of the twentieth century. And it still has no rigorous means of investigating consciousness firsthand, which is the only way we even know that consciousness exists. No wonder science is still so much in the dark in this regard!

When we accept the theory of the continuity of consciousness beyond death as a working hypothesis, meditation on death becomes a great remedy for mental afflictions. It is difficult to be arrogant if you are aware you are going to die. Attachments lose their luster in the face of death. The Buddha said awareness of death and impermanence is the most powerful of all discernments to radically reorient one's life on the path of Dharma.

The Unsatisfactory Nature of the Cycle of Existence

The First Point of the Seven-Point Mind-Training, training in the preliminaries, continues with the third of the "four thoughts that turn the mind"—meditation on the pervasiveness of suffering and discontent in *samsara*, the Buddhist term for the entire cycle of existence in which we are subject to mental afflictions and their results.

When Buddha attained enlightenment, he doubted anyone would believe what he had discovered about the nature
of reality and the human capacity for freedom and spiritual awakening. The Buddha left Bodh Gaya, the place of
his enlightenment, and headed for Sarnath to seek his five
previous companions with whom he had meditated and
practiced austerities for six years. The Buddha considered
them good candidates to be able to fathom what he would
reveal. The Buddha's first teaching was not about bliss. The
first thing he taught his previous companions was the
reality of suffering. First, recognize the reality of suffering.

There are so many happy things to talk about, why talk
about suffering? We all believe we know a lot about suffering. In the Buddha's first teaching on suffering and the
nature of existence, he lifted the surface layer of our strong
habitual tendency to deny suffering. "Recognize suffering,"
the Buddha said and he proceeded to delineate the subtle
levels of suffering.

There are different types of suffering. The first suffering,
"the suffering of suffering," is blatant suffering, physical
or mental. Illness and physical pain are blatant suffering.
There are also the mental sufferings of anxiety, fear, and
unhappiness.

As obvious and omnipresent as blatant suffering is, we
tend to deny it. Young people look at middle-aged people
and their afflictions and think, "That's their problem."
Middle-aged people look at people in nursing homes and
think, "This is for old people." We habitually think the blatant suffering of sickness and aging is something that
happens only to other people. Other people get diseases,
lose jobs, and have car accidents. Denial is the soothing and
false reassurance that the suffering that afflicts other people
won't happen to us.

There is a story about an Australian aborigine who was
caught for stealing, tried, and convicted. When he heard
that the punishment for stealing was hanging, he cried,

"You can't hang me! Hanging is for white people. They're used to it!" Likewise, we tend to think sickness and old age are for people who are used to it.

Also included in the "suffering of suffering" is the blatant suffering of disappointment. Suffering occurs when we want something very much and don't get it. Suffering also occurs when we have something we really want but lose it. For example, you may be totally in love with your significant other, so happy. Then he or she says, "I don't like you any more. Good-bye," and the result is blatant suffering. Blatant suffering includes not wanting something and getting it and also not being able to get rid of something you don't want. The Buddha's first teaching at Sarnath concerned the blatant sufferings of sickness, old age, death, and the many varieties of disappointment we tend to think we are magically immune from. But blatant suffering is only the tip of the iceberg of suffering.

Recently, members of the Mind and Life Institute had a discussion with the Dalai Lama about potential topics for its next conference with Western scientists. One of the topics suggested to His Holiness was to compare Western views and Buddhist views of suffering. Sounds interesting, right? But His Holiness's response was that Western cognitive scientists and psychologists generally focus only on blatant suffering, whereas the Buddhist view is that the real problem with suffering is something Westerners don't regard as a problem at all. So he discarded that topic.

There are two deeper levels in the Buddhist taxonomy of suffering. The next level after the "suffering of suffering" is the "suffering of change." Our stimulus-driven states of pleasure, happiness, and gratification depend on events working out one way and not another and are considered states of suffering. Things go the way you want or they don't and, either way, you suffer. This is one of the views that have earned Buddhists the "sourpuss" label. [ ] having things go your way be suffering? Because [ ] something deeper going on. What the Buddhists are [ ] ing out is that whether you get something you wan[ ] hold onto it; or you get rid of something you don't war[ ] something you don't want to happen doesn't—all th[ ] events are conditioned and subject to change. Buddhis[ ] are very interested in sources and not merely effects, and stimulus-driven pleasures are not considered sources of genuine happiness. Does driving a Porsche, getting rid of a nuisance, or enjoying the fact that your home is not burning down, tap into a source of genuine happiness? If something is a genuine source of happiness, then increased duration and frequency of that stimulus should result in more happiness. But how often does that happen, and for how long? The Buddha's teaching was to look deeper, far beyond the law of diminishing returns, for the genuine source of happiness.

The Buddhist analysis of pleasure appears bleak. The Buddha said that although stimulus-driven pleasures may produce relative well-being, they don't pass the test as genuine sources of happiness. For example, the Tibetan monk Palden Gyatso spent thirty-three years in a concentration camp operated by the Chinese Communists. He was starved and tortured for years on end. Imagine that every Tuesday you got tortured but on one Tuesday, the person who tortures you doesn't come to work because he is sick. A message arrives in your cell, "I cannot torture you today because I don't feel well." What would you experience? Happiness! In a concentration camp when somebody brings you rotten food that fell in the dirt, what is your response? Happiness. Relative to having no food, you are happy. But from a perspective outside the concentration camp, it seems that everything inside is suffering, every moment, including the

as ill because, even on a day
n Gyatso still starved. But
here were good days and
garbage for a meal makes it
e concentration camp, we could
of the prisoner is limited.
ing is that from the viewpoint of an
s gained realization of Ultimate Truth,
xperience is suffering. But this is not dis-
oner in a concentration camp thought that
in the world was also imprisoned in a concen-
amp that would be dismal. If the prisoner believes
are people outside who have enough to eat and are
tortured at all, that is an optimistic and inspiring
nought. The Buddha taught that we are suffering in a type
of concentration camp fenced in by our limited views and
mental afflictions. The Buddha taught that from the viewpoint of one who has experientially realized Ultimate Truth,
we are in the ocean of samsara and everything we experience
is unsatisfactory.

The Buddhist position is that what we experience as pleasure is merely a relative attenuation of our dissatisfaction.
There is nothing wrong with the happiness derived from
stimulus-dependent joys, but from the Buddhist perspective,
these states of happiness are merely a fleeting attenuation
of suffering. When a pleasant stimulus is removed, the mind
falls back into its habitual state, a state that is afflicted, and
a state that is suffering. The true source of suffering lies
deeper in our experience and underneath temporary
attenuations.

There are some simple tests for the Buddhist hypothesis.
In situations of sensory deprivation, when stimuli are removed, boredom, a subtle form of mental suffering, sets
in. Without anything to stimulate the mind in a pleasurable

fashion, we move beyond boredom to loneliness, uneasiness, and unhappiness. Pascal said the primary affliction of modern man is the "inability to sit quietly in one's chambers." Being alone for a sustained period is a type of torture called solitary confinement. In a sensory deprivation tank where stimulation comes only from your mind, over time the mind becomes chaotic and breaks down.

From the Buddhist perspective, situations of solitary confinement or sensory deprivation do not create difficulties. Instead, these situations uncover problems that were already there. What happens when we are alone or sensorily deprived is the same as what is happening all the time but is buried under stimulation. Circumstances are not the cause of suffering. The Buddhist view is that suffering is due to underlying afflictions of the mind. We fall into boredom, malaise, sadness, anxiety, and depression when stimuli aren't coming in not because we are social animals, not because we have bodies, but because the mind is afflicted, though not intrinsically or immutably. What appears as suffering when stimulation is removed is the afflicted nature of the mind, what Buddhists call the "suffering of change." With respect to the afflicted nature of the mind, the suffering of change, everything else is a symptom. The Buddha's teaching that stimulus-driven pleasure is simply an attenuation of suffering directs us to look even deeper for the root cause of suffering.

Blatant suffering, the "suffering of suffering," is obvious as long as you are not in denial. Understanding the "suffering of change" takes some thoughtful investigation. The next level of suffering is the "the pervasive suffering of conditioned existence," or the fundamental suffering of vulnerability, and is deeper still. We are profoundly vulnerable due to the nature of the way we exist. At present there is nothing that makes us immune to the suffering experienced in concentration camps. The layer of skin between the environment and our nervous system is only micrometers thick. The question as to what protection we can have against the innumerable situations that cause suffering and fear has proven to be a dead end for many great thinkers who argue that this is just the way it is; this is the way we are made; humans suffer because we are human. Another argument is that humans suffer because nature can't be controlled. Nor can we control time, so we age, we suffer, we die, no matter what medical treatment we receive. That is the way it is. Suffering is part of reality. As Sigmund Freud observed, "We are so made that we can derive intense enjoyment only from a contrast and very little from a state of things...Unhappiness is much less difficult to experience."[6]

The Western philosophic cornerstone "humans suffer because we are human" is, in the Buddhist view, a non-answer stemming from an incomplete analysis. The Buddhist analysis of vulnerability results in the extraordinary hypothesis that we suffer because we identify with, or "closely hold onto," the constituents of our personal identity: "This is my body. These are my desires, my thoughts, my ambitions, my fears; this is me."

Given that we have a body, thoughts, and feelings, is there an alternative to identifying with them? The Buddhist answer is yes. Realize the nature of your own mind and identity, fathom the nature of your own body, and with the sword of insight, cut the root of suffering. I suspect this is what the Dalai Lama had in mind when he turned down suffering as a topic for an East-West mind science meeting. Blatant suffering? Not so interesting. Stop denying and there it is. Suffering of change? Western science assumes it can't be fixed because the problem is hard-wired. The suffering of vulnerability, what Buddhism considers the key to suffering, is not recognized in the West at all. Why do we have the suffering of vulnerability? Because we grasp onto our body, our identity, our self. Very deep. The key is inside.

A person who is liberated, who has freed his or her mind of all mental afflictions, still experiences physical suffering. The difference between us and an *arhat*, a person who has freed the mind from mental affliction, is that an arhat doesn't identify with pain. Arhats experience physical pain vividly but don't grasp onto it; they can take action to avoid or alleviate pain, but whether they do so or not, the physical pain doesn't come inside. What an arhat does not experience is mental suffering. A *buddha*, one who is perfectly spiritually awakened, has gone a further step. A buddha has no mental suffering of his or her own, but is vividly and non-dually aware of the suffering of others.

Superficially, the arhat who is free from mental suffering can seem to us who lack this realization as numb and detached, in a state of existential anesthesia. A buddha, one who is fully awakened, presents the paradox of being free from suffering and also non-dually present with other people's joys and sorrows, hopes and fears. A buddha taps into immutable bliss, the ultimate ground state of awareness beyond the dichotomy of stimulus-driven pain and pleasure. The mind of a buddha has been purified of all obscuration and from its own nature there naturally arises immutable bliss, like a spring welling up from the earth. With the unveiling of the buddha-nature of unconditioned bliss, there is also a complete erosion of an absolute demarcation between self and other. The barrier is gone. This is why buddhas are vividly and non-dually aware of the suffering of others, their hopes and fears, the whole situation, and at the same time are not disengaged from the purity and bliss of their own awareness. The mind of a buddha doesn't block out anything and nothing is inhibited, and this is why the awareness of an awakened being is frequently described as "unimaginable."

Meanwhile, back in samsara, we are identifying—"This is my body. These are my problems. Your problems are not my problems." Our ground-state is the suffering of vulnerability, a very big problem. Many people assume that after death, the suffering of life is extinguished. Buddhists say that is wishful thinking. The Buddhist position is that whether you like it or not and regardless of your belief system, the nature of reality is such that there is an unbroken stream of consciousness not contingent on this body. Your body will eventually turn into fertilizer but your consciousness carries on.

There are both theoretical and empirical grounds for the continuity of consciousness. There is currently no consensus in psychology, neuroscience, cognitive science, or philosophy of the mind, regarding an empirically based theory of consciousness. This is a major void in the edifice of modern science. Since object-oriented scientific methods themselves present obstacles to the effective study of consciousness, scientists are at odds even about the methodology of studying consciousness.

There are alternatives to the Western methods for the study of consciousness. The philosopher of science Thomas Kuhn observed that in order for a paradigm shift to occur, it is not enough to see that one's present paradigm is flawed. It is important to present a coherent alternative that accounts for what you know and makes intelligible what was previously unaccounted for. If you are in a boat that needs periodic bailing, you won't improve matters by being rescued by a sinking ship—and you don't want just to swim for it either. What you want is another boat, preferably one without any leaks, otherwise your best bet is staying where you are.

The Buddhist hypothesis is that, like the scientific theory of the conservation of mass/energy, there is conservation of consciousness. Consciousness doesn't *arise* from mass/energy, but consciousness is *conditioned* by mass/energy. The brain, sense faculties, nervous system, and environment all condition consciousness. Just as mass and energy take different forms—gas, fluid, or solid—the Buddhist teaching is that under different conditions, consciousness manifests in different ways. Additionally, consciousness is not a by-product of matter, nor does it arise *ex nihilo*, out of nothing.[7]

The Buddhist view is that the brain does not produce consciousness, but it does condition consciousness. The stream of consciousness is a continuity that stores imprints, memories, and tendencies throughout a lifetime. Just as mass/energy changes form rather than disappearing altogether, consciousness changes as it disengages from the physical body.

The Buddhist theory of the origin of consciousness is that consciousness arises from consciousness. The Buddhist hypothesis is that an individual's consciousness does not arise from the consciousnesses of his or her parents. Parents have their own continua of consciousness. Individual consciousness exists prior to conception, arising from a preceding, unique continuum and will carry on after this life.

When individual consciousness disengages from the body, the number of types of embodiments it can enter into is vast. There are states of re-embodiment that are conditioned by intense suffering; another state conditioned by unfulfilled desire; another conditioned by mental dullness; and another by great joy. If in this life as a human, we do not profoundly purify our minds and gain deep realization, we are vulnerable to rebirth in other less favorable realms of existence. The continuum of consciousness is tremendously malleable and can take on a wide variety of forms, some subtle and blissful, some very dense and miserable. There is nothing in this vast spectrum of modes of rebirth that we are automatically exempt from. Since we are no longer incorporated in a human body after death, there is nothing human about us at all. According to Buddhist theory, re-embodiment is propelled by our habitual grasping.

The sobering notion here is that not only is our mind basically in an afflicted state making us vulnerable to suffering, it doesn't get better by itself. If we continue in habitual patterns, there is no way out. When Buddhists say no way out, they mean it. Samsara never runs down. The cycle of existence from rebirth to rebirth is like being a ball in a perpetual motion pinball machine. Merely wishing, "I have been in samsara for countless eons and have had enough," won't get you out. Samsara runs of its own momentum as long as it is fueled by the same habitual patterns. The Buddhist hypothesis is that samsara stops only when we take radical measures and break through the habitual patterns of delusion.

Buddhist psychology states that mental suffering is produced by one of three primary mental afflictions. The first primary mental affliction is delusion. The Buddhist term "delusion" includes the philosophical term "reification" and means mistaking what has no inherent existence as being concretely real. Delusion results in grasping—"I am," "I am autonomous," "I am separate," "I am permanent." The primary delusion of our self as an inherently existent, autonomous entity is the source of all mental afflictions.

Out of delusion, the primary affliction, grows the second fundamental affliction, attachment. Attachment is not simply desire but entails superimposing desirable qualities upon objects and screening out undesirable qualities. The result is craving. Attachment is distorted awareness in which we idealize an object—"If only I could go there, have that job, that spouse, that car, then I would be happy." Idealization creates a fiction that we cling to. When we conflate a person with a superimposed fiction, we might fall in love with the wonderful fiction and later be disappointed that the person "changed."

Anger, also referred to as aversion or hatred, is the third of the three primary afflictions. Anger is the natural complement of attachment. Anger regards its object with superimposed disagreeable qualities, and filters out desirable or neutral qualities. The frequent result of anger is aggression.

The Buddhist hypothesis is that from day to day, from moment to moment, whenever we experience mental suffering, its source is the arousal of one or more of the mental afflictions.

When we experience suffering, we habitually identify the source of suffering as "out there"—other people, situations, traffic, the government. In Buddhism, this is an incorrect analysis, a wrong view. The radical Buddhist diagnosis of our condition is that the source of suffering is mental afflictions. When mental afflictions are catalyzed in any of many ways, we suffer. The actual source of suffering is not "out there." External circumstances and other people merely serve as catalysts to trigger something already within us. The source of suffering is not our job, spouse, children or other variations on the theme "I am suffering because of *them* or *it*." The source of suffering is rooted in mental afflictions.

What about happiness? Once again, Buddhism presents an extraordinary hypothesis. The Buddhist hypothesis is that happiness is your birthright; all you need to do is discover it. When we stop the behavior that impedes natural, inborn happiness, when we stop throwing dirt in the wound, just stop, happiness starts to well up naturally. From a Buddhist perspective, what we need to do is stop making the great efforts smothering the natural happiness that is within us. A good definition of Dharma is: that which enables us to unveil the natural, genuine happiness within.

The purpose of discursive meditation on suffering, the third of the four thoughts that turn the mind, is to become disillusioned with all the mundane pursuits we value.

Pleasure, reputation, comfort are all stimuli that result in relative well-being but do not deal with the fundamental problem, our profound vulnerability to suffering, a problem that continues until we do something about it.

Karma

The last of the four thoughts that turn the mind is karma. "Karma" is the Sanskrit word for "action." In anthropological terminology, "karma" is a thick, theory-laden term. Karma refers to the nature of actions and how their long-term consequences play out over time. According to Buddhism, the universe is not a mechanistic, sterile machine as some philosophies argue. Instead, reality has a moral dimension. Some modern Western Buddhists have shrugged off the significance of karma and the continuity of consciousness after death, claiming that the Buddha simply borrowed these ideas from the Indian culture of his time. Study of the prevalent views concerning the afterlife that were proposed in India during the Buddha's lifetime, however, shows that his assertions were profoundly unlike those of any of his contemporaries. Moreover, he claimed that he had directly observed the truth of his claims in this regard on the night of his enlightenment, and he showed others how they might verify these theories for themselves.[8] Certainly we must consider that the Buddha's assertions in this regard may be wrong. But to claim that he adopted these from others as congenial metaphysical beliefs is simply a sign of ignorance.

The repercussions of karma are deep because they affect not only this lifetime, but the entire continuity of consciousness extending over many lifetimes. The Buddhist belief in the continuity of consciousness from one life to another is backed with logical reasoning. Reasoning alone isn't utterly compelling, but Buddhism does present the continuity of consciousness as a coherent and rational hypothesis, and centuries of Buddhist contemplative experience have produced experiential evidence to support this hypothesis. There are many cases of remembered past lives, foretold future lives and, further, the subjective details of the transitional, or intermediate, state between embodiments, called the *bardo*. Preparation for dying and taking rebirth is a very significant part of Tibetan Buddhist practice.

In 1989, I interpreted for the Dalai Lama in a Mind and Life Conference with a group of neuroscientists in Newport Beach, California.[9] Most neuroscientists believe that the mind is a by-product, or epiphenomenon, of the brain; mind vanishes when brain dies and that is all there is to it. The neuroscientists were disturbed when the Dalai Lama, a very intelligent man, discussed the continuity of consciousness from one lifetime to the next. The scientists pointed out that retrospective accounts of reincarnation, however numerous they may be, are not scientifically compelling due to lack of proper controls. For example, a child's experiences in the first years of life are largely unknown. We can't know for certain what the parents told the child, where he went, or what he saw on television. It was further pointed out to His Holiness that only a prospective study would be impressive scientifically. If scientists interviewed a dying Tibetan yogi and were told by him the specific details of his rebirth and these details were later confirmed by a child reincarnation of the same late yogi, this would be very hard for scientists to explain away as coincidence. His Holiness is very interested in collaborating with scientists on a prospective study of reincarnation.

Continuity of consciousness and karma are not elements of a religious creed Buddhists are required to believe. The extraordinary premise of Buddhism is that the nature of reality can be experientially determined through diligent spiritual practice. Being Buddhist means only that you trust and follow the Buddhist path, critically.

One key to the contemplative exploration of the nature of reality is meditative concentration, the ability to stabilize the mind and enhance its clarity. The refined and stabilized mind is the tool Buddhists use to investigate the whole of reality, from cosmology to the nature of awareness. Such meditative technology gives you access to exceptional states of awareness.

The continuity of consciousness from lifetime to lifetime is not contingent upon any belief or disbelief in reincarnation. From the Buddhist point of view, even if you personally don't believe in continuity of consciousness, there is still continuity. An analogy from physics is that if you roll a ball down a ramp, it accelerates, even if you believe its velocity remains constant. In the future there may be contemplatives, maybe even Western contemplatives, who will take up the prospective challenge of the neuroscientists and die under scientific scrutiny.

If continuity of consciousness is a fact and if, as Buddhists tell us, it is possible to pass through the dying process with complete awareness, then an important question arises. Is rebirth random? Does Nature play roulette so that in one life you are human but in the next, for no reason at all, you are a frog? If there is coherence to rebirth, what is the nature of that coherence? The Buddha's claim was that, from the perspective of an awakened awareness, there is coherence—certain types of actions give rise to certain types of consequences. The coherence is called *karma*.

The fundamental cornerstone of existence as a sentient being is seeking happiness and avoiding suffering. The attainment of enlightenment may be the ultimate goal but in the meantime, a sentient being would rather be well than sick, have enough to eat rather than starve, have harmonious relationships and not painful ones, have a fortunate life rather than a miserable one. We all desire these things. The Buddha taught that certain types of actions give rise to certain types of consequences. The question then becomes: what types of actions give rise to the things we wish for, and what types of actions give rise to the things we seek to avoid?

The natural inclination is to believe that this is easy enough to figure out for oneself. Unfortunately, the undisciplined mind tends to be subjected to delusion. As the eighth-century Indian Buddhist sage Shantideva wrote in *A Guide to Bodhisattva Way of Life*, "Those desiring to escape from suffering hasten right toward suffering. With the very desire for happiness, out of delusion they destroy their own happiness as if it were an enemy."[10] In other words, deluded desires for happiness lead us to engage in actions of attachment that inevitably result in aversion. Our goal is happiness, but our actions lead to suffering.

Continuity of consciousness is a continuum through different states of awareness: sleep, dreams, the waking state, the dying process, the intermediate state, and rebirth. Freud wrote, "in mental life nothing which has once been formed can perish...everything is somehow preserved and...in suitable circumstances... it can once more be brought to light."[11] This statement, taken out of the context of the rest of Freud's views, is reminiscent of the Buddhist theory of karma, actions, and their consequences.

The Buddhist premise is that all actions, including mental actions, leave seeds, or imprints, on a continuum that is not only a *continuity* of experience, but also a kind of *repository*. This continuum is laden with tendencies and configured by experience. When something happens to you, whether traumatic or joyful, the experience imbeds itself in the form of memory, resulting in emotional and behavioral tendencies. In this way, the continuum of consciousness, or mind-stream, is configured by the cumulative effects of parents, friends, education, and our general environment.

The mental continuum is also configured by our actions. Engaging in a certain type of action develops a tendency, a pattern, or habit that is initiated and then reinforced. If the action was difficult at the beginning, it becomes easier as the habit becomes more deeply ingrained. Some habits develop much more easily than others. Responding with irritation when something disagreeable happens is a very easily acquired habit. But irritation and indignation are only two of many possible responses to something disagreeable. When a driver is rude on the freeway, gesturing and firing off a sermon on the nature humanity can get to be a habit. Another option is simply moving out of the way. A habit reinforced by subsequent actions triggered by outside events is one type of karma.

Being held morally, or karmically, accountable for one's thoughts is daunting. Fortunately, there is a loophole. When an unwholesome thought arises, it is grasping onto it, thinking, "I want this ... I want to do that...," that starts the karma meter ticking. If you are meditating, and a disgusting image or desire arises, no problem. A malevolent, jealous, or selfish thought arising in the space of your mind does not accumulate negative karma. No harm is done by the presence of negative thoughts as long as you don't grasp onto them. When thoughts are allowed to play themselves out and vanish of their own accord, your mind remaining like space, there is no accumulation of karma. The problem is having sticky awareness that latches onto negative thoughts with, "How could I be thinking this stuff ... but I like this thought ... Oh, but I shouldn't...." Identification, grasping, is the problem, not the thoughts themselves.

I mentioned a loophole. If thoughts of anger, jealousy, or craving arise that distort the mind, you can choose not to identify with them and create a space around them. You can sever grasping and the accumulation of karma by honing attention to focus right in on the nature of the mental process itself. This is a powerful technique that works if you hit the mark. If you can attend right at the onset, right when the mind begins to be drawn into the vortex of a negative thought, simply by observing the nature of the thought, the karmic effect is cut just as if with a knife. Effective spiritual practice includes developing the attentional skill to remain outside the vortex of afflictive thoughts and emotions without slipping in.

The fundamental moral, or karmic, framework of Buddhism is a list of ten virtues and ten non-virtues. These do's and do not's cover the most common problems in life. Committing an unwholesome or non-virtuous deed plants a seed that can potentially produce a negative impact as it matures in the mind-stream in this lifetime and the ones to follow. In this list of ten, there are three unwholesome deeds of the body, four of speech, and three of the mind. The three of the body are intentional killing, stealing, and sexual misconduct. These three non-virtues are negative because they inflict harm and suffering. The physical misdeeds are behaviors we can make decisions about; we can usually decide not to engage in them. There is nothing metaphysical here.

The next four unwholesome acts concern speech and are more difficult to recognize and deal with than physical non-virtues. The first is harsh and abusive speech. The non-virtues of speech are difficult because, as the Buddha said, nothing in the world is faster than the mind; but the mouth is a close runner-up. Harsh speech engages a mental affliction, frequently anger, sometimes attachment or delusion, and turns speech into a subtle and sophisticated weapon, at times more damaging than a punch to the jaw. Harsh speech includes sarcasm. Tibetans liken sarcasm to throwing a rock covered in fluffy wool—it is initially mistaken for a friendly puffball until it meets its target.

The second type of verbal non-virtue is lying. Lying is intentionally saying what is not true and can have many motivations. Slander or divisive speech is the third verbal non-virtue and an interesting one. Slander may be lying with a twist or it may be the simple truth coupled with a motivation to do harm or create conflict.

Idle gossip, the fourth of the verbal non-virtues, is considered the lightest of all the ten non-virtues but, as one of my lamas remarked, it the easiest way to waste an entire life. Idle gossip is speech motivated by mental afflictions such as attachment, anger, jealousy, pride, and delusion. The net effect of idle gossip is worse than just wasting time; it reinforces mental afflictions and accumulates negative karma.

The next grouping in the list of ten non-virtues is the three non-virtues of the mind. The first is malice. Malice is the intention to inflict harm. Avarice, craving another person's possessions, is the second non-virtue of the mind. The third of the non-virtues of the mind is holding onto false views, which is regarded as the most harmful of all ten non-virtues. "False views" refers to misconceptions about the nature of reality. An example of a false view is the belief that actions have no moral consequences.

Paralleling the Buddhist list of ten non-virtues is a list of ten virtues. These are the flip side of each of the non-virtues. For example, the virtue opposite to killing is protecting life and the virtue corresponding to harsh speech is speaking gently.

All virtuous and non-virtuous deeds place imprints upon the mind-stream that are potent karmic seeds that will ripen in this or a future lifetime. Once karma is imbedded in a stream of consciousness, it is carried from one lifetime to another until it is catalyzed. Just as a plant seed can remain dormant in the desert for decades and sprout to life at the first contact with water, a karmic seed can lie dormant for a long time, from lifetime to lifetime, before a catalyst triggers its ripening.

Another characteristic of karma is that its effect is similar to its cause. For example, if one cultivates a tendency to help those in need, the karmic effect carried into the next life would be being born with an altruistic tendency, being gifted in compassion. Buddhists explain the differences between babies, obvious to any parent, as partly due to karma. This does not deny genetic and environmental influences. Many influences come together in an intricate weave to form this life. The interesting point here is that Buddhists don't consider the mind of an infant to be a blank slate. Due to the influence of past lives, sentient beings are strongly conditioned even before conception. Therefore, cultivating wholesome tendencies is a top priority of Dharma practice.

The view that karma affects the continuum of consciousness from one life to the next is of fundamental importance in Buddhist practice. Many Buddhists acknowledge that attaining buddhahood in one lifetime, although possible, is highly improbable. Understanding karma and its effect on the continuity of consciousness elevates spiritual practice from an all-or-nothing, one-life-only proposition. If spiritual practice has continuity and coherence, if greater kindness, wisdom, and balance have developed and the various afflictive tendencies have declined, then these qualities are embedded in the mind-stream. Even if you don't become enlightened in this lifetime, if you practice Dharma diligently, because of the nature of actions and their consequences, you will be able to pick up where you left off in the next lifetime.

In the Tibetan Buddhist tradition, reincarnations of exceptionally mature practitioners are sometimes identified in childhood. These *tulkus*, which literally means "emanation bodies," are a source of inspiration for Tibetan Buddhists. The recognition of tulkus acknowledges that spiritual maturation is preserved as karmic propensities from one lifetime to the next. This is true not only for tulkus, but for all practitioners.

A third type of karmic effect, and the most difficult to understand, is environmental. The various types of environments encountered in your life are also a result of karma. Being born in a hostile environment, amid plague, famine, drought, war, is a maturation of karma manifesting as an environment. The same reasoning also holds true for a harmonious, beautiful environment.

The Buddhist hypothesis is that humanness is very much contingent upon a human body and we are not thoroughly as human as we believe. When the human body dies, what remain are tendencies. According to the Buddha's teachings, it is difficult to conceive being born in a non-human form because we identify so much with human intelligence and human form. But we have more in common with other realms than we like to think. For example, if cravings dominate your life—"I want a nice car, a bigger house, more of my fair share"—then this is comparable to the life of a *preta*, a hungry ghost. Similarly, leading a life driven by one's "animal appetites," not taking advantage of human intelligence and experience, for all practical purposes, is a human facsimile of living the life of an animal. The general Buddhist teaching is that a life heavily dominated by delusion directs one toward rebirth as an animal; a life heavily dominated by craving leads to rebirth in a hungry ghost realm; and a life heavily dominated by malice or cruelty heads one toward rebirth in a hell realm.

I will give you an example of a rebirth in a Buddhist hell. Keep in mind these rebirths, all of them, are no more substantial than dreams. A Buddhist hell is not a place in the center of the earth or on the back of the moon. If one takes rebirth in a hell, the hell you experience comes into existence, like a dream, at the time you are born there and, also like a dream, seems very real while you are there. One of the Buddhist hell realms is called "again and again revitalized." In this hell, you and all the people around you have weapons. You are in constant hand-to-hand combat, maybe killing a few of the other inhabitants of the dream before someone rams you through with a big spike and you die. But then you come right back to life and fight again. This happens over and over: fight, kill and get killed, come right back. That situation continues until the tendency that propelled you there wears itself out.

In non-human realms, unfortunately, the laws of karma also hold. There is a caveat, however. The greater your intelligence, the greater your understanding and wisdom, the greater impact your actions have. Animals accumulate a small amount of karma for aggression, but a human being with the same behavior accumulates much heavier karma.

The metaphor of the tortoise cruising around in the ocean surfacing for air every hundred years is also descriptive of what is necessary for an animal to be reincarnated in a human realm. From the Buddhist perspective, compassion is rare in the animal realm but it is there. In the hungry ghost realm, compassion is even rarer, and rarer still in the hell realms. However, again there is a loophole. Because of the relative difficulty of compassion in non-human realms, the karmic significance of even a little bit of compassion is great. It is said that in a hell realm, a being who has compassion for another is immediately liberated.

Think of an example from your own life when you felt you were in hell. How difficult was it to feel genuine compassion for someone else? Not impossible, but certainly difficult because we tend to be absorbed in our own feelings and problems. It is not easy for virtue to arise in the midst of craving and obsession, or when the mind is deluded. This is why once you take rebirth in a miserable state of existence it is very difficult to get out.

From the Buddhist perspective, the type of fortune we encounter, happiness or sorrow, is not due to somebody doing something to us. If I win the lottery, it is not because Buddha selected me for a bonus. No god or buddha is responsible for what happens to us. Rather, our circumstances are fundamentally created by previous actions. This is a dangerous statement if misunderstood. A very unfortunate misinterpretation of what the Buddha was getting at in his teaching about karma is the conclusion that other people's suffering is simply their own fault. The Buddha did not teach that a child suffering from disease or hunger brought this suffering upon himself. The Buddhist explanation of suffering is that a deed embedded in the continuum of consciousness eventually gives rise to consequences. The deed may have occurred in this life or many lifetimes ago. This does not imply that a suffering person is morally degenerate any more than suffering the consequences of eating contaminated food does. The suffering we experience is due to karma accumulated under the influence of delusion and mental afflictions. This is true for all sentient beings.

The person witnessing another person's suffering has only one appropriate response: "How can I help?" When karma comes to fruition and causes suffering, the response should never be, "This is your karma. It's your destiny, so I can't help." Your own karma may very well present itself as an opportunity to help a suffering person. Misunderstanding actions and their consequences can be disastrous.

The Buddhist response to the non-virtues we all commit while strapped to the wheel of samsara can be inspiring and encouraging. The Buddhist teaching is that it is possible to neutralize negative karmic seeds embedded in the stream of consciousness. Deeds cannot be undone, but it is possible to purify one's mind-stream so that the impact of karmic seeds will be nullified.

The method used to purify the mind-stream is the "four remedial powers." The metaphor for the effectiveness of the four remedial powers is that of burning a seed. Karma, like a seed, can be scorched in the fire of purification so that it will not sprout. The seed won't vanish, but it will not sprout.

The first of the four remedial powers is remorse, regarding a misdeed as detrimental. Remorse is sincerely focusing on a misdeed, taking responsibility for it, and regretting having done it. Remorse also includes acknowledging consequences. Just as remorse is a step toward nullifying the impact of a negative karmic seed, rejoicing in virtue empowers its positive karma. Tsongkhapa said that the easiest way to empower the mind in virtue is to take delight in virtue. In the same vein, rejoicing about something malevolent, such as congratulating yourself on sarcasm, empowers the negative propensity of the karmic seed.

Rejoicing enhances and remorse helps neutralize the effect of karmic imprints on the mind-stream. Another example: If you give a homeless person five dollars but walk away thinking, "He would have thought I was just as generous if I had given him only two dollars. Then I could have bought myself a coffee and newspaper," that remorse just neutralized the karmic benefit from your five-dollar beneficence.

Remorse is hazardous when conflated with guilt. Remorse is wholesome because it focuses on an event. Guilt is an afflictive state of mind focused on the self as in, "I am an unworthy person." Guilt, a reification of the self around negative tendencies, is simply another mental affliction. Properly directed remorse, on the other hand, can be very helpful for disengaging from unwholesome tendencies.

The second remedial power is reliance. When we have harmed other sentient beings, the remedial power of reliance is cultivating compassion for others; and when we have behaved wrongly toward spiritually realized beings or their teachings, the power of reliance is entrusting ourselves to their guidance.

The third of the four remedial powers is resolve, turning away from misconduct. The power of resolve is stopping unwholesome behavior by the strength of determination and decision.

The final remedial power is purification. This is also called "applying the antidote," and entails doing something that counteracts or neutralizes the negative deed. For example, if the deed involved killing, applying the antidote would be protecting life.

Buddhist tradition teaches that through the four remedial powers it is possible to completely extinguish the potency of even the most virulent deeds. There is no deed so evil that it cannot be purified. Milarepa said that the aim of his Dharma practice was to die without remorse. His point was that if you have engaged in non-virtuous deeds, it is important to purify their karmic imprints on your mind-stream while you have the freedom to do so; purify karmic deeds in this life so that you don't carry negative imprints into the dying process. Crossing the threshold of death is a really bad time for remorse to arise.

The Buddhist scheme also accounts for grace, influence from outside the cycle of suffering, which is a powerful source of purification. It is said that the power of compassion, mercy, and grace of the enlightened ones is infinite. To open ourselves to grace, just as in Christianity and other religions, we need to open to it with faith. If you don't have faith, follow carefully the tenfold law by engaging in virtue and avoiding non-virtue and you will still come out all right.

We have now covered the First Point of the Seven-Point Mind-Training: "First, train in the preliminaries." The preliminaries are four discursive meditations upon the preciousness of a human life of leisure and opportunity; death and impermanence; suffering; and karma. The preliminaries accelerate disillusionment with false dharmas so that we don't have to learn their lessons by long hard experience. At whatever age you start, ten years or eighty, you can get on the fast track to spiritual awakening if you realize at the outset what doesn't work.

Disillusionment with the mundane pursuits of happiness is not enough, nor is fathoming the depth of suffering or the variety of evil in the world. Knowledge of these might make you a good existential philosopher, but it won't give you the inspiration to devote yourself to spiritual practice. Theoretical understanding comes from reading, hearing lectures, conversing, thinking. But theoretical understanding is like a recipe in a cookbook, and a recipe is not the same as a meal. It is only from practicing Dharma that sustained inspiration for spiritual practice is derived. The practice itself nourishes you with a sense of happiness and well-being. Suffering is diminished. The benefits of Dharma are tested by Dharma practice itself.

The Second Point:
Cultivating Ultimate and Relative Bodhichitta

The Seven-Point Mind-Training is a quintessential guide to enlightenment, which is defined in the Second Point as "cultivating ultimate and relative bodhichitta." The Sanskrit word *bodhi* means *awakening*, and one who is awake is called a *buddha*. *Chitta* means *mind*, *heart*, and *spirit*, so I translate *bodhichitta* as *a spirit of awakening*. With ultimate bodhichitta we probe the nature of reality to realize its ultimate nature. Relative bodhichitta is the altruistic aspiration to realize perfect spiritual awakening for the sake of all sentient beings.

The cultivation of relative bodhichitta is like a mountain climber skillfully throwing a grappling hook up to a ledge to which he is climbing. The climber, confident in his hook, puts all his weight on the line, and starts the upward ascent. A skillfully placed grappling hook is a climber's connection with his ultimate destination. Bodhichitta is the grappling hook for the attainment of enlightenment. Bodhichitta is also the basis of continuity of practice. If you die suddenly or become so ill that your capacity for practice steeply declines, bodhichitta—the aspiration for perfect awakening in order to be of service to others—will provide continuity over the lapses in practice and continue to draw you like a magnet toward enlightenment from one lifetime to the next.

After solid grounding in the discursive meditations of the preliminaries, the Second Point of the Seven-Point Mind-Training moves directly to enlightenment itself, the cultivation and integration of ultimate and relative bodhichitta. The Second Point begins the training in formal daily meditation to integrate Dharma into active daily life.

In traditional Buddhist practice, one begins every session by taking refuge, entrusting oneself to the "three jewels": those who have achieved perfect spiritual awakening, Dharma as the path to such awakening, and the spiritual community that is committed to enlightenment. Upon the foundation of refuge, bodhichitta, the highest motivation, is cultivated with the heartfelt prayer: "May my practice be of benefit for the spiritual awakening of all sentient beings." This prayer nurtures our highest possible motivation, enlightenment for the welfare of others.

Once you have achieved stability, reveal the mystery.

The Second Point moves directly to the contemplative investigation of the nature of reality and consciousness itself. The brief mnemonic of the text encapsulates some of the deepest insight practices in Tibetan Buddhism. The insight practices taught here probe the nature of consciousness and its relation to reality, which is the mystery to be revealed. The stability referred to is meditative stability, mental balance, the prerequisite to the contemplative investigation of the ultimate nature of mind and reality. The mind is stabilized and refined into an instrument of investigation, which is the foundation for the cultivation of wisdom and compassion. This is the quintessential method for revealing the mystery.

The hand gesture, or *mudra*, commonly used in the meditative posture symbolizes the goal of the Second Point, the union of ultimate and relative bodhichitta: the right hand, symbolizing compassion, rests on the left hand, which symbolizes wisdom. The touching of the two thumbs symbolizes the union of wisdom and compassion, both the path and the goal of Buddhist practice.

Achieving stability is central to the Second Point of the Mind-Training and has two interrelated aspects. One aspect of stability is faith, or confidence, which is a theme shared by all religious traditions. The other aspect is meditative stabilization, a practice highly developed in the Buddhist tradition.

Faith

In our modern, highly secular world, we are not only overwhelmed with information, but we are cast into an ocean of conflicting religious, philosophical, and scientific claims about the nature of the universe and human existence. No human society in recorded history has ever been presented with such a diversity of views, many of them presented as if with great authority. Now in the midst of this cacophony of voices, we are presented with the teachings of the Buddha and later teachers who have followed the path he revealed. When we first encounter the Buddha indirectly through his teachings, we meet with a stranger from a faraway time and a faraway place. It doesn't get much stranger than that. And when we first encounter Buddhist teachings, many of them certainly do seem strange, for they fly in the face of many views held by our society at large.

The Buddha himself as well as contemporary authentic Buddhist teachers do not present themselves as unquestionable authorities on the nature of reality, nor as masters who instruct us infallibly on how to lead our lives. These teachers offer themselves to us above all as friends, specifically as spiritual friends, and as guides to lead us on an experiential journey in the pursuit of knowledge and personal transformation. But when we first meet them, they are strangers, and it is perfectly appropriate to respond to their teachings with agnosticism and skepticism. After all, when assuming a stance of agnosticism, we are quite realistically acknowledging that we don't know—the first step toward wisdom! And by taking a position of skepticism, we are in effect saying, "I doubt that you know either." Considering the wide range of authoritative claims being made today about everything from the nature of consciousness to UFOs, in many cases such skepticism has to be well founded.

But if we want to know, if we want to make genuine discoveries about matters that are of life-and-death importance to us, we have to move beyond agnosticism. If we are totally convinced that no one else has discovered what we want to know, then we have no one to rely but ourselves. But what are our grounds for being so certain that no one else knows about what we are after? If we are to be skeptical, surely we should start by being skeptical about how much we know about how much everyone else knows! If I'm really agnostic, I have to start with the premise that I don't know whether you might have made important discoveries that I have not. Likewise, just because our Western civilization is ignorant in some respects, it would be silly to assume that no other civilization has made important discoveries where we have not.

When it comes to knowledge, Western civilization has made enormous strides, especially since the Scientific Revolution. We can take great pride and satisfaction in our many discoveries concerning the world around us. But one domain of reality in which we still remain scientifically in the dark is the realm of consciousness. It's just not science's strong point. However, precisely where science is at its weakest, the Buddhist tradition makes its strongest and most astonishing truth-claims. The only way we know of the existence of consciousness is by means of our first-person experience, and the Buddhist tradition has devised many ingenious methods for enhancing and refining this mode of perception so that we can probe more deeply into the nature, origins, and potentials of consciousness. In any early account of the Buddha's life and teachings, it is obvious that he claimed to have made bold discoveries based on his own meditative experience. If you read how he responded to many of the metaphysical assertions of his time, you will see that he wasn't one for simply adopting wholesale the beliefs of his contemporaries.

For example, the earliest account of his enlightenment makes it clear that his claims about the reality and significance of the continuity of individual consciousness after death were based on his own experiential knowledge.[12] In evaluating his claims, we may conclude that he was right or that he was wrong, but there is nothing to imply that he was agnostic or that he lifted these ideas from someone else. His assertions about rebirth and karma were unique in his time. One of his remarkable claims that *was* inspired initially by other contemplatives is that the scope and precision of mental perception can be enormously enhanced by training in meditative concentration. In a broader sense, he claimed that the mental afflictions that beset us—such as hostility, craving, anxiety, and delusion—are not immutable. With training they can be attenuated, and with deep training, they can be eliminated completely.

How do we know whether he knew what he was talking about? Simply put, we don't. We start out as agnostics. But if we want to find out, the only way to proceed is to put the training to the test of our own experience. Here is a time not for skepticism, but for intelligent faith. William James comments in this regard that where preferences are powerless to modify or produce things, faith is totally inappropriate, but for the class of facts that depend on personal preference, trust, or loyalty for actualization, "faith is not only licit and pertinent, but essential and indispensable. The truths cannot become true till our faith has made them so."[13] We will never progress in Buddhist practice, in education, or in any other great venture without such faith, starting with faith in our own ability to gain new knowledge and transform ourselves in meaningful ways.

When we first meet the Buddha indirectly (through his teachings) or a contemporary Buddhist teacher directly, we are meeting with a stranger. But if we cultivate the relationship, over time, we get to know the qualities of the teacher, and he or she may earn our trust. Then the teacher becomes a friend on whom we can rely for matters that are important to us, including matters that are presently beyond our ken. After getting to know a specific Buddhist teacher, if we find him untrustworthy or unhelpful, then we are free to choose another teacher. Likewise, if upon careful examination we find the teachings of a certain Buddhist tradition to be unreliable, we can check out another Buddhist tradition. And if we find the Buddhist teachings as a whole to be unsound, we are free to look elsewhere. A number of my lamas have commented after giving public teachings, "If you find these teachings to be sound and useful, by all means put them into practice. If not, keep on looking!"

At the same time, we need to apply discerning intelligence to our own way of putting the teachings to the test. Do questionable Buddhist truth-claims violate reason or compelling empirical evidence? Or do they just violate our assumptions and what the people around us think? What do we really know, and what have we picked up as untested assumptions and preconceptions from our society? This is a time for self-directed skepticism. And if we put the teachings into practice and find them ineffective, where does the inadequacy lie: in the teachings or in our own implementation of them? For example, the Buddha and many later Buddhist contemplatives claim to have achieved irreversible freedom from various mental afflictions. If we fail to do so, what have we proven? That they didn't either, or simply that we did not practice with sufficient diligence and intelligence?

On the one hand I'm inclined to say there are no easy answers to these questions. On the other hand, there is one kind of response that is relatively easy and untroubling. While we are at sea in the midst of uncertainty about the nature and potentials of our existence, we can cling to agnosticism and skepticism as we would cling desperately to an anchored buoy. This can provide us with a bit of security and an easy answer: "who knows?" Intellectually there seems to be safety here, immune to the ridicule of others. But there's also an immobility to this position. We are at sea in the midst of confusion, and there we remain.

The Buddha is like one who swims out to meet us and shows us the way to shore. He says he has been there, and many discoveries lie in wait for us on land if we will let go of the buoy of our uncertainty, our faint-heartedness, and our skepticism. Of course, there is nothing to compel us to place our trust in him or in any later Buddhist teacher. We can remain agnostic and skeptical as long as we like. But if we choose to accept the challenge of the Buddhist path of contemplative exploration, we need to let go of our insecurities and take the plunge into practice. And this requires that we accept some of the Buddha's assertions on faith as working hypotheses. The Buddhist tradition speaks of three kinds of faith, and this is the first kind: the faith of belief.

How can we believe Buddhist truth-claims when there are so many diverse claims attributed to the Buddha, let alone the many points of disagreement among different Buddhist traditions? Two things need to be borne in mind here. The first is that, according to even the earliest recorded teachings of the Buddha, not all his assertions were meant as definitive truths about the nature of reality. Some of them are called "provisional truths," which are culturally imbedded and are meant more as heuristic devices to help specific individuals or communities at specific points in their spiritual development. But the Buddha and many later Buddhist contemplatives made many other truth-claims, based upon their meditative experience, that were meant to be definitive. That is, they were presented as genuine discoveries about the nature of reality, not just social constructs specific to a particular time and place.

How are we to discern which Buddhist teachings are provisional and which are definitive? Buddhist tradition states that the cultivation of that kind of discerning intelligence is a crucial element on the path to spiritual maturation. Put the teachings to the test of reason and experience, and see what you find. As for the many truth-claims across multiple Buddhist traditions over the past 2,500 years, it would be unreasonable to expect that they would all speak with one voice. Just look at the history of Western science over the past four hundred years! And even today, in any cutting-edge branch of science there are disagreements, many of them quite fundamental.[14] Once again, grappling with such diversity is a central challenge in the pursuit of knowledge. If we're not up to this challenge, we can always slide back to the stagnant comfort of agnosticism.

The faith of belief as a working hypothesis is one kind of faith that is regarded as indispensable in the Buddhist tradition. A second kind of faith entails admiration for those who have achieved high states of spiritual realization and for their teachings. Such faith is not simply a matter of belief,

but rather arises out of one's understanding and appreciation of the noble qualities of such individuals and the truths
they reveal. And a third type of faith in Buddhism is the
faith of aspiration. With the faith of aspiration, the possibility of making genuine, deep discoveries about the nature
of consciousness, its origins, and its potentials becomes
more than a matter of belief. It is more than an appreciation based on understanding. It is a fervent desire to test
the teachings oneself by engaging in the practice. Now is
the time when the extraordinary claims made by the Buddha and later Buddhist contemplatives are truly adopted
as working hypotheses to be tested by experience.

Faith is important but is no substitute for putting spiritual teachings to the test. Does practice help or not? Are
mental afflictions decreased and does genuine happiness
increase? Constant vigilance, assessment, and reassessment
are required to follow a path of spiritual awakening. What
is required is consistent probing, not settling into dogma-
tism or complacency, and continuously testing the path for
its effectiveness. Of course, we are testing not just "the path"
but our intelligence and perseverance in following it, so
we must be equally critical of our own efforts. This brings
a type of stability, or faith, that is in motion, part of the
process itself.

William James addressed the issue of faith in the context
of the dogmatic and materialistic mood of late nineteenth-
century science. At the close of the nineteenth century, many
scientists felt that religious belief was antithetical to the
rational and skeptical stance of science. For example, William Clifford, one of the more prominent nineteenth-century
scientific materialists, attacked religious faith on the
grounds that "it is wrong always, everywhere, and for
everyone, to believe anything upon insufficient evidence."[15]
Many scientists considered religion to be a failure of

intellectual integrity, and faith to be a path of least resistance for those unable to handle the brute facts of science. Some scientists today express the same sentiment, claiming that religious people hold onto their beliefs because of an unfortunate genetic predisposition.

What such materialists ignore, however, is that scientists and religious people alike, without exception, place their faith in some belief system which transcends the scope of their present knowledge. As William James pointed out, whether in scientific research or in daily life,

> We often *cannot* wait but must act, somehow; so we act on the most *probable* hypothesis, trusting that the event may prove us wise. Moreover, not to act on one belief is often equivalent to acting as if the opposite belief were true, so inaction would not always be as 'passive' as the intellectualists assume.[16]

Faith, he asserted, is essential, but as a *practical*, not a *dogmatic*, attitude, and it must go with toleration of other faiths, with the search for the most probable, and with the full consciousness of responsibilities and risks. Specifically, James defended one's right to believe ahead of the evidence only in those cases where (1) much is at stake, (2) the evidence at hand does not settle the case, and (3) one cannot wait for more evidence, either because no amount of evidence can settle the case, or because waiting itself is to decide not to believe.

For many things studied by science, personal beliefs are virtually irrelevant. Whether or not a scientist believes in the existence of intelligent life in other solar systems will have a negligible effect on the data she collects from the Hubbell telescope. In other domains of reality, faith or intuition will significantly influence the reality that is being addressed: parenting, teaching, and almost any domain in which we engage with people. There is an enormous range of experience in which faith and intuition influence the reality about which we have faith.

What about personal reality? Do you have faith that the mental afflictions that cause suffering are genetically determined or do you believe that your mind is malleable and these afflictions can be alleviated? Do you believe that wisdom, compassion, virtue, can be cultivated, or do you believe that the brain's physiology fixes an upper limit on these virtues? Our faith concerning the human potential for wisdom and compassion has an enormous impact on how we lead our lives. Even a small positive intuition that happiness and well-being actually could arise from our hearts and nurture us can have a tremendous influence on life. Alternately, if you have faith that all happiness comes from the outside, this faith will also profoundly influence the choices you make in life.

William James agreed with most scientists that there are things about which we should not have faith. But there are other domains of life in which faith or lack of faith will have an enormous impact. If we have no faith that we can develop insight or develop deeper compassion, it's not likely that we will. In this way, our beliefs often act as self-fulfilling prophesies. We can have faith in our own potential, or we can remain skeptical and agnostic. Some people are skeptical of Buddhist truth-claims because they violate the beliefs of their religion. Others are skeptical of the truth-claims of all spiritual traditions because they violate the beliefs of scientific materialism. And yet others are skeptical of all truth-claims, be they scientific or spiritual, because they violate the beliefs of postmodernism. In Christianity references are often made to "believers" and "non-believers," with Christians being the former and everyone else being counted as the latter. But in reality we are all believers! It is a just a question of *what* we believe.

Meditative quiescence

Faith brings one type of stability. The second type of stability is meditative quiescence, which is the primary meaning of "stability" in the aphorism: "Once you have achieved stability, reveal the mystery." Once the mind is stabilized and finely tuned, the mysterious nature of phenomena, both the objective world and the mind, can be investigated and revealed.[17]

It is remarkable that training the attention, a prerequisite for spiritual maturation in Buddhism, is virtually neglected in the modern West. The West has very noble religious, scientific, and philosophical traditions, but one element that has been extraordinarily absent for at least a thousand years is a well-developed, systematic means of training the attention.

If the instrument used in probing reality is mechanical, a telescope for example, it needs to be in excellent working condition. Similarly, if the mind itself is to be the tool for probing reality, the mind should be in excellent working order. This is what is meant by "stability." Buddhists consider the mind to be in good working order when the mind is balanced and attention is refined.

Techniques for developing the mind's stability have been created and tested in the Buddhist tradition for 2500 years. These techniques address the basic problem of our minds, lack of balance. The Sanskrit word *klesha*, meaning "mental affliction," has the connotation of the mind being twisted or distorted. What the Buddhist tradition is telling us, in plain English, is that our minds are normally screwed up! And it's because our minds are screwed up that we experience so much distress in our day-to-day lives. We get wound up about things we are attached to, things we want and are not getting, and things we fear losing. We get twisted about things we don't like, events we didn't want to happen, and about not getting things we do want. The tendency of the mind to become unbalanced and warped is due to such mental afflictions as attachment, anger, and delusion.

The marvelous scientific technology developed in the West over the last four hundred years doesn't help much in exploring the mind directly, in discovering the inner causes of well-being and suffering, or discovering the essential nature of consciousness itself. The only instrument available for probing the nature of consciousness directly is the mind itself. But as we quickly discover from experience in meditation, our minds are distractible, they get fuzzy, and they fade out. The Second Point of the Mind-Training tells us to refine the mind into a reliable tool by training in stability and vividness, then use the mind to reveal the mystery—the ultimate nature of objective phenomena and mind itself.

Training the attention has two aspects, mindfulness and introspection. Mindfulness is the ability to attend to a chosen object with continuity and without distraction. Mindfulness is different from concentration. Concentration entails condensing the attention to a narrow focus. Mindfulness is a state of stable attention that may be wide open and spacious or tightly focused, as one desires.

Introspection, sometimes called meta-cognition, observes what is happening in the mind, it discerns the quality of the attention. When you are angry, the faculty of introspection observes the anger. When practicing meditative quiescence, if distraction or excitation arises, or the mind starts to fade into laxity, introspection observes these changes. Introspection is the ability to observe the state of one's mind from moment to moment. How is the mind operating? Is it like a car with smoke billowing out from under the hood, or is it cruising smoothly? Do virtues such as compassion and generosity arise easily or do they require a lot of effort? In cultivating sustained attention, if you haven't developed your ability for introspection, then you are not going to notice when you are meditating poorly, and this means you will develop habits of lousy meditation. Habits, good and bad, are hard to break. It is possible to develop a sloppy, lethargic meditation practice with the mind running amuck. To recognize this, and be in a position to remedy it, introspection is crucial.

Compulsive ideation is the mind frothing at the mouth. Stating out loud whatever comes to mind without any social filter could lead to a visit to a mental hospital. But if you can keep the same compulsive thoughts to yourself, this is considered normal. Introspection is the key for harnessing the mind so it can be useful, rather than compulsively spewing random imagery, memories, and ideas. When with introspection you note that the mind is rambling, just draw it back, again and again. If you attend to what is happening in your mind when it is happening, you won't get carried away on the many express trains of imagery and conversation that pass through. The technique is to remain still while your mind is in action. This is very different from the mind burbling on and you burbling along with it. If you notice your meditation fading, from laxity to lethargy to sluggishness to drowsiness, then arouse yourself, even take a break to go out and splash cold water in your face.

Introspection, discerning how the mind is functioning from moment to moment, is crucial in meditation. It is also very important for mental health. In the Tibetan Buddhist approach, the relationship between spiritual awakening and mental health is seamless. Sound mental health is a requirement for spiritual awakening. If you are not in good mental health, even though you may think you are taking a fast track to enlightenment by practicing very diligently, you can wind up exacerbating your own mental problems.

The importance of introspection is also recognized in the West. A friend of mine named David Galin, a psychiatrist and cognitive neuroscientist, comments: "It is more damaging for a person's integration to be out of touch with the dimensions of personal reality through loss of self-monitoring than to be out of touch with the externals through sensory loss or paralysis."[18] Dr. Galin is saying that a deficit in introspection is worse than any sensory impairment. Sensory impairment does not preclude being an integrated, mentally healthy individual, but a deficiency of self-monitoring, or introspection, does.

Astonishingly, many modern philosophers of mind claim that meta-cognition, the mind's ability to self-monitor, is impossible, it can't be done at all. However, people in the health professions recognize that not only is meta-cognition possible, it is absolutely essential for mental health. When the answer to the question, Is the mind healthy and balanced? is no, it is best to pause. Developing the skill of introspection, increasing the ability to check up on one's state of mind, is a specific goal of meditative stabilization.

William James, one of my intellectual heroes, wrote about the importance of attentional stability in education:

> The faculty of voluntarily bringing back a wandering attention over and over again is the very root of judgment, character, and will ... An education which would improve this faculty would be *the* education *par excellence*. But it is easier to define this ideal than to give practical direction for bringing it about.[19]

James explored the relationship between sustained, voluntary attention, and ethics, mental health, and genius. He wondered if there was a way to improve attention and eventually concluded that he just didn't know. However, simply raising the idea of training the attention made William James exceptional for late nineteenth-century Boston. Had William James lived in Tibet, he would have encountered techniques for training attention everywhere.

The Seven-Point Mind-Training, in agreement with contemplative traditions around the world, tells us that the attention can be trained to exceptional degrees and with remarkable results. The Second Point of the Mind-Training implies that not only can attention be stabilized, but that the potential of the human mind is so great that it can be used as an instrument for investigating the ultimate nature of reality.

More than a century ago, James reported on research indicating that it is possible to focus the attention continuously on an unchanging object for only two to three seconds,[20] and this continues to be the position of cognitive scientists today. Without further investigation of basic assumptions, one could get the impression that two to three seconds is the hard-wired upper limit of the brain's capacity for attention.

Since our experiential reality is heavily conditioned by what we attend to, as James pointed out, if we had some control over attention, we would implicitly have some control over our experienced reality. The skill of directing and sustaining attention is more than a marvelous ability; it is the cornerstone of understanding and choosing the reality we wish to experience. The focus of the Second Point of the Mind-Training, once again, is training in stability in order to "reveal the mystery" of the ultimate nature of reality, our own and that of other phenomena.

Buddhism offers many methods of training attentional stability that can be categorized into two basic approaches: control and release. The control approach entails being able to focus and sustain attention on a chosen object at will. The goal of the control model is to become master of one's mind. A Tibetan metaphor for the untrained mind is an elephant in rut, rampaging through experience, driven by its own afflictions and causing havoc. In the control model, the out-of-control elephant of the mind is gradually brought to heel. The criterion for success in the control model of training the attention is straightforward. To assess stability of attention, observe whether the chosen object is held in the attention or not. To assess vividness of attention, observe whether the object is clear or not.

The second approach to meditative stabilization is the release model. Let's take the analogy of a polluted river. The previous model of control is like taking active steps to purify the water in the river by filtration and so on. On the other hand, it is known that even if a river is dead due to excessive, prolonged pollution, if one just stops pouring in more pollutants, the purifying elements in the river itself will begin to reassert themselves. Over time, by releasing the river from continued pollution, it purifies itself. The release model when applied to the mind-stream is similar. Instead of applying specific antidotes to all the toxins in the mind, one simply tries to stop polluting one's mind-stream with grasping onto afflictive thoughts and emotions. This can be done quite simply by maintaining one's awareness without distraction and without mental grasping. In this way, even when mental toxins arise, the mind does not cling to them, and they are swept away effortlessly. In the release model, there is no object upon which to focus the attention. Meditative stability in the release model utilizes awareness itself without reference to any specific object. The release model is a "field stability," maintaining awareness in the field of the mind without latching onto any object. The technical term for the release model is "settling the mind in its natural state."

The control approach to meditative stabilization is most familiar to Westerners and is most easily understood since science is largely based on a control model. The scientific revolution in the West was motivated in part by a religious belief that the mind of God was inscribed in the laws of nature. Deciphering nature's laws was a way to understand the mind of God. But there was another motivation fueling the scientific revolution—the desire to control nature. In some respects, desire for control over nature is positive. When it rains, we like to have a roof that doesn't leak; when it is cold, we like to keep warm; we like being able to prevent and control disease. Where the control model has failed in science is in its lack of balance. We have learned a great deal about the external world, learned to control it to an impressive extent, yet this ability is not balanced by a corresponding knowledge and ability to control our own minds. Without the counter-balance of control over our own minds, our tremendous technological power will remain on a trajectory toward disaster.

In Buddhism, the control model is applied first to one's own mind with a motivation to help others. A secondary concern is controlling the external world. There are many control model types of meditation in Tibetan Buddhism and here I will now lead you through one practice that is ideally suited to balancing the endemic malady of the Western mind—compulsive ideation. This training in breath awareness can be practiced for an entire meditation session as is often done in the Zen and Theravada Buddhist traditions. Or, as in the Tibetan tradition, breath awareness can be used to calm and stabilize the mind in preparation for other meditations.

The Buddha said of this practice, "Monks, this concentration through mindfulness of breathing, being cultivated and practiced, tends to the peaceful, the sublime, the sweet and happy: at once it causes every evil thought to disappear and calms the mind."[21] This remarkable claim, based upon the Buddha's own experience and corroborated by thousands of contemplatives after him, speaks volumes

about the nature of the mind. The breath itself is not a pleasurable object, nor is it a virtuous one. It is simply neutral,
like a stream of pure water uncolored by any additives. Yet
when the attention is focused on the breath, by the simple
fact of the mind abiding in a state of clear awareness, disengaged from perceptual and conceptual stimuli that arouse
either craving or aversion, a sense of sweetness and joy begins to bubble up and afflictive thoughts disappear. The
mind is indeed being controlled, but, like the polluted river
that quickly purifies itself when toxins are no longer
introduced into it, the mind quickly reasserts its intrinsic
equilibrium, joy, and serenity. This is one of the most as-
tounding and significant discoveries about the mind that
anyone has ever made, and it deserves special attention in
our society. How remarkable that happiness can be found
without pleasurable sensory and intellectual stimuli, and
that the mind can be calmed without drugs.

The Practice of Mindfulness of Breathing

Relaxation. When you first sit down to meditate, the mind
tends to be rambunctious. The first goal is to somewhat
subdue the mind, keeping the body as still as possible. Sit
comfortably so that your spine is erect and your abdomen
can expand freely during the in-breath. You can sit either
on a chair with your feet flat on the ground or on a cushion
on the floor. Hands can be in your lap or on your knees. Let
your breath move easily. In this meditation, your eyes are
open and your gaze is cast down resting in the space in
front of you. Let your gaze be vacant without focusing on
any visual image. Let the muscles of your face and around
the eyes relax. Sit quite erect, and let your shoulders and
arms relax.

Three calming breaths. To complete this initial relaxation
process, take three slow deep breaths. Breathe first into the

abdomen, then expand the diaphragm, and finally breathe up into the chest. Breathe out slowly and gently through the nostrils.

Counting the breaths. Breathe into the abdomen so that the abdomen expands during the in-breath and contracts gently during out-breath. Focus on the sensation of the passage of air around the nostrils or upper lip. At the end of an exhalation, just before inhalation, mentally count "1." After the second exhalation, count "2" and continue counting. The counting is a cue, not a focus of attention. The attention remains on the breath and the sensation of air around the nostrils or upper lip.

An alternative technique while attending to the breath is to bring awareness into the field of the body as a whole. This field includes the tactile sensations of the entire body, where you feel your buttocks against the chair or the ground, your feet, legs, thighs, torso, shoulders, neck, and head. Bring your awareness into the field of tactile sensations, and briefly at the end of the first exhalation and just before you inhale, count "1" mentally. During the entire course of the inhalation and exhalation, simply be present, resting your awareness in your body and on the sensation of breath.

Introspection. Add introspection to breath awareness. Introspection is an intermittent, inwardly directed cross-current during mindfulness, which is maintained as constantly as possible. See if you can discern from moment to moment what is going on in your mind: what is the quality of attention? Other than mindfulness of the breath, what is going on?

Remain relaxed, and in this way count the breaths 1 to 21. If you don't make it to 21 with continuity, start again at 1.

Stabilizing the attention by focusing on the breath is an example of the control model meditation practice. The attention is engaged by holding onto an object, and when that object is lost, the attention must be redirected again, over and over. The control model of training the mind is practiced widely in the Hindu, Buddhist, and Taoist traditions.

Stabilizing the attention using a mental image. In Tibetan Buddhist practice, breath awareness is frequently used in preparation for other ways of stabilizing the mind. Tibetan Buddhists often train the attention by creating a mental image and attending to it with continuity and clarity. To practice this technique, also a control model, first become familiar with your chosen image by concentrating on a physical representation of that image. Then mentally recreate the image and attend to it.

A metaphor for the mind when you first try to stabilize the attention is a bucking bronco—climb on and two to three seconds later you are thrown off. Focus again and get thrown again. With persistence, continuity develops. The wild stallion can be trained.

When you first try stabilizing the attention, it seems that mental agitation is worse than before you made any effort at all. But the mind was always scattered. You were just not aware of it. If you acknowledge that one of the goals of meditating is to witness the condition of the mind and re-alize that stability develops gradually, you will not be disappointed.

The control model, fastening your mind onto a chosen object, a mental image, or your breath, has been practiced in the Buddhist tradition for more than 2500 years. Many people using this technique have been monks and nuns. When you live as a monk, as I did for fourteen years, espe-cially in retreat, you can actually control your mind to a considerable extent. During a solitary retreat, you have a lot of control over your environment. You know exactly how much rice you have left. Apart from the rats, nobody takes your food. Living in a monastery, the control model also can work well. Mastery of the control model is a matter of technique and practice.

A common aphorism in the cloistered environment is: "Noise is a thorn to the meditator." Gen Lamrimpa, a highly accomplished Tibetan meditator, once told me that if he heard a jarring sound while in deep *samadhi*, like cans banging, the first time it happened it would shock him but he could settle back again. But another loud noise would shatter his meditation. He said that when his meditation was shattered by noise, he would diffuse his awareness and start all over again. The cumulative wisdom of centuries of cloistered contemplative practice is that noise disrupts meditation.[22]

The cloistered environment stands in stark contrast to the uncontrolled environment of everyday active life in the modern world. When I was a graduate student living in a family housing unit at Stanford University, I meditated early in the morning. At about 7:00 outside our window, a group of little girls would begin shrieking and driving their plastic tractors and tricycles across the bricks. I was meditating and these girls were disturbing my peace. I got to feeling pretty sorry for myself so I phoned my lama, Gyatrul Rinpoche, and asked for advice. He gave me a one-liner, "Just view it." This was not just Rinpoche's way of telling me to quit whining, but a reminder of the more encompassing teaching to embrace obstacles in practice. And carry on. We can't always control our environment, but we can embrace it, the good, the bad, and the loud, and integrate it into Dharma practice.

Release Model

The main practice of the release model is called "settling the mind in its natural state."[23] "Natural state," note carefully, does *not* refer to the mind's customary state. There is nothing natural about our ordinary state of mind. The typical state of the mind is distracted, carried away by one thought after another. In this state, when the mind focuses, it is grasping, identified with thoughts, memories, hopes, fears, and emotions. This usual state of our mind is like roaming the six realms of samsara, from anguish to bliss and everything in between. The practice of "settling the mind in its natural state" is a very simple and direct practice to begin to break free from the bondage of this compulsive cycle.

The quintessence of the release model for training the attention is to let awareness come to rest without distraction and without grasping. "Without distraction" means not being carried away by whatever drifts through the space of the mind. "Without grasping" means not identifying with or mentally grasping onto any of the events or emotions that come along. Let events arise, play themselves out, and vanish without intervention.

The release model is quite different from the control model that fixes mindfulness with continuity on an object, the breath, or a mental image. In the control model, mindfulness is like a rope that is tied to an object. In the release model of "settling the mind in its natural state," the rope is released and mindfulness settles into the space of mental events. The practice of mindfulness of breathing releases the mind from attractive and unattractive perceptual and conceptual stimuli that arouse craving and aversion; and in so doing, the mind already begins to heal naturally. But in that practice, there is still grasping onto an object, so in that technique, practiced as a means of cultivating quiescence, delusion is not counteracted. In this practice of "settling the mind in its natural state," one releases grasping of all kinds, onto neutral sensations as well as onto negative and positive thoughts and emotions. The self-healing of the mind goes deeper. In releasing all such dualistic fixation on mental and sensory objects, primordial awareness begins to shine through the veils of obscuration with greater and greater brilliance.

To practice settling the mind in its natural state, sit with your eyes open, your gaze resting in the space in front of you, without being focused on any object, and draw your attention into the field of the mind. The gaze is important. Disengage the attention from external objects and pay attention to your mind. Shapes and colors arise in the field of vision, sounds in the field of hearing, and there is also a field of experience that is accessible only to the mind— thoughts, imagery, feelings, memories, and imagination. Let your awareness come to rest within its own domain, within the field of the mind, without extending itself out to the various sense fields. See if you can draw your awareness into the field in which these mental events emerge, play themselves out, and vanish. Let your body be as still as a mountain and let your awareness be as open and friction-free as space. Let the breath be natural and unforced.

Bring your awareness into the field of the mind and attend closely. Allow the natural limpidity and luminosity of your own awareness to emerge, shining a bright light in the space of your own mind. Let your awareness hover right in the immediacy of the present, without slipping into thoughts concerning the past or speculation about the future. For all manner of mental events that arise, including emotions that we so easily identify with, see if you can let your awareness remain at rest, non-interactive, and non-judgmental, keeping awareness in a state of stillness like empty space. Observe whatever arises. Observe the nature of each of the phenomena—emotions, imagery, memories, thoughts—without grasping onto their referents. Attend fully to the very nature of the mental phenomena without giving any effort to creating, sustaining, or stopping these events. Let them be, arising, playing themselves out, and dissolving of their own accord. See if you can perceive the origin, duration, and mode of disappearance of mental events without conceptual elaboration. The crucial point is to perceive the mental events without grasping or identifying with them any more than space identifies with the birds and insects that fly through it. Let your awareness be completely at rest even when your mind is in motion.

The pragmatic benefits of developing attention, cultivating the ability to direct attention at will and focus on what is constructive and helpful, are easily appreciated. A few years ago, I heard a woman diagnosed with metastatic breast cancer speak about the devastating effect she experienced upon reading about her prognosis in a magazine. She said she couldn't get the statistics out of her mind. All hope she had of overcoming her disease by positive thinking, diet, and behavior had vanished. This is a classic and tragic example of being tortured by one's own mind. Her final comment was, "I wish I knew how to meditate," and my immediate, silent response was, "I wish you had started earlier." A Buddhist aphorism is, "Your mind can be your greatest friend or your greatest enemy." Unfortunately, in her case, it was an enemy.

I'll use an analogy to compare the release model of settling the mind in its natural state to the control model of meditation. If seismologists could figure out a way to release tectonic tension through a lot of little earthquakes and thus prevent a large sudden one, we would all be grateful. That would be good control. The control model in science has proved beneficial for controlling certain natural disasters, epidemics for example. Descartes expressed this model for science when he predicted that by knowing the forces and the actions of material bodies, we could "make ourselves the masters and possessors of nature."[24] But the release model is equally valuable. Recall Henry David Thoreau's famous statement, "In wildness is the preservation of the world,"[25] and John Muir's remark, "In God's wildness lies the hope of the world—the great fresh unblighted, unredeemed wilderness."[26] Nature, powerful, majestic and beautiful, works well all by itself; don't try to fix it. The preservation of wildness is analogous to the release model. How impoverished we would become if we tried to control everything and how vulnerable we would be if we had only wildness.

Both the control and release models develop attention. The control model utilizes grasping; the release model entails letting go from the core of awareness. In the release model, thoughts, ideation, imagery, memories, are not a problem to be controlled or snuffed out. The gushing fountain of thought is not the problem. The problem is grasping. This is a more subtle practice than the control model. Is it really possible to attend to something without latching onto it? Settling the mind in its natural state requires a light touch, like a bee just barely touching the flower while it drinks its nectar. The bee does not control the flower. The great benefit of the release model is that it is an ideal practice for an actively engaged life in which there is little control over the environment.

One of the metaphors Tibetans use for the technique of practicing "without distraction and without grasping" is of an unhurried grandpa at a park watching other people's children play. The mothers hover over the kids. The grandpa watches closely but does not intervene. Not intervening while observing vigilantly is the crux of the practice. An excellent word for this quality of awareness is "limpidity." Limpidity has the dual connotation of complete transparency, like air or glass, and also luminosity or brightness. Limpidity describes a pool of water in the desert emerging from a spring in the fine sand, the bright sun shining through the water. The pool is limpid, completely transparent and luminous. Anything that appears in the water, even a speck of dust, becomes brightly illuminated. This is the defining characteristic of the natural state of awareness—it is limpid, clear and luminous and, like space itself, not the least bit sticky.

There are profound reasons for engaging in attentional practices. Buddhists regard ignorance as the root of suffering, and ignorance has two parts. One type of ignorance is failure to attend to our actual nature, the nature of our own awareness. Not attending to who we actually are is a form of ignorance. A second kind of ignorance is identifying with things that we are *not*. We mistake as "I" and "mine" things that in fact do not have a self in them, cannot be an "I" or "mine." These two errors are the essence of ignorance, the root of samsara, the source of suffering.

Buddhism offers a working hypothesis: the myriad of thoughts and emotions that arise in the mind, the entire array of mental phenomena that we habitually identify with so strongly, is not our true identity. Identifying with these phenomena is what is meant by ignorance. In the quiescence meditation practices I have described, identification is arrested and replaced by a limpid, vigilant awareness, and the habitual tendency to grasp onto "I" and "mine" is arrested.

Dismantling ignorance by overcoming the identification habit with awareness—is this all there is to spiritual practice? No, this is not enough. There is a complementary practice that I will mention briefly here and describe in more detail later. The corollary practice to attending vigilantly without identification to our own body, feelings, and mind is attending frequently and closely to the minds, bodies, feelings, and experiences of others. This is the basis of compassion. What we attend to becomes our experienced reality, and as we attend to the situations of other people, this will expand the scope of our own reality. As we start to diminish our fixation on our own concerns and attend more to other people, balance is achieved.

It is said that the awareness of a buddha is completely even, like the ocean, taking in equally the joys and sorrows of all people, friends, loved ones, relatives, and those never met. This is the meaning of a statement made by so many of the world's great spiritual teachers, "Love your enemy." It doesn't mean love the person you hate. You can't do that. Love those who hate you.

Meditative quiescence, with its two qualities, stability and vividness, is attainable. You can get there. There are many plateaus of development, but once true quiescence is achieved, the mind can be focused on a chosen topic effortlessly, without distraction, for at least four hours. Once quiescence is attained, you can create a mental image and sustain it with a clarity virtually equivalent to seeing it with your eyes. At this stage of attainment, the attention remains in the mental realm, not seeping out into the physical senses. In the deepest stage of quiescence training, the senses go dormant while the mind continues in a high state of stable vigilance.

Buddhist descriptions of attaining meditative stabilization are very precise. The achievement of quiescence entails an experience of bliss throughout the body and mind, an extraordinary lightness, as well as a dexterity of the mind. When mental and physical bliss subside a bit, there is a state of clear, serene awareness. Buddhists say that the quiescent mind is attentive, aware, and in excellent working condition. From the Buddhist perspective the undisciplined mind, prone to laxity, excitation, and distraction, is dysfunctional.

The Tibetan lama Geshe Rabten, under whom I trained for years in India and Switzerland, said that before his monastic training his mind was like a stag with a great rack of antlers trying to make its way through a dense forest. He would struggle, get stuck, struggle again, one hindrance after another. Over the course of his formal twenty-four-year monastic training, he said his mind became progressively less like an entangled deer and more like a monkey gliding through the jungle from one vine to another. When this buoyancy and malleability arise, the mind is ready for anything. It slips skillfully through previous hindrances.

Tibetan contemplatives report that a finely honed mind can probe the nature of awareness directly; you recognize it. As you probe deeper, you see for yourself that this phenomenon of consciousness is not reducible, not a mere epiphenomenon of matter. Consciousness has the nature of luminosity, emptiness, and cognizance. The cumulative experiential finding of the Buddhist contemplative tradition is that consciousness is a fundamental constituent of reality that maintains its own unbroken continuum.

Achieving quiescence does not take the same amount of time for everyone. Tibetans describe a superior, middling, and inferior ability for quiescence. A person of superior abilities, after becoming well-grounded in the preliminaries, might require three months of intensive effort under skillful guidance. For people of middling abilities, six months is average. For people of inferior abilities, about one year of intensive effort is necessary. If quiescence isn't achieved in one year, Buddhist contemplatives recommend returning to the preliminary practices, with a special emphasis on the cultivation of compassion.

The achievement of attentional stability has a parallel in the evolution of Western science. The breakthroughs in science in the seventeenth century were possible only in dependence upon developments in technology. Using a telescope that had been invented in the early seventeenth century, Galileo discovered spots on the sun, craters on the moon, and moons orbiting Jupiter (contradicting the Aristotelian cosmology of his day that the sun had no flaws, the moon had no pits, and no celestial bodies had moons). Relying on the astronomical data of Tycho Brahe, a Danish astronomer who developed technology to precisely measure the movements of the planets, Kepler was able to discover that the planets travel in elliptical orbits, not perfect circles as Aristotle and Europeans after him had believed for centuries.

In astronomy, as in other sciences, breakthroughs are often the result of the refinement of tools of observation and measurement. The Seven-Point Mind-Training states that the basic tool of discovery is our own mind, finely honed by training in attentional stability. The discovery to be made by our minds, the "mystery revealed," is the essential nature of awareness itself. The mystery remains a mystery only as long as it is veiled, obscured by ignorance.

The same mystery addressed by the Mind-Training receives a very different approach by modern science, which views consciousness simply as an epiphenomenon of matter. The materialism of science leads to the assumption that mental states are by-products of the brain, and therefore knowledge of neurophysiology should lead to understanding feelings, experiences, subjective states, and consciousness itself. What scientists investigate are correlates between brain and mind functions, but this knowledge should not be equated with understanding consciousness itself. Upon careful examination, it doesn't even shed any light on the nature of the actual phenomenon of consciousness. While it is commonly assumed that these brain correlates produce their corresponding consciousness states, this conclusion is not demanded by the empirical scientific data. On the contrary, as William James pointed out more than a century ago, evidence for mind/brain correlations may indeed imply that the brain produces mental events, or that it has the lesser role of simply releasing or permitting them, or that it merely transmits them, as light hits a prism, thereby transmitting a spectrum of colors. But with their bias toward materialism, most cognitive scientists simply assume that the first hypothesis is correct, despite the lack of compelling scientific evidence.

The centuries-long Buddhist tradition of investigating the nature of consciousness is summed up in a statement from *The Cloud of Jewels Sutra:*

> All phenomena are preceded by the mind. When the mind is comprehended, all phenomena are comprehended.... By bringing the mind under control, all things are brought under control.[27]

These words present us with a challenge, not a dogma. The extraordinary hypothesis of Buddhism is that the refined mind can fathom the nature of reality and consciousness itself, with the most extraordinary results.

Regard all events as if they were dreams.

As we engage with this practice, we move beyond meditative quiescence to contemplative insight into the nature of our experienced world. What the Mind-Training refers to with the simple mnemonic, "Regard all events as if they were dreams," shakes the very foundations of our existence. Niels Bohr's comment about quantum mechanics—"Those who are not shocked when they first come across quantum theory cannot possibly have understood it."[28]—is equally true of these teachings. For example, after Geshe Rabten completed his twenty-four years of formal monastic training, he spent years in solitary meditative retreat in the mountains above Dharamsala. Much of this time he spent meditating on the true nature of the phenomenal world, and when I asked him about his experiences, he replied, "If I should tell others about what I have seen, they would think I am crazy!" Those who study the Buddhist theory concerning the dreamlike nature of reality and are not shocked cannot possibly have understood it.

Buddhist practices for the cultivation of contemplative insight into the nature of reality are designed to overcome our fundamental ignorance about the nature of our own identities and reality as a whole. And this insight, when unified with the stability and vividness of meditative quiescence, is said to bring one to nirvana, an irreversible state of freedom from all mental afflictions and their resultant suffering. Some Western Buddhists, however, have recently called this claim into question, stating that Buddhist accounts of irreversible spiritual awakening, or enlightenment, are misleading.[29] This conclusion is based on the personal experiences of a number of Western meditation teachers who have dedicated as much as forty years to their spiritual practice. Those interviewed concurred that their realizations and awakenings do not last. They pass, and those meditators have found that they invariably return to the world of change, and this brings with it the wounds of pain.

As long as we are embodied, we are certainly immersed in a world in which all conditioned phenomena are in a state of flux. This includes, of course, our own bodies and minds. But the important question is: does our engagement with the ever-changing world necessarily trigger our own mental afflictions of attachment, anger, and delusion? The Buddhist assertion is that these mental toxins are responsible for all the mental suffering and fear we experience, and when the mind is purified of these afflictions, all mental distress vanishes and even physical pain is experienced in such a way that the mind remains tranquil. So when the Buddhist assertion of the possibility of nirvana is refuted, what exactly is being called into question? Are mental afflictions, as understood in Buddhism, not really at the root of suffering? Or if they are, is there no possibility of being forever healed from these afflictions? In other words, if we accept the premise that we suffer because our minds are distorted by these afflictions, are we intrinsically screwed up, or only habitually screwed up?

The observation that many senior Western Buddhist meditators have not achieved any lasting state of liberation should lead us to question not only the authenticity of traditional accounts of achieving nirvana, but also the nature of our own spiritual practice. I have heard many Western Buddhists' reports of their deep insights into the nature of reality through the practice of insight meditation, but I have never heard any of them report that they have accomplished quiescence as it is described in authoritative Indian Buddhist treatises on this practice. On the other hand, I have heard one Tibetan contemplative, Lobsang Tenzin, give a personal account of his fifteen years of intensive, continuous meditation in solitude, resulting in what he called "a state of immutable bliss that was constant, carrying through both during and between his formal meditation sessions." I have never heard of any Western Buddhist who has dedicated him- or herself to such awesome practice under such adverse circumstances. But if, through diligent practice, *one* person can achieve a state of permanent liberation, this holds out the possibility for others who have not yet risen to that level of insight.

The Buddha himself made it very clear that the achievement of nirvana depends upon the union of both quiescence and insight, for without the stabilizing influence of quiescence, all insights will be fleeting, and their transformative and liberating effects will not last.[30] However, a recent school of Buddhist meditation, originating in Burma, has proposed that achievement of the high degree of attentional stability of genuine quiescence, or meditative stabilization, is not necessary for the realization of nirvana. It is enough, they claim, to realize the ultimate nature of reality, or nirvana, with the support of mere "momentary stabilization." Many Western Buddhists have followed this advice, and even the most senior of them, it seems, have not achieved any lasting state of liberation. The very notion that a momentary glimpse of the actual nature of reality, or even many of them, should be enough to permanently overcome the fundamental affliction of delusion seems dubious. As an analogy, if a person is suffering from acute paranoia, a mere glimpse of the groundlessness of his fear will not likely heal him forever. Why then should anyone expect that a mere glimpse into the true nature of reality as a whole will forever overcome our delusions, which are far more deeply rooted than any psychosis?

If we are to exercise healthy skepticism, we should be just as skeptical of our own spiritual understanding and practice as we are of the reports of enlightenment of those who have preceded us. Otherwise, instead of ascending to the heights of Buddhist contemplative realization, we are prone to slip back to the commonplace Freudian assumptions that humans are inevitably subject to suffering due to "the superior power of nature, the feebleness of our own bodies and the inadequacy of the regulations which adjust the mutual relationships of human beings in the family, the state and society."[31] The Buddha claimed to have made an extraordinary discovery, and his findings have purportedly been corroborated by many later generations of Asian contemplatives.

If we are to make this discovery for ourselves, let us bear in mind the observation of the historian Daniel J. Boorstin, who refers to "the illusions of knowledge" as the principal obstacles to discovery. The great discoverers of the past, he declares, "had to battle against the current 'facts' and dogmas of the learned."[32] The Buddha encouraged his followers to be skeptical of his teachings and test them both rationally and experientially. The dogma of our society is that to be human is to be intrinsically subject to mental affliction and suffering. Maybe the time has come to wage a sustained battle against that dogma.

If all we are after is a temporary alleviation of our mental afflictions and the resultant suffering, there are a great number of avenues we can pursue. And if Buddhist meditation is presented as just one more way to achieve a transient easing of our distress, with no hope of a complete and irreversible cure from all mental afflictions, then it is reduced to the status of one more matrix of psychological techniques. But this was not what the Buddha himself was pursuing in his quest for enlightenment, and it is not what he claimed to offer to the world.

Within Buddhism, there are various ways to set out on the path of contemplative insight. In this Seven-Point Mind-Training, we are first encouraged to "regard all events as if they were dreams." To explain this aphorism, I will draw from the teachings of the Dzogchen (Great Perfection) and Mahamudra (Great Seal) contemplative traditions of Tibetan Buddhism. When you first encounter such teachings, if you don't sense that they challenge the foundations of your worldview, or that there never was any foundation at all, then you are not getting it. The Seven-Point Mind-Training makes very strong statements about the nature of reality. If these statements are wrong, they are enormous mistakes. If they are correct, they are profound solutions.

When, in an earlier story I told about Gyatrul Rinpoche, a lama in the Dzogchen tradition, and his advice to me to "just view it," this was a loaded statement. The meaning is "apply your understanding of Dzogchen, the Great Perfection, to all that you experience." We all embrace a view of reality, sometimes without ever consciously choosing it. A common view of Western culture is that reality is the world just as it appears to us. If I look at Jack sitting ten feet away from me, his body looks like a big chunk of matter existing totally separate from me. I am here and he is there and there is a vacuity between us. The environment I experience also seems to be totally out there and independent of anything I think, say, or perceive. From what I can tell from appearances, if I were to drop dead, that reality would not change at all.

Appearances suggest that perceived phenomena exist independently of perceptions. Most of us, by default, live by this philosophic view. Appearances inform us that subject and object are separate and therefore, when people treat us badly, we target them as radically separate from ourselves and retaliate.

From the history of scientific discovery, we might anticipate that there are deeper realities than appearances would lead us to believe. Some of the views of twentieth-century quantum mechanics run profoundly counter to many of the assumptions of classical physics. The Seven-Point Mind-Training likewise presents a working hypothesis radically counter to ordinary subject-object experience. The injunction to "regard all events as if they were dreams" encourages us not to view things as if they were real, as if they existed objectively from their own side. We assume that reality neatly corresponds exactly to how it appears. The Mind-Training points to something deeper.

The Buddhist criterion for reality is that any hypothesized entity must be verified by critical analysis or careful observation. If probing into the nature of something causes it to disappear, this implies it wasn't real in the first place. There are ten classic Buddhist metaphors for the nature of phenomena. One metaphor is a mirage. A desert road that looks wet, if investigated, will be found to be dry. A mirage suggests a reality that isn't there. A second metaphor is a rainbow. A rainbow is not really an illusion, but the more closely you inspect it, the more it fades from sight. Although it appears to exist objectively, out there in the sky, upon careful examination we find this isn't so.

What about reality as a whole? Will reality disappear as we investigate deeper and deeper? The easy answer is of course not. I look at Jack, who seems to be here. When I shake him by the shoulder, he tells me to stop. Is that adequate proof that Jack is here?

Try the same proof in a dream. If I were dreaming and said, "Jack, are you really there?" he could say, "Yes." I could do a reality check by touching his shoulder, and I would feel something firm. But this is a dream and feeling something tangible in a dream doesn't mean that there is matter there. In a dream, Jack could appear, I could even touch him on the shoulder, but he would not exist independently from my dream.

Let's move from Buddhist analysis to philosophical realism. Realism assumes that there is a real, physical world out there, atoms, planets, and stars, from quarks to super clusters of galaxies. Almost all scientists until the end of the nineteenth century accepted the assumption that the phenomena known to science are "out there, existing independently in the objective world." There were a few doubters, but scientific realism, the belief in reality being "out there" waiting to be discovered, was the working assumption of science. Realism has theological underpinnings: in the beginning, God created the world and human beings were created on the sixth day to discover what God

had already made. The theological premise of scientific realism is that the world is out there waiting to be discovered.

Then came quantum mechanics in the twentieth century.
Scientists, working under the reductionist premise that to
understand something it is necessary to reduce it to its basic components, started probing into what they thought
would be the ultimate nuggets of physical reality, the final
indestructible ball bearings of the Reality Machine, what is
really there. Reductionism, the sensible assumption that has
propelled most of science, is not unique to the West. The
Vaibhashika school of Buddhist philosophy states that only
fundamental constituents are real and the rest of phenomena are simply subjectively biased configurations. At the
turn of the century, physicists were astonished to find that
the fundamental components of physical reality seemed to
depend on the mode of questioning and method of measurement. The fundamental constituents of reality "out
there" did not seem to exist independently of systems of
measurement. As physicist Bernard d'Espagnat recently
commented,

> It seems we are forced (by physics, not philosophy!) to acknowl-
> edge that we *cannot* know mind-independent reality as it is. In
> other words, the world described by science must be consid-
> ered as being a picture of mind-independent reality, not as it
> really is, but *as it is seen through the selective and deforming lens of
> our own sensory and mental structures.*[33]

The unexpected findings in physics undermined the
philosophical stances of scientific realism and reductionism.
Empirical results began to accumulate from the double-slit
experiment, the delayed-choice experiment, and a variety
of other experiments indicating that some of the deepest
assumptions underlying Western science up to the twentieth
century were just wrong.

Albert Einstein and Niels Bohr, adversaries on many issues in physics, made similar statements about the defining

role theory plays in science. When quantum mechanics was in its early stages of development, Einstein remarked to a young Werner Heisenberg, "on principle, it is quite wrong to try founding a theory on observable magnitudes alone. In reality, the very opposite happens. It is the theory which decides what we can observe."[34] Einstein was pointing out that it is the conceptual framework that makes data intelligible and determines what emerges into experience. Similarly, Niels Bohr wrote, "we must remember ... all new experience makes its appearance within the frame of our customary points of view and forms of perception."[35]

A more radical view of physics asserts that in order for phenomena to shift from a state of being merely possible to being tangibly real, consciousness is instrumental. Awareness of an event is the actual trigger that makes potentia transform into physical reality. This is a minority view in physics today, but a minority view held by some very brilliant people. A more conservative view is that the world consists of elementary particles that do not exist independently of measurement, and the measuring device chosen determines the kind of phenomena that emerge from a potential state to an actual state. Whether a photon is a particle or a wave is determined by what the instrument measures. Reality doesn't exist independently of the system of measurement and interpretation.

Another theory in physics concerning the relationship of subject to object states that we co-create the universe by posing questions. Specific questions are posed through specific systems of observation, measurement, and experiment. Setting up an experiment is a physical enactment of a question which evokes a reality that otherwise would not exist.

Hilary Putnam, a philosopher at Harvard, has stated a similar idea in philosophical terms. He suggests that human beings are like characters in a novel of which we are also the authors. We are writing a novel that does not exist independently of its authors. An analogous Buddhist idea is "creating karma," referring to the process of engaging conceptually and creatively with the world we experience.

There is significant common ground between Buddhist contemplative wisdom and twentieth-century empirical science. Since 1987, a series of dialogues has been in progress between Western scientists and the Dalai Lama in the Mind and Life Conferences. Niels Bohr advised his scientific peers when they encountered the implications of quantum physics, "Be prepared for a big surprise," but most of science continues rolling along in the rut of scientific materialism as if the most profound discoveries of quantum mechanics had no broader implications. The empirical discoveries that imply our interdependence with the nature of reality do not just apply to tiny particles; they affect all of reality. The implications of these discoveries, however, have been somewhat contained, like an earthquake held temporarily in check.

The nature of our interdependence with reality may seem like a head trip for people who can do the math. How do these radical statements touch experience? Physicist Nick Herbert wrote:

> The source of all quantum paradoxes appears to lie in the fact that human perceptions create a world of unique actualities— our experience is inevitably 'classical'—while quantum reality is simply not that way at all... Since physics assures us that our lives are embedded in a thoroughly quantum world, is it so obvious that our experience must remain forever classical?[36]

Research in quantum mechanics discovers a reality inconsistent with gross appearances. Physical reality appears like it's made up of tiny, hard, objective, independent granules of stuff, but physics says this isn't the case. Yet even the physicist who does the research, or a philosopher of physics who understands the implications of the research, experiences life—home, job, family—in an ordinary, non-quantum way. In experience, nothing has shifted.

Is disassociating the understanding of quantum physics from the experience of everyday life necessary? If our understanding can dive into the depths of the quantum mechanical view of the nature of reality, does our everyday experience have to be left wading around in a pre-quantum view of the world? How can experience and understanding be reconciled? Generally speaking, physicists don't seem to have much interest in integrating the insights of quantum mechanics into daily life. But integrating insight into experience is exactly what Buddhist contemplative practice is all about. Gaining insight and saturating every aspect of existence with that insight is the specialty of generations of Buddhist contemplatives. How deeply the insights of quantum physicists and those of Buddhist contemplatives actually coincide remains to be seen. It certainly deserves careful investigation.

Buddhists, like physicists, probe reality. Buddhists send an analytic probe right into the nature of experience and mind itself. Does an observed phenomenon exist purely objectively and independently of the perception of it? By penetrating analysis, it can be discovered that it does not; instead, there is a subjective component to phenomena without which phenomena don't exist at all. For example, a room appears to be totally "out there." On probing, we find that the room as we perceive it is contingent upon our visual faculties. Likewise, sounds that we hear are dependent on our ability to hear. At this point we are involved in a psychological truism. Keep on probing. There is light; photons exist. Sound waves really ripple through various media at finite speeds. A sound wave as described in physics appears to your conceptual mind but what you actually *hear* is quite different. You may have felt a shock wave from a jet breaking the sound barrier, but you have never perceived a sound wave move through the air, just as you have never seen a photon zipping along at 186,000 miles per second. Light waves and sound waves as they are theorized in physics are concepts that are created within the context of a conceptual framework.

The Middle Way philosophy of Buddhism makes this point: investigate anything—mind, matter, cosmos, space, time—probe its objectivity, as something that exists without any trace of subjective influence, neither conceptual nor perceptual, and the result will be that you find nothing. Using the stabilized mind to probe the nature of phenomena leads to the discovery that everything is interdependent. In other words, the way phenomena appear is not at all the way they actually exist.

The Mind-Training says, "Regard all events as if they were dreams." How do dreams appear? The most productive method to explore dreams is by being aware of dreaming while dreaming. Start by reflecting on how things appear in dreams. Let's take as a working hypothesis, as Buddhists do, that dreams emerge from your unique psyche and past and are not part of a big generic dream that belongs to everybody. In Buddhist theory, dreams are a flowering of mental propensities, or seeds, an idea that corresponds roughly to the Western theory of the contents of the subconscious. Suppose I dream that I am speaking before a group of people. From a waking perspective, I would say that the people in this dream don't exist independently from the dream. Yet when I am dreaming, people appear to be just as objective and separate from me as people seem during the waking state. In a dream, if somebody insults me, I get angry just as though this person exists objectively. In non-lucid dreams, demarcations between subjects and objects appear very real. When I get happy in a dream, that happiness is not significantly different from the happiness I experience in the waking state. If someone punches me in a dream, it seems very real. While there seems to be an objective environment, in a dream objects and environments actually exist in relationship to me, the dreamer. Dream and dreamer are interdependent.

In the Buddhist analysis, there is an analogy between the non-lucid dream state and our usual waking state. What we assume to be absolutely real in a dream and in the waking state is not as it appears. The Buddhist analysis of our deluded waking state goes deep into the analogy between waking and dreaming. From the perspective of the waking state, it is easy to agree that what appears real and concrete in the dream is illusory, despite the fact that from within the dream it can be proved to be "real." In my dream, I can touch Jack or ask him if he is real and he will say yes. Within the context of a dream, that is good proof. From the perspective of the waking state, I see that objects in the dream have no objective existence, but are dependent on me, the dreamer. Within a dream you can be absolutely positive you are not dreaming. The exception to the delusion of mistaking the dream-state to be real is to be aware, within the dream, that you are dreaming.

From the relative state of being awake, it is possible to reflect upon the dream-state as being a state of delusion. The Buddhists push past the state of relative wakefulness to actual wakefulness. The word "buddha" means "one who is awake." From the perspective of a buddha, the normal "awake" state is a relative dream state and, additionally, the dream is deluded. Those of us who have not yet become buddhas can begin to appreciate the relationship between dream and dreamer by practicing lucid dreaming.

The daytime practice of dream yoga is what the Mind-Training refers to as regarding all phenomena as if they were dreams. No leap of faith is required to immerse yourself in the radical and intuitively sound hypothesis that phenomena have a dreamlike quality. This hypothesis is not unique to Buddhism and is found in a number of other contemplative traditions. Working with the dream-state analogy, imagine the relative perspective of a more awakened state (a buddha-like state), and realize that right now you are dreaming. The daytime practice of dream yoga entails pondering, "In this waking state, relatively speaking, I am fast asleep. Apparent reality is a dream and all of my assumptions about absolute demarcations, subject/object, self/other are profoundly mistaken." A proficient lucid dreamer has dreams that are completely clear and, while dreaming, is aware that objects and individuals in the dream are nothing more than appearances of the mind. Absolute demarcations vanish. The environment in a dream and the persona of yourself in a dream are expressions of your own mind. The dream analogy to the ordinary waking state is a practice, not a philosophy.

The purpose of the Seven-Point Mind-Training is to provide sufficient wisdom and practice, synthesized in one teaching, to achieve spiritual awakening. Buddhists do not assume that humans are hard-wired to perceive and respond to reality in fixed ways. Instead, the Buddhist hypothesis is that the mind is malleable and what is required to change perception and response is consistent behavior.

When you wake up in the morning, note that the waking state has a dreamlike quality and reflect that, from an enlightened perspective, the waking state itself is a dream. In our dreamlike ordinary waking perspective, the distinction between subject and object is exaggerated. This means that sentient beings whom I experience as "other" are not absolutely other. "Otherness" is a convention. The sense of absolute objectivity and absolute subjectivity is part of the dream. The daytime practice of dream yoga, "regard all events as if they were dreams," is to sustain the sense that, from an awakened perspective, this relative waking state is a sleeping state.

There is also a nighttime practice of dream yoga, and some people are fortunate in having a natural knack for it. There are several techniques to develop the ability to dream lucidly. The best one for people with active minds is to settle the mind in its natural state while falling asleep. Visualization techniques tend to lead to insomnia from the effort required to maintain a visual image. Settling the mind in its natural state rests the mind in its own natural limpidity, not trying to do something, not intervening. Lying on your right side, called the lion's posture, is most effective for inducing lucid dreaming. Lying on the left side or on the back is not as effective, and the worst position is lying prone.

The optimal mental state in which to induce lucid dreaming is to maintain limpid, fully conscious awareness and observe yourself falling asleep. Dr. Stephen LaBerge, who has done extensive research into lucid dreaming, confirms what Buddhists have said for over a thousand years: it is possible to enter the dream state with complete consciousness, possible to maintain lucidity throughout the course of a dream, possible to emerge from a lucid dream back into deep sleep, and possible to maintain limpid awareness and eventually emerge into the waking state.

To begin the practice of dream yoga, start by noticing early morning dreams when sleep tends to be lighter and of higher frequency. Emerge from sleep holding the story line of a dream; then, maintaining the thread of the story, reenter the sleep-state right into a lucid dream. As you are preparing to sleep by settling the mind in the natural state, do so with the aspiration to recognize the next dream as a dream. Buddhists and lucid dream researchers agree that such intention to recognize a dream as a dream is very helpful.

The aphorism "Regard all phenomenon as if they were dreams" is a statement regarding the nature of reality. To awaken, practice yoga in the dream, both the waking dream and the sleeping dream.

We imagine that, from the perspective of a buddha, the ordinary waking state is dreamlike. There is another perspective from which this is true—the deathbed. When we know full well that we are about to die, and reflect back on our life with all its experience, joys and sorrows, anxiety, all the stuff we are attached to, life may appear as having no more substance than a dream. Whether our time is long or short, this is a profoundly authentic perspective on the nature of a life. Life is a flash of lightning in the dark of night. It is a brief time of tremendous potential. The deathbed view of life has a direct practical benefit in day-to-day relationships. Atisha, who was a monk, gave this pithy counsel to distressed married couples: Your spouse is going to be dead soon. You are going to be dead soon. Be nice to each other.

The Seven-Point Mind-Training packs the profound teachings and techniques of Buddhism into aphoristic statements. The Mind-Training is constructed of steps of insight, one after another. The lines of the Mind-Training encode practices that have tremendous practical application. The challenge is to awaken.

Examine the unborn nature of awareness.

Direct the mind right into the nature of awareness itself and examine that which is "unborn." "Unborn" awareness is primordial awareness.

As long as you are alive, you can practice breath awareness. At any time and in any circumstances, as long as you breathe, you can practice breath awareness. In the Buddhist tradition, during the gradual sequence of dying, the mind continues through a number of experiences after the breath has stopped. After breath has ceased, even though the senses have shut down, and for all practical purposes you have lost your body, you can still observe the mind. After the breath stops, you can still meditate. As the dying process progresses, eventually you lose your mind also. The "mind" you will lose is the mind that is conditioned by life, the mind filled with memories, experiences, hopes, desires, emotions, conceptual faculties of recognition, and imagination, the same mind trained in meditation.

What is left after losing breath, body, and mind is what the Buddhists call "unborn awareness," or "the clear light of death." Unborn awareness is awareness in its primordial state, unstructured by experience or by a human brain and nervous system. The primordial nature of awareness is not structured by a sense of subject versus object. Unborn awareness is also not conditioned by being a good or bad person or even by being human. For centuries, contemplatives who have maintained continuity of awareness throughout death and subsequent reincarnation have described the details of the death experience, including the nature of unborn awareness.

All of us will have the same opportunity as contemplatives to experience primordial awareness at death. We have no choice. We will lose our breath, our bodies, and our minds, and primordial awareness is what will be left. We will have an opportunity to ascertain the unobscured, unborn nature of awareness when we die; but whether we will be able to make use of this opportunity is another question. If we are offered a meal but don't know how to open our mouth, we cannot eat. Death offers us primordial awareness on a plate. Will we be prepared to take the opportunity of ascertaining it, tapping into this wellspring of wisdom, compassion, and power? Whether or not unborn awareness is ascertained during death is contingent upon whether it has been ascertained during life.

The way to ascertain unborn awareness during life is to practice.

"Examining the unborn nature of awareness" is the meditative practice of turning the attention in upon itself to observe the observer. The three meditation techniques of the control model (using an object such as the breath to develop attentional stability), the release model (settling the mind in its natural state), and examining the unborn nature of awareness (observing the observer), when practiced daily and in sequence, form a foundation for effective practice, integrating Dharma into daily life.

The practice of observing the observer delves into the unborn nature of awareness itself, dismantling the dichotomy between inside and outside. On the practical level, it is a potent antidote for a broad range of mental afflictions. When you get angry, anxious, or are craving something, when you feel jealous or conceited, practice observing the observer. This one practice drives a spike right through the heart of these afflictions, causing them to evaporate like mist.

Meditation

Sit upright, diaphragm open, chest up, shoulders nice and relaxed, breathing down into your belly. Soften all of the area of the face, especially around the eyes. Bring your awareness into the space in front of you, directing the line of your gaze along the line of your nose without focusing. Let your visual awareness hover restfully in what Tibetans call "the space in between." For a minute or two, draw your attention inwards. As soon as a thought, recollection, imagination, or any other mental event arises, be present with it and aware of it. It doesn't get away without being noticed. You detect it swiftly, without impeding it. Whatever arises in the mind, you are right there in the present, not slipping into memories or imagination but hovering right at the entrance of the mind where mental events emerge. Rest there, for a minute or two, settling the mind in its natural state.

Now move into insight practice, examining the unborn nature of awareness. This practice is from the *terma*, or treasure teaching, *Natural Liberation: Padmasambhava's Teachings on the Six Bardos*. This *terma* was discovered by Karma Lingpa in the fourteenth century in a cave on Gampo Dar Mountain in central Tibet and is attributed to the eighth-century Indian tantric master Padmasambhava. He gave this quintessential instruction:

> While steadily maintaining the gaze, place the awareness unwaveringly, steadily, clearly, nakedly and fixedly, without having anything on which to meditate, in the sphere of space. When stability increases, examine the consciousness that is stable. Then gently release and relax. Again place it steadily and steadfastly observe the consciousness of that moment. What is the nature of that mind? Let it steadfastly observe itself. Is it something clear and steady or is it an emptiness that is nothing? Is there something there to recognize? Look again and report your experience to me![37]

Padmasambhava's directions are to observe, articulate what is observed, and then return to further observation. He continues:

> Steadily place your mind in the space in front of you and let it be present there. Examine well: what is this thing of yours that you have placed here today? Look to see if the one who is placing and the mind that is being placed are one or two... If there is not more than one, is that one the mind? Observe: what is the reality of the so-called mind? ... Let the one who is pondering, What is the mind like? observe that very consciousness and search for it. Steadily observe the consciousness of the meditator, and search for it. Observe: in reality, is this so-called mind something that exists?[38]...observe whether it is an emptiness that is nothing. If you say it is an emptiness that is nothing, then how could an emptiness that is nothing know how to

> meditate? What good is it to say you cannot find it? If it is noth-
> ing at all, what is it that brings forth hatred? Is there not
> someone who thinks the mind has not been found? Look
> steadily right at that.[39]

Bring the meditation to a close.

The practice of examining the unborn nature of awareness deepens and extends formal daily practice beyond the confines of this body, these conditions, this life. The practices in the root text of the Seven-Point Mind-Training—cultivating meditative stabilization, settling the mind in its natural state and examining the unborn nature of awareness—in Atisha's time of the eleventh century were based on centuries of cumulative contemplative experience aimed at achieving enlightenment in a single lifetime. I am convinced that these practices are just as applicable to contemporary Western life as they were to other cultures in other centuries.

There is a deep, gradual shift from training the attention with breath awareness, to settling the mind in its natural state, to probing the nature of awareness itself. The Dalai Lama once was asked, "What is the point of your practice?" and answered, "I am preparing to die." This was not a morbid statement. Death is an extraordinary experience, if we prepare to take advantage of it. Awareness of the clear light of death, unborn awareness, can be sustained for hours or days, in some cases for weeks, in rare cases for months. The Mind-Training advises us to prepare for death by examining the unborn nature of awareness during life.

Buddhists are concerned with knowledge that shifts and transforms perception, not knowledge for knowledge's sake or knowledge that has no impact on life. Many people experience some of the short-term rewards of meditation such as increased balance of mind and mental clarity. Many people also notice, usually retrospectively, that the balance gained in meditation is easily lost. The practice of examining the unborn nature of awareness follows the practice of regarding all phenomena as if they were dreams and moves into insight practice aiming for the deepest reality that can be accessed. It is through such practice that one can achieve a transformation of perception in which the fruits of meditation become stable and are no longer lost.

A hard fact, repeated over and over in the Tibetan Buddhist tradition, is that insight practices are impossible to fathom thoroughly without a platform of meditative quiescence. Accomplishing meditative quiescence means overcoming mental agitation, distraction, sluggishness and laxity, and being able to effortlessly focus awareness exactly, vividly and with stability for at least four hours. From the Buddhist perspective, awareness that stable and vivid is the defining characteristic of a functional mind. A scattered and dull mind, even though it can get by, is an afflicted mind.

Meditative retreat isn't necessarily the only or best solution to the problems of practice. In 1988, I helped a highly accomplished Tibetan contemplative, Gen Lamrimpa, lead a one-year retreat for about a dozen people. Externally, everything was done right, homes were sublet, cars put up on blocks, money was saved to be off work for a year. We had a cook and we had a great place. Yet when some of the participants devoted themselves full-time to meditation, their mental afflictions just got worse. Whether in retreat or in active life, the central issue is how to live so that daily life supports rather than erodes spiritual practice, and the Seven-Point Mind-Training addresses this problem.

The First Point of the Mind-Training has already told us how, in the four preliminary practices: by attending to those aspects of reality that will inspire us to release the grasping of mundane concerns and reorient priorities toward spiritual practice. The Seven-Point Mind-Training then teaches meditative stabilization, settling the mind in its natural state, the insight practices of regarding phenomena as dreamlike and examining the unborn nature of awareness.

Primordial awareness, which is referred to as "unborn awareness" in the Mind-Training, is also referred to as the clear light nature of the mind, or *rigpa* in Tibetan. *Rigpa* is awareness that is beyond subject/object duality. Düdjom Lingpa, a great Dzogchen master who lived in the latter part of the nineteenth and early twentieth century, said it is extremely important to understand the difference between mind and unborn awareness. The difference is that mind is locked into structures, conditioned, saturated with conceptual frameworks, distinctions between subject/object, existence/non-existence, good/bad, up/down, Buddha/ordinary sentient being, samsara/nirvana, etc. Mind is not only saturated with conceptual frameworks, it reifies itself and its objects, assuming them to have their own intrinsic nature. We believe in a personal identity and when we look at another person, we believe also in his absolute identity separate from our own. The mind works in conceptual frameworks and reifies the results.

Mind, configured by conceptual frameworks, contrasts with unborn awareness. The experience of unborn awareness entails a spacious dissolution into a great expanse with no object, without obstruction and without intentionality. Unborn awareness is the effortless realization that all phenomena, the self included, lack an independent, self-sufficient nature.

The dualistic mind and unborn awareness are very different. The former is awareness that has become deluded. To penetrate the nature of mind is to see that it never was anything other than unborn awareness. To use the Tibetan metaphor, unborn awareness is like water; mind is like ice, and yet ice is nothing other than water in a different form.

The Mind-Training says "examine," not speculate, debate, or study. This aphorism of the Second Point is short and feisty. Every word has meaning. There are two approaches to this aphorism in the Tibetan tradition, both legitimate, both lead to insight, ultimate bodhichitta.

One approach is "theory before practice," which puts theory first and meditation second. In the Tibetan tradition, this means gaining a thorough conceptual framework such as Madhyamaka, Dzogchen, or some other view. Once the theoretical base is in place, you are ready for meditation. This is a good approach and after about four years you might have so much knowledge of the philosophy that you can teach it. But understanding doesn't mean you have insight.

In the "experience before theory" approach, theory arises from experience itself. For the deep questions raised in insight practice, methodology with no theory whatsoever won't work. The approach of Padmasambhava is to provide just enough theory to push deeper while maintaining experience as the leading edge. This approach is direct and ideal for people who don't have years to spend in study or in solitude.

Insight practice is similar to scientific research. Just as there is no way to understand physics or chemistry without spending time in the lab and no way to understand math without doing problems, you have to practice meditation to gain insight.

One might expect that by doing insight practice, consciousness itself will become apparent. Padmasambhava examines this assumption by asking whether the visual, auditory, and other appearances in the mind are identical with consciousness. If consciousness is not the same as these appearances, what is its nature? What actually happens in insight practice is that one just sees more appearances. But not seeing consciousness is not the same as its absence. The teaching advises us to keep probing.

Recall the two approaches of theory first versus experience first. Karma Chagmé, a seventeenth-century master of the Mahamudra and Dzogchen lineages, distinguishes between them by using the metaphor of gathering firewood. You can gather firewood by snipping off all the branches of a tree one by one, so that the tree shrivels up and dies. This long, difficult process is similar to the approach of the monk who spends twenty years studying Buddhist philosophy, eventually graduating with a massive theoretical framework, spends the next twenty years in retreat, and finally devotes the rest of his life to teaching. The second approach, experience first, heading right to the heart of practice with just enough theory, is ideal for people who can't afford the time investment required for theoretical acquisitions. The experience-first approach cuts the tree down starting at the root. This can save a lot of time.

One of the best-known aphorisms of the Buddha is, "Anything that is born dies." Anything that is created is destroyed. In Buddhist cosmology, eventually all of the billions of world systems will be incinerated, leaving not even ash behind. A human life, all relationships, anything that is produced will come undone. Yet, nirvana, liberation, is called the "deathless state" and can be attained in life. Human beings are born and they die. Mind arises and passes, yet in the midst of its ongoing flux there is unborn awareness. That which is unborn does not die. To ascertain and dwell in the unborn nature of awareness is to achieve the deathless state. This can be done during life. What is required is faith enough to practice. Becoming familiar with the unborn nature of awareness during life improves the chances of ascertaining the clear light of death while dying. In ascertaining unborn awareness during death, everything that is conditioned, everything that is born and will die, is released. In this ultimate release, one is deathless, outside life and death.

Unborn awareness is not separate from mental events; it is the fundamental nature of that which is arising all the time. It presents us with a challenge: by *not* looking for something else, you can focus into that which already is.

The Seven-Point Mind-Training begins with incremental steps to develop insight, also called wisdom, or ultimate bodhichitta. The first step is to achieve meditative stability, or quiescence. We have discussed two methods for developing quiescence: the control method of breath awareness and the release method from the Dzogchen tradition of settling the mind in its natural state. The next step is to cultivate insight by directing awareness in upon awareness itself and examining closely. Insight into the essential nature of awareness itself and the nature of all phenomena is the ultimate spirit of awakening, or ultimate bodhichitta.

Even the remedy itself is free right where it is.

The Second Point of the Seven-Point Mind-Training continues the pursuit of ultimate bodhichitta: "Even the remedy is free right where it is." This quintessential line refers to the non-inherent nature of all phenomena.

What is the problem and what is the remedy? The central problem is delusion, a false way of engaging with reality. The principal delusion is reification—mistaking our selves and phenomena as being inherently real and independent. We reify our minds and we reify subject and object. Reification profoundly segregates self from other and apprehends phenomena as being independently existent. Founded on the sense of "I am real," "I am independent," "I have a body and mind," there arises a strong sense of "you are totally separate and unrelated to me." This is the problem.

The perception of others as totally separate from ourselves encourages others to perceive us in the same way. This is the effect of delusion. According to Buddhist psychology, reification, the absolute dichotomization of self and other, self and object, is the basis of craving. I crave a nice car, a fine reputation, a certain person, and believe that if I had these things I would be happy. Alternately, we might believe something is getting in the way of our happiness. Reification is here too—"It is so-and-so's fault, it's the weather, politics, traffic." With reification, aversion, hostility, and resentment settle in.

The emotional imbalances of craving and aversion arise from the same cause: reifying the intrinsic, independent existence of our selves and other phenomena. From the central delusion of reification, also called "ignorance" in Buddhism, craving and aversion arise. In Buddhist psychology, the three primary afflictions of ignorance, craving, and aversion lead to all other mental afflictions.

How does the central delusion of reification begin? Dharmakirti, a great seventh-century Indian Buddhist logician, said reification starts by grasping onto self, then grasping onto others, and the result is mental affliction. Grasping onto self is the first step of delusion, the core of ignorance. If you are concerned that life is short, look to the root of the problem right where it starts, with "I am." Who says, "I am"? Turn in and look.

The remedy to the delusion of reification is wisdom. Wisdom arises from insight. Insight arises from practice, and the technique that focuses on the central issue, reification of self, is observing the observer. This stage of meditation is reached by first training in quiescence by practicing the control model of meditation, like patiently training a wild stallion. Then, practice the release model of training the attention by letting go of identification and settling awareness on the nature of awareness itself. Next, turn in and observe the observer. Alternating between the control and release approaches to training the attention and then releasing identification is a powerful method for fathoming the essential nature of awareness itself.

From a Buddhist perspective, the problems in the world, from small interpersonal ones to huge geopolitical ones, are fundamentally the results of delusion. Therefore, the ultimate remedy is wisdom. Wisdom can be cultivated just as compassion and patience can be cultivated. One facet of wisdom is intelligence. Buddhist practice seeks to cultivate intelligence by testing Dharma conceptually and experientially. Another type of wisdom is primordial wisdom, a kind of innate wisdom that isn't generated. You can't pollute or purify primordial wisdom, you can't acquire it and you can't lose it. Primordial wisdom isn't cultivated; it is unveiled.

There are two types of wisdom, both of which are remedies for delusion. The first can be cultivated and rises and declines, just like patience, loving-kindness, compassion, and many other conditioned qualities. The goal of the cultivation of intelligence is to unveil primordial wisdom, which is the very nature of awareness itself. Even the remedy, wisdom, when its very nature is unveiled, turns out to be primordial wisdom itself, "free right where it is."

There is a metaphor for the relationship between cultivated and innate wisdom. Imagine a child who grows up separated from his mother. Years later, when the child and mother meet, they recognize each other instantly. The same is said to be the case of cultivated and innate wisdom. Cultivate wisdom, and when primordial wisdom is unveiled, the two meet like mother and child. The child is intelligence, which is cultivated, and the mother is primordial wisdom, which is present all along. The ultimate remedy for delusion, primordial wisdom, was never acquired, and therefore is described as "free right where it is."

The practice of settling the mind in its natural state gives some sense of how thoughts themselves are naturally released. You don't release thoughts by applying a remedy. Rather, when you simply stop grasping onto them, you find that thoughts and mental events are released in their own state right where they are. A thought that arises in the open space of awareness has nothing to grate against, nothing to grasp onto; it simply arises and plays itself out like a cloud or rainbow forming and dissolving in the sky.

When I was practicing settling the mind in its natural state in retreat, Gyatrul Rinpoche, my spiritual mentor, told me, "When the mind is settled in its natural state, even if all the malevolent forces in the world should arise to torment you, they could not harm you. And even if all the buddhas and bodhisattvas should come to surround you, they could not benefit you. Since there is no target, you are beyond needing their benefit. You don't need a blessing from outside your mind, because when your mind is settled in its natural state, it is its own source of blessing."

In the quiescence practice of settling the mind in its natural state, you may get to a point of hitting a ceiling beyond which you can go no further. The ceiling is reification of self, of "I" the observer, "I" the meditator. You observe ideas and events arise and pass, but what is not released is "I." Thoughts are released, even emotions may be released, but "I" is not released. Therefore, abiding in a state that is non-conceptual, a state in which you are not grasping onto thoughts, is not enough to radically liberate the mind so that it doesn't revert to its habitual delusions.

For liberation, the cultivation of insight is necessary. What is required is to turn inward, probe right into the nature of awareness itself. What is doing the probing? Wisdom, which is cultivated and strengthened by probing into the nature of reality. "Even the remedy itself is free right where it is" means that even the intelligence that probes is free. There are two ways of looking at this. One is that even the mind that is observing and meditating does not have an inherent identity of its own. The mind seems to exist as something in itself, but when you probe right into its nature, not only are thoughts found to be merely appearances arising as dependently related events, but even "I," the observer doing the meditation, is discovered to be an appearance that is reified. Even the remedy, the "I" penetrating through delusion, does not have its own intrinsic independent existence.

All phenomena exist in a state of interdependence; nothing exists independently. This includes awareness. When I first met Geshe Rabten in 1971, he had completed his monastic training and was meditating in retreat in a cowshed in the mountains above Dharamsala. One of the topics of his meditation was the lack of inherent existence of all phenomena. He meditated on the one pillar that held up the roof of his cowshed and got to a point where the pillar no longer seemed to exist as a real entity. He felt he was not there as a real entity either. It was then that he told me about his meditation, saying that if he were to describe his experience, people would think he was crazy, and if they didn't think he was crazy, they were not getting it.

Everything is interdependent. This friendly statement just begins to skim the surface. What Buddhist contemplatives are saying is that in the whole universe right down to the subatomic level, nothing exists purely objectively or purely subjectively. We can say, "Oh, it's mere appearance. I get it." We can focus in and observe that nothing exists in the mind purely subjectively or objectively, that there is profound interdependence. But when we really experience this, our perception of the world as a whole is profoundly altered.

The line in the Mind-Training that Atisha brought to Tibet might have been, "Even the remedy itself is devoid of inherent nature." This would be a straightforward, specific statement meaning that the remedy has no separate, autonomous identity, or nature. But that is not the line Atisha used. The aphorism here is, "Even the remedy itself is free right where it is." We are seeking to get out of suffering, and we arrive as a last resort at the Dharma. We are about to apply a remedy, a "fix-it," when the Mind-Training says, "even the remedy," just like everything else, "is naturally free right where it is" as soon as you release grasping. This does not simply mean being devoid of intrinsic existence. The word "free" means that by penetrating right through the nature of intelligence to primordial wisdom, which has never been anything other than pure, has never been anything other than free, you are free right where you are. In other words, the meaning of the remedy being free is that cultivated wisdom penetrates through to primordial wisdom, which has been free and pure all along.

When we observe the mind, we notice how we reify the events of the mind. By reifying anger and other mental impurities, we empower them. Reification is like blessing afflictions, "Dominate me" and giving them the invitation, "Hit me." This is delusion at work. Imagine sitting on a lawn, resting in your own nature, and a truck comes along and dumps a lot of garbage next to you. Is your response, "This is mine!"? Not likely. Similarly, we don't need to identify with anything that is dumped in the space of our awareness.

It gets worse. There is another level of delusion. After we have reified, "This affliction is mine," we construct a personal identity based upon the reification of what never existed: "I am an angry person. I am a nice person. I am a selfish person. I am paranoid. I am a jerk. I'm wonderful!" This is another level of delusion. It is a tragedy to live life acting out of an assumed identity that doesn't exist.

The Mind-Training tells us that the innate nature of mind is pure: the remedy itself is free right where it is. How do we assume a false identity? Suppose a hypnotized person is told he is a kangaroo. In his trance, he jumps around like a happy kangaroo until someone asks, "Where is your pouch? Where are your big feet?" If he hadn't been so involved in being a kangaroo, he might have noticed that he doesn't look much like a kangaroo. Some basic questioning of his identity might snap him out of his kangaroo delusion. Like a man believing he is a kangaroo, we identify with ingrained suggestions about our identity. When we identify with the mental afflictions, we suffer.

There is a parable in the Tibetan tradition similar to the New Testament parable of the prodigal son but with an interesting twist. Karma Chagmé relates this story in the book *Naked Awareness: Practical Instructions on the Union of Mahāmudrā and Dzogchen*,[40] and I will paraphrase it here:

In the center of the land of Orgyen dwelled a wealthy and powerful king, his queen, his son the prince, and his wise minister. The kingdom was powerful, the palace was huge, and the king's reign was tremendous. But the prince was foolish and immature.

On one occasion, the prince went to a festival near the palace and became entranced by an illusionist. Illusionists plied their trade using three ingredients: deep concentration, some kind of physical substance, and mantras. These three elements were masterfully spun together to create very persuasive and realistic illusions. The prince, entranced by the illusionist's apparitions, suffered near total amnesia and forgot his identity. When he looked around, he failed to recognize his ministers and started wandering. The prince wandered for years as a beggar suffering the misery of being homeless. The heir to the throne being lost, the king grew old and the kingdom fell into decline.

After years of wandering, the prince came to the door of his former wise minister to beg for food. The prince was dirty and his clothes were in tatters, but the minister recognized him and tried to persuade him of his true identity: "You are the prince! Come home! The king awaits you."

The prince, believing himself to be a worthless beggar, did not believe the minister and refused to enter his father's palace. The minister explained what had happened with the illusionist and how he had wandered off. In doing so, the minister challenged the prince to examine his identity: Who were his parents? What was his birthplace? What was his true identity?

The prince was dumbfounded. He couldn't answer a single one of the minister's questions. When he examined his identity, he could find no answers because he had reified his identity as a beggar. The prince, stunned at what he *didn't* find, asked the minister to reveal his personal history and actual identity. The prince then understood instantly and was enthroned.

In an instant, while not discarding his identity as a beggar, he stopped living in the manner of a beggar. The misery of being a vagrant disappeared by itself and the kingdom and the subjects without exception came under his rule and they lived in great joy and happiness.

The beggar prince is symbolic of the nature of our true identity. The young prince symbolizes the state of mind that neither realizes the actual nature of awareness nor is deluded by the momentarily arising expressions of the mind's creative power, a state of mind that neither grasps nor is illuminated, a mind that has not yet penetrated to its essential nature. The minister symbolizes the spiritual mentor, endowed with realization, who teaches out of compassion. Just as the prince did not recognize his true identity and became a beggar, we fail to recognize our own true identity and wander "like beggars" in the cycle of existence. Just as the minister recognized the prince and restored him to the position of royalty, the spiritual mentor serves as guide to recognizing the true identity of one's mind, primordial wisdom.

The aphorism "even the remedy itself is free right where it is" refers to the insight that penetrates to primordial wisdom. This simple but potent line says two things. One is that by attending to and reifying mental phenomena, which are frequently afflictive, we grasp onto mental phenomena as "I" and "mine." This is the foundation upon which we construct and reify a sense of personal identity. We construct a sense of who we are out of identification with mental afflictions and other qualities and habits. This sequence of errors is the enormous problem that causes so much suffering.

The second implication of this aphorism is that by identifying with that which is not our "self," we fail to recognize our actual nature. By failing to attend to our actual nature, we fail to realize it. This is similar to the hypnotized man so busy jumping around believing himself to be a kangaroo that he doesn't notice he is actually a human being.

The word used in this line is "free." What happens if you free mental afflictions by releasing them? Shantideva, the eighth-century Indian Buddhist author of *A Guide to the Bodhisattava Way of Life*, was referring to mental afflictions when he wrote, "Once the affliction that dwells in my mind has been expelled, where would it go, and where would it rest and attempt to destroy me?"[41] After you stop empowering the afflictions by identifying with them, you see that the primordial nature of your own awareness has never been anything other than pure. If you can intuitively affirm, even tentatively, that the essential nature of awareness, your own intrinsic primordial wisdom, is none other than the mind of the Buddha, then primordial wisdom invites you to dwell in that quality.

At the point when grasping onto a false identity is released, practitioners of Vajrayana Buddhism use visualization and imagination to assume an identity commensurate with primordial wisdom, the identity of a buddha. Without understanding the lack of an inherent nature of one's ordinary identity, this practice can be not only silly but dangerous. In Vajrayana practice, any sense of superiority is an indication that delusion is being enhanced and the practice is being done incorrectly. Suffering is the result of doing misguided practice with all the good intentions. One example from my experience was a fellow who spent months in intensive Vajrayana practice, assuming the identity of a buddha. Eventually he came to regard himself as superior to everyone around him and was abjectly miserable. This was a state of affliction reached with great effort in mistaken practice.

There is a very practical way to take the danger out of spiritual practice, particularly ones that use imagination. When practicing, settle the mind in its natural state and when probing inward, remember the parable of the prince. Before he recognized his true identity as a prince, under the guidance of his mentor he carefully investigated his identity as a beggar and found that it didn't exist.

The parable of the prince is analogous to the practice of probing in, then releasing. When you think, "I am thinking this, these are my thoughts, this is who I am," investigate the origin of the thoughts. What is their location, who is it that observes them? Investigate. What is the nature of the meditator who is striving so diligently? The result is a not-finding. In that emptiness of not-finding, there is a spaciousness free from personal ego in which the ordinary sense of personal identity has vanished. In that spaciousness there is space for something of boundless proportions to be present, which is, in fact, already present. Primordial wisdom is already there. Primordial wisdom is not something you will get someday. It is already within you. It is just not being recognized.

His Holiness the Dalai Lama advises practitioners of Vajrayana to meditate on the emptiness of their own identity first. Otherwise, there is no point in doing such visualization practice. Retaining one's own identity while imagining that one is a buddha is a major delusion. To be free of danger, first completely dissolve your ordinary sense of ego. In the spaciousness that results, assume the identity of that which has been present all along. Don't worry about assuming the right, perfect identity of a buddha. It is not going to be right. We can't clearly imagine what buddha-mind is like. The point is to be less wrong as we proceed. Just as a hypnotized man has to recognize he is not a kangaroo in order to recognize his human identity, we have to dissolve the delusion of self-identity, the ego, before entering into the spacious, primordially present identity of buddha-mind.

Enlightened awareness is a quality of awareness that is free of reified divisions of self/other, subject/object; it is boundless, spacious, and all-embracing. Enlightened awareness perceives the lack of inherent existence of all phenomena. It is an awareness that is implicitly, naturally, imbued with boundless non-discriminating compassion. As much as you can imagine that, you experience a facsimile of enlightened awareness right now.

The great benefit of Vajrayana practice is that by imagining yourself as the embodiment of a buddha, you can draw from your own awareness qualities of that buddha and these very qualities are experienced more and more vividly. The more deeply you imagine the quality of compassion, the more you tap the reservoirs of compassion within you. Imagination is an invitation that draws qualities forth from a source that is fathomless. If you lack the intuitive affirmation of primordial wisdom, or buddha-mind, or if you believe that in no sense whatever are you a buddha, then there is no point to doing Vajrayana practice.

Vajrayana practice is based on intuitively affirming the awakened state and taking the awakened state itself as the path to awakening. The truth of the path, its validity, is realizing the awakened state.

In meditation, you can assume the identity of a buddha by intuitively affirming the presence of buddha-mind. Buddha-mind saturates your own mind, like oil saturates paper. The choice is to either attend to the "myness" coagulating the self, or open the door to engaging with the enlightened awareness that innately suffuses all your mental states.

Recall the parable of the prince, "While not discarding his identity as a beggar, he stopped living in the manner of a beggar." This means that in assuming the identity of a buddha, you do not stop being who you are. This is not really assuming a new identity, but neither is it being who you always believed yourself to be.

The essential nature of the path is resting in the universal ground.

This aphorism refers to a mind free of conceptualization, relaxed in a state free of grasping onto self, others, subject, object, past, present, future, or anything else. This practice of resting in the universal ground is similar to settling the mind in its natural state, but the meaning is not the same.

"Settling the mind in its natural state" is initially presented as a quiescence practice, a precursor to the insight practice introduced here. Quiescence practice follows a technique, frequently attention on the breathing, to calm the mind so that the mind can then "settle in its natural state." At this point, whatever thoughts arise are observed with clarity and without grasping or any other intervention. Contemplative adepts report that quiescence practice commonly leads to experiences of bliss, clarity, and non-conceptuality, but the qualities of quiescence alone are founded on an unstable equilibrium.

The attainment of quiescence alone does not enable you to fathom the depths of the mind or sever the root of delusion. The profoundly ingrained tendencies of locking onto conceptual frameworks and reification have not been eradicated. With quiescence practice alone, these deep habits just become latent. In other words, it is possible to achieve quiescence, a state of bliss and clarity, in which delusion is not apparent, not because it has been eradicated or overcome, but simply because it has become dormant.

The Tibetan Buddhist tradition reports rare and exceptional individuals for whom the practice of settling the mind in its natural state alone has been sufficient to attain full awakening. For these few, it is possible to penetrate immediately to the absolute nature of the mind. But for most of us quiescence alone is not enough. "Settling the mind in its natural state," which is a quiescence practice, is not enough. It is necessary to vigorously explore the origins of mental events, where they take place, how they dissolve, and then to penetrate the nature of the observer. What is required for most of us is a very rigorous training that includes a phase of active investigation in close dialogue with an experienced spiritual mentor who challenges our habitual tendencies of reification. Most of us need to investigate the deeply rooted belief that there really is a world "out there" and a self "in here" engaging with it. Grasping and reification are extremely tenacious.

By progressing in the practice through investigation, insight is gained into the nature of awareness itself, and grasping ceases. The stage of penetrating through all conceptual frameworks and reification to insight into the primordial nature of awareness is called the "breakthrough." At the point of breakthrough you are ready for the practice encoded in the aphorism "the essential nature of the path is resting in the universal ground."

Maitripa, a great Indian *mahasiddha,* or contemplative adept, summarized breaking through to the universal ground:

> All great, all-encompassing realities are primordial, and their nature is not fabricated. If you do not seek, but settle your mind in the inconceivable absolute space of phenomena, that is meditation. Meditating while seeking entails a deluded state of mind.[42]

"Meditating while seeking entails a deluded state of mind" is an interesting statement! Maitripa is saying that universal truths are timeless and not contrived by human thought. Insofar as one is seeking, there is a sense of "I am looking for something," which reaffirms the superimposition of the conceptual frameworks of subject/object, this/that, I/you. In the stage of breakthrough, the conceptual framework of seeking itself is challenged. Maitripa's advice is that there is a point when you need to let go of everything. If you skip the rigors of insight practice and merely abide in the quiescence practice of settling the mind in its natural state, chances are you will hit a low ceiling. But with insight practice, you can penetrate through the sense of division between subject/object and meditator/object of meditation. Once this barrier is broken through with insight, Maitripa says stop probing. After breaking through to non-conceptual, non-dual awareness, the essential nature of the path becomes simply resting in the universal ground.

In the cultivation of quiescence, the relationship between mindfulness and introspection is important. In practice, when you approach the achievement of quiescence, the mind is no longer prone to excitation but is fearlessly calm, stable with vivid clarity. The mind flows single-pointedly like a laser. While in meditation, there is no danger of the mind slipping into laxity. Awareness is directed and focused, effortlessly. At this point, introspection has completed its job and meditation is at a turning point. The mind is functional, smooth, free of laxity and excitation. At this point, the intervention of introspection, checking up with "how am I doing now?" becomes an impediment. When quiescence is achieved, relinquish introspection, release grasping so deeply that introspection itself is released. Until this point, continuity of attention could only be sustained with effort, but once quiescence is achieved, you no longer attend to an object—you release it. You release the object you attend to.

Many of the themes of quiescence practice are analogous to events that take place in insight practice. However, only insight meditation fully supported with quiescence is radically and irreversibly transformative. In the state referred to as "the universal ground," habitual grasping is released deeper than a state of abeyance; it is completely severed right at the root. In the Dzogchen, or Great Perfection, practice a distinction is made between minor emptiness and great emptiness. This is a crucial distinction. In Dzogchen practice, you probe right into the nature of awareness to observe the observer. What is found is an absence and in that absence there is luminosity, a clarity or limpidity, but no agent, nothing from its own side. You observe an absence of an observer, an absence of an intrinsically existent, self-sufficient observer observing an observed object. The absence of an intrinsic and autonomous observer is called "minor emptiness." It is called "minor" because there is still grasping. What is being grasped onto is the absence of an observer, an absence dependent upon engaging with a conceptual framework. The meditator may not be reifying concepts, but the "absence" is apprehended only within the context of a conceptual framework. When even the notion of "emptiness" or "absence" is released, the essential nature of the path is resting in the universal ground. The essential nature of the path is a state of awareness that is beyond the notion of emptiness or non-emptiness; beyond existence or non-existence; beyond past, present, or future, and beyond subject/object. The essential nature of the path is Great Emptiness.

There is another level here. The awareness that suffuses our minds right now, as far from enlightenment as that may seem, is none other than the universal ground. Gyatrul Rinpoche sometimes chided me, saying, "When you were a young man, you went to India, going from one teacher to another. Then you went off to Switzerland, back to India, then to Sri Lanka, then you come here. You are still going here and there. What you don't recognize is that what you are seeking is always with you!"

The path to enlightenment has many facets, but the Mind-Training tells us that "the essential nature of the path is resting in the universal ground." The term "universal ground" is my translation of the Sanskrit word *alaya* and the Tibetan equivalent *künzhi* (*kun gzhi*). "Kün" means all, or everything, and "zhi" means basis, or ground. You may be familiar with the Sanskrit term *alayavijñana*, sometimes translated as "storehouse consciousness," with the term *vijñana* meaning "consciousness." In the Yogachara school of Buddhist philosophy this refers to the stream of consciousness that carries on from lifetime to lifetime, acting as a repository for memories, habitual tendencies, and karmic seeds. That is one meaning of *alaya*. But that is not the meaning Atisha is referring to here. The great fourth-century Indian Buddhist sage Asanga stated that when quiescence is accomplished, one should relinquish mindfulness and simply be present in a state of awareness without form, without any sense of subject and object. Here awareness is drawn into itself, disengaged from the senses, a state in which the mind is free of appearances and there is not even a sense of having a body. In this state of quiescence, the mind is vivid and clear. Quiescence is spacious, serene, without form and substance. Like a mountain cabin in the recesses of your mind, quiescence is a nice place to hang out. The problem is that quiescence in itself is not transformative. Once you have achieved quiescence, you have disengaged from whatever tendencies you have for anger, craving, jealousy. But that is all. Quiescence is ethically neutral, neither virtuous nor non-virtuous, and implicitly conditioned. Quiescence is subliminally structured by your past habitual tendencies that carry on from one lifetime to another. This ongoing consciousness is sometimes called the foundation of samsara, the basis for the cyclic existence of birth, aging, sickness and death, life after life. This is the substrate of the *samsaric* stream of consciousness that holds the whole show together. But this consciousness is a only a facsimile of that which the Mind-Training refers to as "universal ground."

The "universal ground" of this aphorism of the Mind-Training is the ultimate universal ground, the Great Emptiness, which is the foundation of both samsara and nirvana. This "universal ground" is the "one taste" that pervades the entire phenomenal world and absolute reality. This is the realization of complete openness, natural perfection, and absolute spontaneity, in which one fathoms the falsity of one's previous reification of such dualistic constructs as subject and object.

Let me draw a parallel with an analogous type of breakthrough. At a recent Mind and Life conference with a small group of distinguished physicists, His Holiness the Dalai Lama was struck by the depth of insight physicists have gained by probing into the nature of phenomena, right down to particles of light. One physicist, Anton Zeilinger, described how when he probed deeply, he found that nothing existed objectively and independently. Instead, all quantum events arose within the context of a system of measurement. The Dalai Lama was amazed that physicists have so deeply penetrated the nature of phenomena. And this physicist was also amazed that Buddhist contemplatives have come to similar conclusions without the aid of modern science and technology.

There are two related meanings of the word "dharma." It often refers to spiritual practice, but it also means simply phenomenon, any phenomenon. Photons are dharmas. The essential nature of phenomena is called in Sanskrit *dharmata*, meaning "dharma-ness," the very state of being existent, or simply reality-itself. Reality-itself is in the nature of the objects of investigation, and this is where physics goes stunningly deep. Quantum theory addresses profound questions about the nature of reality. Penetrating into the nature of any "dharmas," whether mental processes, images, outer phenomena, atoms, or photons, is to ascertain *dharmata*—reality-itself.

Buddhists also engage in research. Buddhists investigate the mind experientially, probing the nature of mind to discover the nature of the observer. The result is a "not finding."

By investigating the nature of the observer, contemplatives penetrate beyond mind (Sanskrit: *chitta*) to *chittata*, or "mindness," the mind-itself, the essential nature of the mind, the very state of being aware.

The pursuit of contemplative insight entails probing both the nature of objective phenomena (both mental and physical) and probing inward to discover the nature of the subjective mind. This is the prerequisite to the experience of the breakthrough. "Resting in the universal ground" is a state of awareness in which *dharmata* and *chittata* are no longer perceived as distinct from each other. Now one realizes that the real nature of objective phenomena has never been separate from the real nature of subjective awareness. This is a universal truth, simply called *tathata*, or suchness, for it is finally beyond all articulation. The Buddhist explanation for the surprising findings of quantum mechanics is that the essential nature of the photon is none other than the essential nature of the mind of the physicist who is probing the essential nature of the photon. The more profoundly we study external phenomena, the more clearly we see the reflections of our own minds.

Nothing we conceive or perceive exists independently of our conceptions and perceptions. All subjects and objects arise together, and nothing whatsoever exists independently of the conceptual framework within which it is conceived. This is a radical statement with deep implications. For example, if nothing has independent existence, not even a photon, how can scientific researchers distinguish between good and bad research? As long as you believe there is something out there, you can assume good research will accurately reveal what is out there. But if there isn't anything really out there existing independently of all conceptual frameworks, are we creating the world of physics as we go along?

If phenomena do not exist independently of the conceptual framework in which they are identified, does this mean reality is determined by belief? Such radical relativism is the conclusion of neither Buddhist contemplatives nor physicists. There are different domains of relativity. Someone who is an enemy to me may be a good friend to someone else. Such truths are contingent upon perspective. This reroutes us back to a central issue of Buddhism: reification. Reification is taking something that is true relative to ourselves and believing it to be true independently of ourselves.

Just as there are personal truths, there are cultural truths. There are truths in Western culture that don't hold for Indians or Africans. Until around the mid-twentieth century, anthropologists routinely considered cultures that didn't share Western beliefs to be "primitive." It took decades of exposure to other cultures to realize that many "primitive" cultures operate with a set of assumptions different from our own and have a different basis of rationality.

Beyond personal and cultural truths, consider whether there are truths that are dependent on species. A dog's reality has a strong olfactory component. To a dog, apples may appear gray, not red. Just as human reality is anthropocentric, dog reality must be canine-o-centric. In the Buddhist worldview, with its many types of sentient beings, realities arise in relationship to specific individuals, cultures, and species.

Science attempts to penetrate beyond the limitations of the relative experiences of the individual, culture, and species to what is really out there. Science discovers laws that can be stated mathematically. When Galileo declared that God speaks in the language of mathematics, he was expressing a belief held by most scientists, then as now, that science penetrates beyond anthropocentric understanding to what is really out there.

Buddhism addresses the same question. The Buddhist answer to the question of whether it is possible to enter an unconditioned state of awareness is yes. In accomplishing meditative quiescence, the mind shifts from the physical realm in which experience is dominated by the senses to a realm of archetypal forms, called the "form realm." The form realm is beyond human senses, culture, and conditioning, but is accessible while having a human body. This, I expect, is the realm in which the laws, patterns and mathematical truths of nature exist. The Buddhist claim is that a human being can, by means of deep meditative concentration, access the realm of archetypal forms, and even formless dimensions of boundless space, consciousness, nothingness, and a state of being that transcends the concepts of discernment and non-discernment.

As one shifts from personal to cultural to pan-human realities, and even to universal realities in the archetypal realm, all of these realities arise together with a mind that is able to access them. In all of these cases, the tendency is to reify. Mathematical expressions of the laws of nature are reified by the mind that accesses them as if they are independent of the mind. The Buddhist premise is that neither the constituents of the physical world nor the mathematics of natural laws exist in and of themselves. This *doesn't* mean that archetypes or mathematical laws of nature are merely concepts of an anthropocentric view of nature. But Buddhism claims that it is possible to go even beyond the form realm and the formless realm to the universal ground, which absolutely transcends all conceptual frameworks. This is stated in the Mind-Training as: "The essential nature of the path is to rest in the universal ground." On this theme Padmasambhava declared:

> Astonishing! The ongoing awareness and clarity called *the mind* exists, but does not exist even as a single thing. It arises, for it

manifests as *saṃsāra* and *nirvāṇa*, and as a myriad of joys and sorrows. It is asserted, for it is asserted according to the twelve vehicles. It is a label, for it is named in unimaginable ways. Some people call it *the mind-itself*. Some non-Buddhists call it *the self*. The *śrāvakas* call it *personal identitylessness*. The Cittamātrins call it *the mind*. Some people call it *the middle way*. Some call it *the perfection of wisdom*. Some give it the name *tathāgatagarbha*. Some give it the name *Mahāmudrā*. Some give it the name *ordinary consciousness*. Some call it *the sole bindu*. Some call it *the absolute nature of reality*. Some label it *the universal ground*.[43]

Padmasambhava lists some of the many contemplative traditions within Buddhism: *śrāvakas*, Cittamātrins, Mādhyamikas, and proponents of the *tathāgatagarbha* theory, as well as non-Buddhist schools. He points out that the many names for "the mind" refer to the same reality; many points of view converge toward the same truth. This is analogous to the universal truths of science that are independent of the cultural background of the researcher.

Contemplative practice has many parallels to scientific research. Just as scientific investigation leads to knowledge that transcends culturally conditioned beliefs, so does contemplative investigation. In the following passage, Padmasambhava discusses the universal ground, or essential nature of awareness:

To introduce this by pointing it out directly, past consciousness has disappeared without a trace. Moreover, future realization is unarisen, and in the freshness of its own present, unfabricated way of being, there is the ordinary consciousness of the present. When it peers into itself, with this observation there is a vividness in which nothing is seen. This awareness is direct, naked, vivid, unestablished, empty, limpid luminosity, unique, nondual clarity and emptiness. It is not permanent, but unestablished. It is not nihilistic, but radiantly vivid. It is not one, but is manifoldly aware and clear. It is not manifold, but is indivisibly of one taste. It is none other than this very self-awareness. This is a real introduction to the primordial nature of being.[44]

The primordial nature of being, the essential nature of awareness itself, is without form and yet is neither inert nor static. Padmasambhava challenges us to replicate these findings:

> The mind-itself is certainly empty and unestablished. Your mind is intangible like empty space. Is it like that or not? Observe your own mind!
>
> Empty and void but without a nihilistic view, self-arisen, primordial wisdom is original, clear consciousness. Self-arisen and self-illuminating, it is like the essence of the sun. Is it like that or not? Observe your own mind!
>
> The primordial wisdom of awareness is certainly unceasing. Uninterrupted awareness is like the current of a river. Is it like that or not? Observe your own mind!
>
> The dispersing discursive thoughts are certainly not being grasped. This intangible dispersion is like a hazy sky. Is it like that or not? Observe your own mind!
>
> Recognize all appearances as self-appearing. Self-appearing phenomena are like reflections in a mirror. Is it like that or not? Observe your own mind!
>
> All signs are certainly released in their own state. Self-arising and self-releasing, they are like clouds in the sky. Is it like that or not? Observe your own mind![45]

The Seven-Point Mind-Training begins the probe into the nature of reality using the dream analogy. Within the context of the dream there is a distinction between self and other that cannot be ignored. This is true in life and death as well. When I die, I will reap the consequences of my karma, not someone else's. Yet, from the perspective of the awakened state we realize that the apparent distinction between self and other is a manifestation of something deeper. It is merely an illusory expression of a primordial state of awareness that transcends all distinctions between self and other. The Buddhist position is that there is a nominal truth of "I" and "you," but there is no transcendent real "I" that is independent from its label. It is the conceptual designation of "I" that evokes a referent, creating the apparent discrete qualities of entities.

The Buddhist position is that conventional reality is evoked by the process of conceptual designation. First we designate the self with the sense of "I am," and then the self is reified. William James noted that when we lack a term for something, it is very difficult to engage with it. A label is a vehicle for engaging with its referent. The meditations of the Seven-Point Mind-Training use labels— "minor emptiness" and "great emptiness" are examples—to draw out a reality. The Mind-Training goes deeper, however, in probing beyond the labels to dwell in reality itself.

Between sessions, be an illusory person.

Phenomena, once investigated, are found to be without permanence or stability and are like illusions. This being realized, the Mind-Training addresses the ongoing challenge of contemplative practice to maintain a seamless connection between meditation and the rest of life. In the aphorism "Between sessions, be an illusory person," the words "between sessions" refer to the post-meditative state, the hours of the day when you are not in formal meditation. The remaining points of the Mind-Training are critical in helping us protect and nurture the fruit of formal practice during active life.

The challenge of contemplative practice is to achieve the greatest possible benefit from the quality of awareness and insight resulting from meditation. Just as polluting the environment and then cleaning it up is like following a big elephant around with a shovel and bucket, meditation can clean up after everyday life. In daily life we get stressed out, circle around in mental afflictions and then a warning light flashes, "Need to meditate." Meditation can get us re-centered and tuned-up so that we can go out and jump in the mud again. In retreat, when one is spending twelve hours a day in formal meditation, the post-meditative state is a small fraction of one's overall time. But when living an engaged and active life, meditating only one or two hours a day, integrating formal practice into daily life is critical. The Mind-Training directly addresses the problem of "between sessions," how to integrate the fruit of formal practice into the rest of life.

The challenge is to integrate practice into life like advanced yogis, so that there is no difference between formal meditation and active life. At the other end of the meditation spectrum is the person who has hardly dipped a pinkie into meditation thinking, "I don't need to meditate. I regard all of life as meditation." It is very difficult to transform one's entire life into meditation if no time is actually spent meditating!

By settling the mind in its natural state, a sense of well-being will spring forth from the very nature of awareness, and virtues will arise easily. In meditative stabilization, virtue flows unimpeded. Mental afflictions can still arise but, like fish swimming upstream, are easily swept away.

There is a reality deeper than quiescence. Probing the nature of awareness leads to recognizing the absence of any subject separate from its environment and, further still, that awareness is conceptually completely unstructured and primordial. Primordial awareness is the straight track to enlightenment. More accurately, it is enlightened awareness itself. It is none other than your own buddha-mind. If you can constantly ascertain the essential nature of your own mind, you don't need to do any other Dharma practices. However, it is nearly impossible to rest for a sustained period in buddha-mind, because we have so many habit patterns that lead us astray. The core problem again is reification, grasping onto events and ourselves as being inherently real.

The practice of "between sessions, be an illusory person" is extraordinary because it concerns both physical and mental reality. This sequence of practices of the Second Point of the Mind-Training is aimed at the cultivation of ultimate bodhichitta and began with "regard all events as dream-like"—all that looks real consists merely of appearances. When you examine your mind, the real "I" who seems to be engaging in this examination dissolves, leaving an emptiness. What remains is simply empty appearance. Now, emerging from formal meditation and entering active life, how will you engage with others? "As if you were an illusory being" dwelling in an illusory environment.

The entire environment we perceive around us arises, in part, in dependence upon our sense faculties. The environment we experience does not truly exist "out there." Sight is dependent upon visual faculties, hearing is dependent upon auditory faculties, and tactile sensations depend on nerve endings. Psychologically, all that we experience is dependent upon ourselves. We do not experience anything purely objectively. The arising and perceiving of experience is co-emergent between ourselves and the world around us. Yet, the deep belief persists that the world really exists "out there" now and eons before we were born.

The Buddhist hypothesis extends beyond the psychological. The Buddhist hypothesis is this: that which is perceived arises in dependence upon the perception of it. Things are empty of independent, inherent existence. What appears to exist "out there" is empty of objective existence from its own side. This does not mean that nothing exists apart from our perceptions. Rather, it means that by probing the nature of existence of anything we experience perceptually or conceptually, we find that nothing exists by its own independent nature. Another way of phrasing this is that appearance extends all the way down to the root and there is nothing beyond the appearances. Appearances extend down to quarks; nothing is there purely objectively and nothing is there purely subjectively. This is the Buddhist hypothesis.

In *A Guide to the Bodhisattva Way of Life,* Shantideva raises a serious qualm regarding the Madhyamaka view, which is the view of the Seven-Point Mind-Training, that it is possible to realize the illusory nature of something and still crave it.[46] For example, when you're watching a movie, you may know perfectly well that what you are watching is an illusion, but you may still become afraid when someone is about to get killed. Knowing a movie is fiction doesn't inhibit any of the emotions of fear, joy, sorrow, or lust. Mental afflictions as well as positive emotions continue to arise even when we are aware that something is an illusion.

Shantideva discusses this problem using a simile relevant in eighth-century India—illusionists who created apparitions with the power of their samadhi, magical substances, and mantras. Recall the parable of the prince who forgot his true identity when he became entranced by an illusionist. Shantideva's dialogue challenges the Madhyamaka position by noting that when a magician conjures up a beautiful woman, his subject may feel craving for her even while knowing that she is an apparition. Using a modern example, the realization that TV is "just an illusion" doesn't prevent us from getting angry, afraid, or filled with desire when we watch it.

Shantideva's response to this qualm is that simply having a glimpse of emptiness, some fleeting experience of the illusory nature of phenomena, will not eradicate mental afflictions because of the tremendous power of our habitual response patterns. This points once again to the necessity of achieving quiescence as a foundation for the cultivation of insight. The tendency of reification continues on by the powerful momentum of habit even when we know for certain that what we are dealing with is an illusion. When we see something attractive, our mind reflexively grasps.

Shantideva points out that realizing emptiness once or twice is not enough. A bit of insight into the illusory nature of phenomena will not eliminate mental afflictions. What is necessary to eradicate afflictions at their root is to become more and more accustomed to realizing emptiness. Only drenching yourself in the awareness of emptiness will gradually erode the underlying habits resulting in attachment and aversion.

In his book *Natural Liberation*, Padmasambhava describes the dream yoga technique of the "impure illusory body."[47] This pertains to the aphorism "between sessions be an illusory person." The impure illusory body practice is seeing your own body and that of others as being nothing more than matrices of appearances, displays having no substantial reality. Padmasambhava describes the "the mirror practice" for overcoming the reified sense of "I" that becomes offended or hurt: Dress attractively and stand in front of a mirror. Imagine that you are young and attractive. If you are a woman, say to yourself in the mirror, "You are drop-dead gorgeous!" If you are a man say, "You are ruggedly handsome!" Lather it on. Imagine other people praising your physical appearance. Observe if this elicits something like happiness in you. Observe carefully and then immediately turn in and try to observe that which is thinking, "I like this." Then do the opposite. Look your worst and say to yourself in the mirror, "You are disgusting." Imagine other people being abusive to you. Again, immediately turn in and observe that which is hurt and thinks, "I don't like this." In the mirror practice, your goal is to elicit something and then try to identify its target. The object is to recognize that the target is in fact no more substantial than the reflection in the mirror.

Padmasambhava elaborates further, pointing out that what we take as a real and substantial self is merely a matrix of dependently related events and, apart from delusive appearances, there is no real body, no real mind, no real person. Delusive appearances seem to be substantial from their own side. When you investigate, whether as a quantum physicist or as a Buddhist meditator, you discover that the substance that was expected to be there is not found. The meditator dwells in the awareness that things appear more substantial than they are.

The Seven-Point Mind-Training practice of "between sessions, be an illusory person" tells us to imagine the body as being like an illusory apparition throughout the day. Imagine your own and others' speech to be like echoes. If you are standing next to a canyon and someone a hundred yards away shouts an obscenity to someone on the far side, but the echo comes back to you, you know not to take it personally. It is devoid of content, a voice merely ricocheted off a rock face. There is no substance to the event itself and there is no target. The practice of living as if you were an illusory being is to maintain this awareness throughout the day so that even if people speak in an offensive way, there is no target. All speech is like an echo. All mental events are like a mirage, with no corresponding objective reality. Mental events that seem real, memories that torture us, thoughts that unnerve us, images that frighten us affect the mind as they do only because we grasp onto them as being real. Instead, practice regarding mental events as mere appearances, in which case there is no basis upon which mental afflictions can arise.

Padmasambhava sums up the practice of living as if you were an illusory being by emphasizing that the most powerful corrosive to the armor of Dharma practice is the reification of the eight mundane concerns: seeking material acquisitions and avoiding their loss, seeking pleasurable stimuli and avoiding unpleasant ones, seeking praise and avoiding blame, maintaining a good reputation and avoiding a bad one. The sign of a mature Dharma practitioner is the equalization of these eight mundane concerns. Every transformative path emphasizes the importance of equalizing these four dichotomies until they become of one taste.

There is another interpretation of the line, "between sessions be an illusory person." The practice I have just described is called the "impure illusory body" because it presents an ontological challenge to the reality in which we participate, showing it to be matrices of dependently related events. This practice is called "impure" to distinguish it from another "illusory body" practice, "cultivating the pure illusory body."[48]

The practice of the "pure illusory body" can't be accomplished with intelligence alone. The heart of this practice entails the cultivation of a vision of all physical appearances as being embodiments of enlightened consciousness. Everything mental, verbal, and physical is experienced as being the continuous flow of nothing other than the Buddha's mind, speech, and body.

The intellectual objection to this practice concerns the lack of evidence that this is the actual nature of reality. Great Buddhist intellects such as Nagarjuna and Tsongkhapa have battering-ram syllogisms as powerful tools to pulverize reification. But there is no syllogism that demonstrates that everything is buddha-mind.

There are many things that we believe because we perceive them. But what is the experiential evidence that all forms are none other than forms of the Buddha, all sounds none other than the speech of the Buddha, and that all that arises in the mind is none other than the creative play of primordial awareness? This is not what we see when we look around us. The practice of the "pure illusory body" is based neither on logic nor on ordinary perception. The practice of the "pure illusory body" is based on primordial wisdom.

Within each of us, there is a capacity for the intuitive affirmation of truths deeper than surface appearances, truths not dependent on sensory confirmation. What allows for this intuitive affirmation is primordial awareness. The practice of the pure illusory body affirms the presence of buddhas everywhere. Practicing the pure illusory body is recognizing that the wisdom, compassion, and power of the buddhas is present and active in every moment. How would reality ideally present itself so that one could swiftly attain enlightenment? The blessing and power of all the buddhas is saturating us inside and out at every moment. At the same time, we are preoccupied with the eight mundane concerns thinking, "I didn't get as much money as I deserve ... This is all his fault ..." and so forth. After a while, we die. We missed our opportunity to attend to the blessings of the buddhas. The view of the practice of the pure illusory body is that the buddhas are always trying to get our attention and bring us to enlightenment. We fail to pay attention.

William James said that what we attend to becomes our reality. Samsara never wears out. We are deeply habituated to perceiving everything that happens to us as either good or bad fortune, and if we attend to the eight mundane concerns, they become our reality. In the meantime, we could be on a fast track to enlightenment. The view of the practice of the pure illusory body is to recognize that every single moment offers the best which all the buddhas have to offer. This is as good as it gets, right now.

Recall the man who thought that he was a kangaroo. The man who was hypnotized into believing he was a kangaroo might imagine himself as a human being in order to realize his true identity. Similarly, we deeply believe we are real, suffering individuals with limitations, and we can use the power of imagination to work out of this delusion. Examine appearances and concepts, recognize them, dissolve them. Recognize that there is no core identity, no intrinsic individual who is limited, suffering and deluded. In the absence of intrinsic ego imagine, "I am perfectly awakened here and now." The practice of "the pure illusory body" is also called "pure perception" and is accomplished by the power of imagination.

The practice of pure perception is effective when it is practiced a lot. In pure perception, look beyond the surface and imagine that other people are none other than expressions of buddha-mind. We can choose to focus on positive attributes. What we attend to becomes our reality and if we attend to the buddhas in situations, in things, in other people, it is the buddhas we engage with and the reality of the buddhas that becomes our reality.

Using imagination to perceive reality is a paradoxical concept, so I'll elaborate with a couple of examples. How does the practice of pure perception apply in marriage—in what way is a husband an illusion? In a Buddhist context, "illusion" is an ontological description and does not diminish the value of the person or relationship. What "illusion" means is that you, the other person, and the relationship do not exist as independent, self-sufficient, autonomous little globules of reality. "Illusion" means entities are appearances and there is no concrete reality behind the appearances.

When samsara, ordinary existence with all its ups and downs, is viewed as just appearances, the question arises whether appearances themselves have meaning or value. There is no logic or empirical evidence to answer this question. It can only be answered by engaging in dialogue with our own primordial wisdom.

I will relate an event from my life. When I was twenty years old and trying to make sense of existence, I came across a book on Dzogchen by Evans-Wentz entitled *The Tibetan Book of the Great Liberation*. This was my introduction to Buddhism and it zapped me. I wanted to trace it to its source. At the time, I was hitchhiking in Norway and wrote in my journal, "I've got to seek guidance from a wise old man," the archetype of wisdom for me at that time. The next morning, I started hitchhiking and ended up in the wilderness between Bergen and Oslo. Nobody picked me up for four or five hours. Finally, I gave up and walked against the current of the traffic, dangling my thumb behind me. A black VW driven by a little old man pulled over. I threw my guitar and backpack in the back seat and hopped in. Within five minutes I learned that he was a Buddhist monk named Sugata—there couldn't have been more than a handful of Buddhist monks in all of Europe at the time— and that he had lived in Nepal with Tibetans. We became good friends and corresponded for years.

It is perfectly legitimate to interpret this encounter as a coincidence. However, my intuition says that this wasn't one isolated, remarkable, amazing event. My intuition says that if I clear the dust off my eyes, I will see everyday events that are just as powerful and meaningful. All of life, every day, all the time is designed to bring us to enlightenment if that's what we're seeking. Appearances are suffused with utterly magnificent meaning.

The Buddhist rationale legitimizing the use of imagination is that everything exists in dependence upon conceptual designation. We influence the reality we experience by choosing what we engage with and how we engage with it. What we attend to and how we attend to it determine the nature of the reality that rises to meet us.

In the Tibetan Buddhist tradition it is said that when those who have purified their minds look at their environment, they view a Pure Realm, a domain that is none other than a creation of the mind of the buddhas. One Buddhist belief is that it is possible to take rebirth in a realm that is a figment of the Buddha's imagination, where one can continue practicing Dharma and attain enlightenment. If you suspect that you may not attain enlightenment in this lifetime, belief in Pure Realms provides a very attractive safety net. However, if you perfect the practice of pure perception in this life, wherever you are at any time, now or after death, is none other than a Pure Realm.

There is another approach to the illusory body practice. If you look for evidence of the blessings of the buddhas but see only samsara, if you are unable to affirm the primordial wisdom latent within you, apply yourself to the continued cultivation of virtue. By gradually purifying the mind, cultivating virtue, the dust is cleared off the eyes. By cultivating virtue and purifying the mind, primordial wisdom will gradually emerge into the bright light of consciousness.

The aphorism of the Mind-Training is, "Between sessions, be an illusory person." Another analogy is found in dream yoga. In a lucid dream, you regard yourself as being present. People can hear you speak. You can touch them. In a lucid dream this is recognized as only an appearance; there is nothing real, no substance, no real "I." In dream yoga practice, the stage beyond learning to transform the contents of the dream is letting the dream be. It is just a dream. Buddhist experience in dream yoga shows that transforming dream contents can catalyze the material of the psyche on deep levels. Dredging the depths of the mind brings up impurities, from this lifetime or past lifetimes. When the subconscious starts getting dredged, Buddhists warn us to be prepared for a roller coaster ride of incredibly vivid nightmares. In the practice of letting the dream be, when a cobra is about to bite your neck, don't do anything, even though as a lucid dreamer, you could. Don't do anything. Let the dream be, and let the cobra sink its fangs into your neck, knowing full well that there is no one who is harmed because you are dreaming. The cobra is not real either. Whether you are being pushed into a fire or over a cliff, let the dream be. Use the power of insight to release yourself to the things that scare you most deeply. You are not harmed. This enormous breakthrough occurs in the dream-state while cultivating awareness with intelligence. In your waking state, however, don't walk in front of a speeding truck unless, by the power of your waking-state meditation, you can transform that truck into a marshmallow, as you can in a lucid dream.

There is a close analogy between lucid dreaming and the practice of living as if you were an illusory being. In a lucid dream, while perfectly aware that you are dreaming, you can engage with events while recognizing that they have no substance. Nothing is reified. This same awareness can be brought into every-day life. Observe that in situations in which you become upset or start craving something, invariably the objects of your attention have been decontextualized. In these situations, subjective input is being ignored and the offending situation, act, or person, appears in isolation. Since nothing exists in isolation, this is delusion. This may be the way reality appears, but this is not the way reality actually is.

A frequent theme of Dzogchen practice is "all things appear but are non-existent." All these things around us, including myself, appear. When you investigate their actual nature, you discover there is no essence to be found. This is the meaning of "between sessions be an illusory person."

This point marks a watershed in the Seven-Point Mind-Training. The emphasis so far has been on developing meditative quiescence and contemplative insight, gaining greater understanding into the nature of objective reality and of awareness itself. If this is all you ever knew about Buddhism, you would be left with a very unbalanced impression. So far I have only discussed one of the two primary aspects of Tibetan Buddhist practice, the cultivation of insight, or ultimate bodhichitta. According to Buddhist tradition, one must realize the nature of reality to attain liberation. But wisdom alone is not enough. As His Holiness the Dalai Lama has cautioned, if your spiritual practice includes only the kinds of practices discussed so far, you may be derailed into an indifferent state of disengaged, uncaring, and isolated inner peace.

The remaining points of the Mind-Training are aimed at complementing and integrating the wisdom of ultimate bodhichitta with the compassion of relative bodhichitta. These remaining points show how to transform all motivations into the highest motivation of achieving spiritual awakening for the benefit of all sentient beings. The remaining points provide practical guidance for life, how to speak and act throughout the course of the day and night so that your entire life supports spiritual practice. Just as meditative practice flows into life, giving it depth, meaning, joy, wisdom, and compassion, so life can support meditative practice. With the next aphorism, the Mind-Training begins to balance the cultivation of wisdom with the cultivation of compassion.

Alternately practice giving and taking.

With the simple line, "Alternately practice giving and taking," the Mind-Training begins its second major theme, the cultivation of relative bodhichitta. Investigating the nature of the mind and other phenomena develops ultimate bodhichitta, the remedy for the delusion at the root of samsara. Wisdom, or ultimate bodhichitta, is one aspect of enlightenment; relative bodhichitta, stemming from loving-kindness and compassion, is the other. The practice of giving and taking, known in Tibetan as *tonglen,* is the first of several practices in the Mind-Training designed to cultivate relative bodhichitta.

During his travels in Tibet, Atisha was occasionally known to express a touch of irony. Atisha was a scholar from the sophisticated civilization of classical India, who lived the final seventeen years of his life in rough, wild, and backward Tibet. Buddhism had been introduced to Tibet in the seventh century but had degenerated to a considerable extent by the time he was invited there by the Tibetan King Yeshe Ö. While many Tibetans expressed their deep admiration for bodhichitta, Atisha noted that this altruistic aspiration for enlightenment was often reduced to a mere liturgy. This led him to make the ironic comment that only Tibetans know how to develop the spirit of awakening, bodhichitta, without cultivating loving-kindness and compassion. Modern Buddhists may heed this same cautionary note. The fruit of authentic bodhichitta arises only from the fertile soil of the prior cultivation of the "four immeasurables": loving-kindness, compassion, empathetic joy, and equanimity.[49]

A central theme of Buddhism concerning the relationship between the practices of relative and ultimate bodhichitta is: "Wisdom without skillful means is bondage. Skillful means without wisdom is bondage." The central element of "skillful means" is compassion.

This is a critical point, especially for Westerners. When we begin Buddhist practice, we tend to go whole-hog for the powerful insight practices that have no counterpart in Christianity, Judaism, Islam or in Western philosophy or science. It is easy to go overboard on the wisdom side of Buddhist practice. It happens in Zen. In Theravada practice, the overwhelming emphasis is on insight practice, or vipassana. A Tibetan Buddhist practice based exclusively on Dzogchen or Mahamudra also becomes unbalanced. The Buddha's warning about cultivating insight alone is that wisdom without skillful means is bondage. With rare exceptions, the cultivation of wisdom alone will not lead to enlightenment. At worst, it becomes a dead end.

In other spiritual traditions, Christianity for example, the cultivation of love and service is very much in the forefront. Altruism is considered a noble quality, and in the secular world many people place a high priority on being of service to others. Yet, people in service professions are especially prone to emotional burn-out. Buddha's analysis of this problem was, "Skillful means without wisdom is bondage"—altruism needs to be balanced with insight and wisdom.

An imbalance of either compassion or wisdom results in bondage. Serving others without a deep source of wisdom and insight to draw upon will lead to exhaustion. Alternately, pursuing wisdom without cultivating compassion will lead to a disengaged, self-centered barrenness, another kind of burn-out.

Buddhists speak of both renunciation and compassion as virtues. These two terms may seem antithetical to each other, but they are actually closely related. Fifteen minutes of watching the evening news is enough to make one feel that the problems of the world are so overwhelming that one might just as well not do anything. Giving up, or withdrawing, is not what Buddhists mean by renunciation. The attitude, "Everything is rotten so I'm going to leave the world behind and become a buddha," leads to a deep chill. The deep chill can happen in the Zen, Theravada, and Tibetan

Buddhist practice; no tradition has a monopoly on unbalanced practitioners.

There is a danger of lack of balance also in the practice of meditative quiescence. Imagine achieving quiescence. There is a sense of physical well-being, a nice feeling in the heart, the mind is serene—as long as nobody interferes. This is the slippery slope of quietism, an extreme state in which happiness arises only when no one is bugging you. I once read about a Christian mystic who had fused his breathing with the Jesus Prayer. Hour after hour, day after day, month after month, he saturated his mind with the Jesus Prayer. As long as he recited the prayer, bliss arose. When he became very adept in this practice, he found he no longer wanted to deal with people at all because they interfered with his bliss. In Buddhism, this is called the extreme of quietism.

Balance is the central theme of the Seven-Point Mind-Training. Enlightenment has two wings, wisdom and compassion. With only one wing, either wing, you fly around in circles, if you get off the ground at all.

Buddhist teachings are described as non-theistic because they don't subscribe to the notion of a creator god separate from creation. Nevertheless, when the Buddha was asked how one can become one with God, he didn't answer, "There is no God! Attain *nirvana!*" Instead, he encouraged the questioner to cultivate the four immeasurables, also called the four "divine abidings" of loving-kindness, compassion, empathetic joy, and equanimity. Developing these four is an indispensable, direct foundation for cultivating relative bodhichitta.

The first immeasurable opening of the heart is loving-kindness. His Holiness the Dalai Lama has often remarked, "My religion is cultivating a good heart." The theme of cultivating a good heart is described in many ways in Buddhist teachings. In 1997, I served as an interpreter for a Mind and Life conference with the Dalai Lama and a group of distinguished physicists. Throughout the five days of the meeting, we discussed such fascinating topics as quantum physics, the space-time continuum, space particles, the big bang, and the expansion of the universe. At the end of the five-day meeting, His Holiness concluded, "I was very happy to spend this time with you. In reality, what is most important is to have a good heart." And these brilliant physicists agreed!

His Holiness often points out that debates about the existence of a creator god, buddha-nature, the inherent existence of phenomena, and whether the nature of the world is dualistic or not, all lead to endless discussions. No matter what realization people have, there will always be disagreement on certain subjects. There will never be a time when representatives from all the world's religions and philosophies meet and agree on the big topics of philosophical and metaphysical doctrine, let alone the smaller points. However, there is one thing on which there is agreement among religious and secular people all over the world: the value of loving-kindness and compassion. Who disagrees? No one. Loving-kindness and compassion are at the heart of spiritual practice.

There is a big difference between loving-kindness and attachment. They are at odds with each other, and this requires some close attention because they are routinely conflated. The confusion arises because in the West "love" often refers to attachment, one of the three core afflictions in Buddhism. But "love" is also sometimes used synonymously with "loving-kindness," a primary Buddhist virtue.

Buddhists often use the term "loving-kindness" instead of simply "love," recognizing the confusion between the virtue and the affliction. I've heard people say that they love their mother, spouse, friends, children, the beach, sunny weather, their homes, and their vehicles. What is the common denominator? Should we cultivate all these kinds of love? Buddhists carefully distinguish between the "love" of loving-kindness, the virtue, and the "love" of attachment, which is an affliction and a root cause of misery and conflict throughout the world. Conflating the two is like mistaking a spoonful of dirt for a spoonful of medicine.

Loving-kindness is the heartfelt yearning for the well-being and happiness of others, based upon a similar yearning for oneself. Loving-kindness is concern for a subject with feelings, a subject who, like oneself, can be hurt or gladdened, a subject who wants to find happiness and be free of suffering. In Buddhist terminology, you cannot have loving-kindness for a motorcycle unless you believe it is a sentient being. Having loving-kindness for chocolate, weather, situations, locations or any other inanimate entity is deluded.

Loving-kindness is for sentient beings only. When I look at someone, he appears to my mind as an object. Loving-kindness is not for objects. How can I have loving-kindness for sentient beings when they appear as objects? Loving-kindness arises when there is empathy. I can't empathize with objects as such, because they don't feel anything. Objects only have a surface dimension, so it is natural only to like or dislike objects. Sentient beings have a dimension of experiencing that makes them subjects. As you attend to your own feelings, your own subjective desire to find happiness and be free of suffering, you realize you are not alone. Sentient beings are all in the same boat with the same bottom line: all of us, as subjects, want to find happiness. Loving-kindness, based on empathetic understanding, is only for subjects. When you are engaging with a subject, recognizing the subjective dimension of another sentient being, only then can there be loving-kindness.

Attachment is for objects. Attachment involves focusing on an object's surface, a chocolate surface, a car surface, a woman surface, a man surface. Attachment isn't concerned about its object's dimension of subjectivity. Attachment plus projection is the source of a lot of what is mistaken for love. Infatuation occurs when there is a projection of desirable qualities upon an object, resulting in an investment of self. This same process disempowers oneself because happiness is projected outside onto an object of attachment. A house, job, bank account, girlfriend—if any of these are lost, there goes happiness. But our happiness is never in an object, never outside us. Happiness is a state of mind. When we create an idealization of something, accentuating the positive, pumping up the neutral, ignoring the negative, this is, unfortunately, called love.

A human being—an immensely complex, multi-dimensional phenomenon made up of feelings, desires, hopes, fears, personal history—who becomes the object of infatuation is flattened to a surface: "This person (my loved one), gives me happiness. The figure, the face, the voice... so attractive. I have to have it." This is attachment. Attachment operates with the motivation of finding self-gratification in an object. How does attachment express itself? To a motorcycle: "I own you." To a person: "I love you." Attachment is totally self-centered and engages with objects for one's own satisfaction. The early stages of attachment may be happy, but later there is disappointment as projections weaken and idealization wears thin. Given time, the object of infatuation appears changed, even disagreeable. Aversion sets in and you can't stand the former loved one. Aversion, like attachment, is also deluded.

Attachment is the most subversive mental affliction because it easily takes on the guise of something genuinely good—loving-kindness. We revere people who emanate genuine loving-kindness. Attachment is the pretense of loving-kindness. Attachment is very tricky.

Geshe Rabten told me how to test for attachment in relationships, whether friendships, family, or romantic.

Relationships are complex. Most are based on more than just attachment, but few relationships involve pure, unconditional love, without any attachment whatsoever. Therefore, most of our relationships are a mixture of love and attachment. The reason there is anxiety in relationships is not because there is so much love, but because there is so much attachment. The test of love versus attachment can be done when you perceive that a person you love changes for the worse. What happens? If the love is genuine, feelings of love grow stronger. If the love was really attachment, there is withdrawal.

A friend of mine told me that just before he and his former wife called it quits, they were sitting across from each other at the breakfast table. He was irritated and resentful as he glared over his newspaper, thinking, "You are supposed to be giving me happiness and you are not doing it!" She was very likely thinking the same thing. This was attachment.

Since I was a monk for fourteen years, I am frequently asked to compare attachment to love and asked how to develop loving-kindness without attachment. Immeasurable loving-kindness includes everyone, without a sense of some people being closer to you and some farther away. That sounds possible in principle for a monk living in a monastery, but how can you—or *should* you—possibly avoid having a special sense of closeness to your family?

Happily, there is a non-monastic approach to the cultivation of loving-kindness. One of my Tibetan mentors, the late Tara Rinpoche, a wonderful Tibetan lama who became a monk when he was a child, vividly clarified the strategy for cultivating loving-kindness in lay life. This strategy is a bit different from that of a monk. The lay strategy is to begin with the affection you feel for loved ones, and refine it, just as you might refine gold. In the beginning stages, the chances are that our relationships are a mixture of attachment and genuine love. We want something from the other person: happiness, fulfillment, affection, and these hopes and expectations are an indication of attachment, dealing with objects. But we also truly care about the other person's well-being. So the Buddhist challenge is to nurture genuine loving-kindness in such relationships and purify it by gradually diminishing the affliction of attachment, which results in less conflict, misery, and anxiety in our relationships. As your love for your own children, for example, becomes more and more unconditional, extend that love to your children's friends, their parents, and finally extend this loving-kindness out to all beings.

Recall again William James's principle that what we attend to becomes our reality. We have a choice about what we attend to in our relationships. Do you want to attend to others' defects and mistakes? By selective attention, we can find that the object of our attachment becomes less desirable. Alternately, we can attend to the humanness, the subjectivity of the other person and those qualities we admire, and this will naturally lead to increased appreciation and affection.

Virtually all our relationships start out as a mixture of attachment and genuine love, a mix that gives rise to a lot of unnecessary suffering and anxiety. The lay approach to cultivating loving-kindness is to sift out attachment and purify loving-kindness. This process then can extend to other relationships that are less intimate. In fact, there is no real difference between people close to us and people we don't know. As you develop unconditional love for your children, you realize other children also want to find happiness and be free of suffering. Start with the mix of love and attachment, purify it, and expand out in all directions, like water flowing evenly over an alluvial plain. In *A Guide to the Bodhisattva Way of Life*, Shantideva prays, "May I be a protector for those who are without protectors, a guide for travelers, and a boat, a bridge, and a ship for those who wish to cross over."[50] By following this bodhisattva ideal, you become the unknown friend of everyone you meet.

The distinction between loving-kindness and attachment is enormous. Attachment is an affliction. Loving-kindness is a crucial aspect of spiritual awakening.

The Meditative Cultivation of Loving-kindness

The cultivation of loving-kindness is taught in many ways in the Buddhist tradition. I will describe one technique based upon the writings of the fifth-century Indian Buddhist sage Buddhaghosa.[51] This meditation should be practiced after the usual preparation of sitting in an appropriate posture, taking three cleansing breaths, and cultivating meditative stability, for example by counting twenty-one breaths.

The first step of this practice is to reflect upon the antithesis of loving-kindness, which is anger and hatred. In a non-moralistic way, consider the repercussions of these afflictions. Anger is draining; it takes effort. In retrospect, anger rarely seems justified, nor is it usually effective in solving problems. When you stand back, you see that what you seek is happiness and that what you want to do is solve problems. The Buddha's comment on hatred was, "Hatred never ceases through hatred: hatred ceases through love; this is an eternal law."[52] In this phase of the meditation, investigate the effects and efficacy of anger for getting what you want. As the Dalai Lama often comments, "If you must be self-centered, at least be intelligent about it!"

The most direct method for bringing an end to anger is cultivating loving-kindness. The next phase of the practice is to bring forth the yearning: "At all times, regardless of circumstances, may I be free of anger, hatred, and all varieties of aggression and malice." To bring more power to this meditation, imagine that your yearning has come to fulfillment right now. Imagine encountering situations that have aroused anger in the past and imagine responding to them without anger.

In this meditation, use wholesome desire focused on the well-being of others and yourself to empower imagination. Bring forth the yearning: "May I be free of all mental afflictions." Bring forth the yearning: "Regardless of the situation, may I not fall into the trap of afflictions, but simply deal with the situation free of anxiety, with intelligence and effectiveness." Imagine this to be true right now. Bring forth the desire to be free of the attachment that gives rise to fear and anxiety. Imagine being free of all fear and anxiety in the present, past, and future. Imagine being free of the attachment that gives rise to fear right now.

The next phase of the meditation is to bring forth your most meaningful aspirations and envision a life that would be truly one of fulfillment, happiness, and meaning. Allow the wish to find genuine happiness to arise. Imagine being truly well and happy regardless of the external circumstances. Imagine right now that your deepest yearnings have been fulfilled.

Now bring to mind a living person whom you admire. Contemplate this person's qualities that inspire admiration. With this person in mind, bring forth the yearning: "May you, like myself, be free of all anger, resentment, and hatred, and abide in serenity, without the turbulence of mental afflictions." Imagine that it is so. As you wish to be free of anger and find happiness, wish this also for the person you admire. Let the field of your awareness embrace all the people in your immediate environment with the thought: "May you, like myself, be free of all suffering and be well and happy." Imagine this to be so for each person. Expand your awareness to the surrounding community, to thousands of people, each with desires for happiness, each wishing to be free of suffering, just like yourself. Continue to gently expand your awareness in all directions, extending to all sentient beings on earth, who all have in common the wish for happiness and the wish to avoid suffering, the thought, "May each one be well and happy." Imagine this to be so. This concludes the meditative cultivation of loving-kindness.

Loving-kindness is an especially valuable practice for Westerners, especially Americans, who tend to specialize in self-deprecation. In 1990, I was interpreting for another Mind and Life meeting with the Dalai Lama and a group of cognitive scientists. The vipassana teacher Sharon Salzberg was also one of the participants, and she asked His Holiness about the validity of cultivating loving-kindness for oneself. She commented that she had found this practice very useful in teaching Westerners, for many of us suffer from low self-esteem, self-denigration, and the feeling that we are not even deserving of happiness. There was a long discussion back and forth until it became apparent that the Dalai Lama had a hard time fathoming what we Westerners meant by "self-effacement, lack of self-esteem, self-hatred, self-contempt"! It seemed to take a long time for him to understand these Western afflictions, and in the course of this conversation he learned the meaning of a word that has no equivalent in Tibetan: "guilt." When he learned the nature of these psychological maladies and their prevalence in the modern West, he finally concluded, "In answer to your initial question about beginning the cultivation of loving-kindness directed toward oneself, and whether this has a place in Buddhist practice, yes it does." And he burst into laughter.[53]

Loving-kindness should be directed first toward oneself. If there is no loving-kindness toward oneself, the chance of experiencing genuine loving-kindness for others is remote. The Buddha put it this way, "One who loves himself will never harm another."[54] Focus first upon yourself, wishing, "May I be free of animosity, affliction, and anxiety. May I live happily." Using the power of your desire, imagine it is so.

Next, gradually expand the field of your concern so that at no time is there any hypocrisy. The Christian injunction, "Love your enemy," is very difficult. Buddhism's "Love those who harm you" is just as tough. If you try too soon to bring forth loving-kindness for those who have wounded you or your loved ones, the effect will be very weak or you may simply succumb to hypocrisy. Therefore, the traditional formula used in this meditation starts with loving yourself. Bring forth acceptance and affection for yourself and then extend it to another person, recalling that person's kindness and his or her virtues that inspire affection and admiration. Bring forth the same wish with an underlying empathy—"like myself, so with you."

After you consider yourself, bring to mind a dearly loved friend and cultivate the same thoughts of loving-kindness. Then consider a person you know but toward whom you are indifferent. Regard this person now as you do your loved and admired friend. With loving-kindness wish and imagine: "May you be happy." Finally, consider a hostile person as you did the indifferent person, and extend loving-kindness to him also. In this way, meditate repeatedly until the barriers among the categories of friend, neutral person, and hostile person vanish. This is the meaning of "immeasurable" loving-kindness.

The final phase of this practice applies to a person you consider an enemy. This is difficult. In Buddhism, "enemy" does not refer to a person you hate. An enemy is a person who you feel is your adversary, who wishes you harm. An enemy is a person who would be happy if you got hit by a truck or at least lost your reputation. In this practice, when you focus on an enemy, this is a person who may have harmed you, taken advantage of you, slandered you, or a person who is going after something you have or want. The practice is to wish that person happiness. If you wish to develop unconditional love, practice until all the distinctions between dear friend, casual friend, stranger, and enemy dissolve.

When you meet resistance in this practice, be honest. It is easy to feel loving-kindness for some people, but for others, no way. When you bring a person to mind, there may be fear, dread, contempt, anger, some feeling diametrically opposed to loving-kindness. The mind might just stop. This is a universal problem and you have to backtrack to deal with it. To break down this habituation, dissolve the caricature of the enemy by recalling his or her inoffensive qualities of behavior. When we focus on a person as being contemptible, we tend to focus on just afflictions and misdeeds. But no one is devoid of good qualities altogether. When we view a person as 100% disgusting, nothing else, we feel justified in our contempt. When we feel aversion, we tend to edit the big picture down to a cartoon. But nobody is a cartoon. To dissolve the cartoon, attend closely. There is more going on.

An enemy is a person who has harmed us or those we love, intentionally or not, by cheating, abuse, deceit. If our response is hatred, the enemy wins. The enemy wants to do damage, and if our response is to contort our hearts in anger, the effect of the enemy's action is compounded. The person who wishes us harm should be very satisfied if he not only got us with the first punch of his aggression, but doubles his score with our self-inflicted resentment. In the long run, our own anger and resentment cause us greater suffering than any damage inflicted by someone else. When our response is hate, our enemy has hit a home run. On the other hand, we can stop the game and say, "You have offered me the gift of your hatred, but I choose not to accept." This is possible.

After an encounter with an enemy, the hurt that continues is not due to the damage he inflicted. The enemy has a life and eventually will go off to do something else. After an encounter with an enemy, the source of ongoing suffering is the *true* enemy, anger. Shantideva writes, "Enemies such as craving and hatred are without arms, legs, and so on. They are neither courageous nor wise. How is it that they have enslaved me?"[55] Of all mental afflictions, there is none more virulent and pernicious than anger.

Anger, the true enemy, is a special case. Anger deludes us because it nearly always seems to be justified. The fault always seems to belong to someone else. Some people who have suffered great adversity provide inspiration and guidance in dealing with anger. Palden Gyatso, who spent thirty-three years in concentration camps in Tibet being tortured and starved, told me, "The Communists took my life. They got me when I was a young man, took the heart of my life. Now I am an old man and will die soon." Yet he said this without hatred. When I interpreted for him during a demonstration outside the Chinese consulate in San Francisco, he called up to the gray walls and closed shutters, "What are you afraid of? Come out and speak with us. We wish you no harm. We don't hate you!" How could he say, "We don't hate you," after thirty-three years in a concentration camp? Palden Gyatso sees events in a context broader than the personal events of a single life.[56]

The Buddha described the benefits of cultivating loving-kindness in this way:

> One sleeps in comfort, wakes in comfort, and dreams no evil
> dreams. One is dear to human and non-human beings, deities

guard one; fire, poison and weapons do not affect one; one's
mind is easily concentrated; the expression on one's face is serene; and one dies unconfused. Even if one achieves nothing
higher, one will be reborn in the Brahmā World.[57]

When an obstacle to the cultivation of loving-kindness
appears, for example anger toward an enemy, the cause is
reification. A target has been created that doesn't exist. This
is where insight, wisdom, integrates into the practice of loving-kindness. Insight is the powerful method to overcome
the fundamental obstacle to the cultivation of loving-kindness, reification. Examine closely. Is the target of your anger
a person's body or mind? Investigate and recognize that
the reified object you hate doesn't even exist. If insight practice doesn't take you all the way to this realization in one
step, Buddhaghosa suggests you can still begin to heal your
mind by giving a gift to your enemy. At all costs and with
skillful strategies, break the habit of reifying the enemy.

The immediate cause of loving-kindness is seeing the
lovable qualities in others. Westerners sometimes get the
impression that Buddhist loving-kindness is an "I love the
world, it's my neighbors I don't care about" type of love.
Tibetans describe loving-kindness as the mind *becoming*
love, like the feeling of a mother whose child rushes home
into her arms after being away at summer camp. Loving-
kindness succeeds when animosity subsides and it fails
when it produces attachment.

In the Buddhist tradition, for all its emphasis on non-
violence, oddly enough a prominent metaphor for spiritual
practice is warfare—identifying and vanquishing the true
enemy. Buddhaghosa wrote of the "near" and "far" enemies
of loving-kindness. The near enemy of loving-kindness is
attachment. In cultivating loving-kindness, the affection
that arises can very easily slip over into attachment. Attachment is the "near" enemy because, while its actual
nature is that of a mental affliction, it masquerades as "love."

The "distant" enemy of loving-kindness is its diametric opposite—malice.

The cultivation of loving-kindness, the "giving" referred to in the Mind-Training's aphorism "alternately practice giving and taking," is a very effective practice for active, everyday life. I once practiced the cultivation of loving-kindness during an extended solitary retreat in the high desert. Each time I practiced, I would bring to mind dear friends, neutral people, and some who had treated me badly. But after doing this quite a number of times, my recollections of these people became rather flat, as if I were bringing to mind mere images, but not really attending to actual people. The practice became superficial. In my experience, the cultivation of loving-kindness is most effectively done while actively engaging with other people in their day-to-day lives. When you open your heart to others, the practice is very real.

The complementary practice to the cultivation of loving-kindness is the cultivation of compassion. This is the heartfelt wish that oneself and others be free of suffering and the sources of suffering. Loving-kindness is the wish for well-being, and compassion is the wish for freedom from suffering. Loving-kindness and compassion naturally give rise to and support each another.

The first phase of the cultivation of compassion entails reflecting on the effects of compassion. When you have felt compassion, what have been the effects? What influence have compassionate people had on your life? Conversely, when you experience indifference or worse, a sense of cruelty, what has been the effect? When you witness individuals, communities, governments or nations acting out of indifference or vengeance, what has been the effect?

The next phase of the cultivation of compassion is vividly bringing to mind a person or a group of people who are suffering or an individual or group who are causing suffering. Empathize with the suffering and let the wish naturally arise, "May you be free of suffering and the sources of suffering." Imagine it to be so.

In 1992, I visited Samye Monastery, the oldest monastery in Tibet, a beautiful place, which has been rebuilt after it was destroyed during the Cultural Revolution. An old yogi named Tenzin Zangpo from Eastern Tibet was visiting Samye at the same time and was giving teachings on Shantideva's *Guide to the Bodhisattva Way of Life*. I am very interested in learning from the experiences of advanced contemplatives, so I requested to meet him. I asked the old yogi questions about meditative quiescence, but he kept emphasizing, "For deep meditative practice, before attempting to achieve quiescence, first cultivate compassion."

The importance of compassion can be determined experientially. When mental balance and serenity arise in meditative practice, observe what happens to that sense of well-being under the influence of anger or irritation. Mental balance always gets destroyed. It is not possible to abide in meditative equipoise and be resentful at the same time. The balance of the mind crumbles in the face of anger. And there is something worse.

Imagine doing a long retreat for months on end, practicing meditation eight to twelve hours each day, aimed at the goal of developing deep attentional stability and clarity. Imagine that you accomplish quiescence, with the ability to sit for hours on end with your mind totally focused, effortlessly, vividly and without excitation, wherever you direct it. Once you have achieved such a state of meditative stabilization, if your mind should succumb to the affliction of malice, a thought diametrically opposed to loving-kindness, the Buddha claimed the mind can become a terrible weapon of destruction. Therefore, as you develop the power of concentration, make sure that your mind is less and less prone to the influence of afflictions. Just as there is evidence supporting the belief in the positive power of prayer, take the advice of the Buddha on the opposite point: negative thoughts have power and concentrated negative thoughts can be very dangerous.

Just as attachment is frequently mistaken for love because its superficial display may be similar, anger can look like compassion. When we see someone being victimized by another we think, "Punish the bad person. Rescue the good person." This is the same solution victimizers have and they also feel justified. Anger can be mistaken for compassion when the latter extends only to "good" people, while we hold "bad" people in contempt and feel fully justified in doing so. In the Buddhist perspective, attachment for some and hatred for others is just one more manifestation of an afflicted mind.

Compassion is difficult. Compassion means wishing that both victims and victimizers be free of suffering and the sources of suffering. This is important because when we're filled with righteous indignation, wrath and anger pose as compassion. But anger is not compassion any more than attachment is love.

I was first taught *A Guide to the Bodhisattva Way of Life* in 1972 by the Tibetan lama Geshe Ngawang Dhargyey. This monk, who so wonderfully embodied what he was teaching, said the bodhisattva way of life is one in which you empathize more and more deeply with the suffering of all those around you, not just your family and friends, but the whole world with its myriad sentient beings. Why should we take on this suffering of others, adding to the burden of our own personal problems? Shantideva responds, "I should eliminate the suffering of others because it is suffering, just like my own suffering. I should take care of others because they are sentient beings, just as I am a sentient being."[58] When I heard this I was struck with the math: in cultivating the bodhisattva way of life, one develops a greater and greater capacity for empathizing with the suffering of more and more sentient beings. Every airplane that crashes, every natural disaster, every war—you would need to multiply the number of victims by hundreds to account for all the loved ones whose lives were shattered in each such tragedy. There is so much suffering. If the Buddhist path of liberation entails developing compassion, and compassion entails deeper and deeper empathy with the suffering of more and more sentient beings, where does it end? This is a path of joy? The bodhisattva path would seem to lead to infinite suffering. I asked Geshe Dhargyey to reconcile buddhahood, the bliss of spiritual awakening, with its non-dual awareness of all the suffering in the world. He responded by pointing out that I was extrapolating from a very small pool of experience: "You can't take your own experience and multiply it infinitely to calculate the mind of a buddha. The crucial element that you haven't taken into account is wisdom."

Compassion can be unbearable without wisdom. His Holiness the Dalai Lama has profound empathy for the Tibetan people, who look to him as their refuge and source of hope. How is it possible for him to be happy as long as the Tibetan people suffer? This is compassion balanced with wisdom. Insight taps into a joy that allows one to embrace suffering without being overwhelmed by it. Compassion without wisdom is bondage. Wisdom without compassion is bondage. Compassion and wisdom are the two wings of enlightenment.

The primary realization of insight is emptiness. You can be deluded about a lot of things—the nature of space/time, black holes, the origin of the universe—but if you are deluded about your own nature, who you are, and act on the basis of that delusion, you will constantly suffer repercussions. To end the suffering caused by delusion, apply the remedy of insight into your own personal identity. If the object of all our tender loving care, the inherently existent "I," doesn't even exist, we need to know that.

Tsongkhapa was once giving a discourse in Tibet on the lack of inherent existence of all phenomena, including the self. When a teacher speaks out of deep experience, the words have a special power. A monk in the audience suddenly started to freak out, feeling he didn't exist at all, and in desperation he grabbed onto his collar. Tsongkhapa chuckled and released the monk from his panic by commenting that he had established the conventional reality of his own identity on the basis of his collar!

The Tibetan Buddhist tradition warns about penetrating the nature of selflessness before the mind is ready. If the mind is not adequately prepared, when there is a glimmer of insight into the profound reality of the emptiness of one's own personal identity, it will be experienced as a *loss* of a cherished treasure. However, if the mind has first been nurtured with compassion, then when some realization of personal identitylessness is glimpsed, this insight will be experienced as a *discovery* of the most precious of all treasures. Whether the realization of emptiness is perceived as a loss or a discovery depends on the degree of one's preparation. Insight in the context of compassion is a wonderful discovery. Wisdom without compassion is bondage—insight into the emptiness of personal identity without compassion can be perceived as a loss of self and lead to terror.

If we are empty of inherent existence, in what way do we exist? From quarks to galactic clusters, how does the physical world exist? The Madhyamaka Buddhist view is that we exist as dependently related events. I am a sequential matrix of events. Reading this book is an event.

We are all events. The corollary of emptiness is dependent origination. The two are really of the same nature, just viewed from two different perspectives. Something existing independently, in and of itself, is never found under even the most penetrating analysis. The realization of wisdom is that all phenomena exist as dependently related events. Realizing that existence is inextricably and fundamentally interdependent with everything and everyone leads naturally to acting in ways that take into account all those connections.

Shantideva gave a marvelous metaphor that appears in other religious traditions as well: "Although it has many divisions, such as its arms and so on, the body is protected as a whole. Likewise, different beings, with their joys and sorrows, are all equal, like myself, in their yearning for happiness."[59] The notion of all sentient beings being like a single human body is an excellent metaphor for interdependence. When your nose itches, the compassionate finger helps out and gives it a gentle scratch.

Cultivating compassion primes the pump for the realization of the profound interdependence of all phenomena. We are not independent things that somehow become related. We are the relations. This is why the cultivation of wisdom must go hand-in-hand with the cultivation of compassion.

In 1992, when I went to India with the group of neuroscientists to do research on the effects of meditation, one of our interests was compassion. In the mountains above Dharamsala there are yogis who have spent years cultivating compassion, and we spent some time with a young monk who had been in retreat for six years. Richard Davidson, a psychobiologist from the University of Wisconsin who has done pioneering work correlating shifts in expression with emotions, explained to the young contemplative that he

would see a video called "Compassion in Exile," which con-
tains explicit footage of Tibetan demonstrators being beaten
by the Chinese military. We had hauled electronic equipment up the side of the mountain to video the young monk's
face while he watched. As the monk watched the video,
we didn't detect any change of expression in his face at all,
no grimace or shudder, no expression of sadness. After we
turned off the cameras, we asked him to tell us about his
experience. He said, "I didn't see anything that I didn't already know goes on all the time, not only in Tibet but
throughout the world. I am aware of this constantly." It
wasn't that he didn't experience compassion while watching
these brutal scenes. Rather, his compassion was so constant
that seeing these images on a video monitor provided him
with no new stimuli to arouse his compassion beyond its
steady state.

The Buddhist concept of compassion is deeper than
episodic responses to isolated events. The first phase of cultivating compassion is contemplating the advantages of
compassion and the disadvantages of its absence. One
meditates on the benefits of compassion, then considers
compassion's far enemy, cruelty. Indifference is simply an
absence of compassion. When we feel cruelty, the polar opposite of compassion, we deal with subjects, just as we do
when we experience compassion. When the mind is dominated by cruelty, we recognize that a subject can be made
to suffer and we wish him to suffer. Contemplating the benefits of compassion, the disadvantages of its absence and
the disadvantages of its opposite, cruelty, is part of the
preparation for the direct cultivation of compassion.

The first step of the main practice of cultivating compassion is focusing on a person who is in misery. As you imagine
being in this person's shoes, bring forth the wish, "May
you be free." The next step, without which the whole

meditation winds up being superficial, is more difficult. Focus on an evil-doer, a person who brings grief to others, and wish also for him, "May you be free of sufferings and its sources." A response of contempt, hatred, or disgust toward an evil-doer is not compatible with Dharma. The struggle for most of us is not to give in to our deeply habituated knee-jerk reactions to evil, hypocrisy, and dishonesty. This phase of practice, cultivating compassion for the evil-doer, is one of the litmus tests of Dharma. It is relatively easy to feel compassion for those who suffer. But arousing compassion for a malicious person is an indication that we are making some progress on the path.

Geshe Rabten spent twenty-four years in a monastery, about ten years in the mountains in meditation, and roughly the last fifteen years of his life teaching. I first received teachings from him when he was still in retreat in the mountains above Dharamsala. He made a statement about compassion that was difficult to grasp: an evil-doer is even more worthy of compassion than a physically impaired person. Having compassion for the disabled is quite easy. However, from the Buddhist perspective of emptiness and dependent origination, the person in good health, capable and energetic, who lives his life as an evil-doer, is especially deserving of compassion because he is leading a way of life that will result in misery not only for others but for himself for lifetime after lifetime.

After focusing on a suffering person, then an evil-doer, next focus the practice of cultivating compassion on a loved one or friend with the same wish, "May you be free of suffering and its causes." Next, focus on a neutral person. Finally, focus your compassion on a person in the special category of "enemy," one who wishes you harm, and cultivate compassion for this person also. Cultivate compassion by focusing on the different categories of people—evil-doer, loved one, neutral, and hostile—until barriers break down and compassion flows evenly. Practice until compassion flows smoothly like a river over a flat plane in all directions, not just in the path of least resistance. Wish for all kinds of sentient beings, "May you be free of suffering and its causes."

Remember that the near enemy of loving-kindness is attachment. Attachment is the near enemy because it persuasively masquerades as the real thing, loving-kindness; likewise grief is the near enemy of compassion, for it can easily be mistaken for compassion. If I discover tomorrow that I have terminal cancer and have only three months to live, you are not going to make my day by crying on my shoulder. I will gain no benefit by your being sad for me. Grief is the near enemy of compassion.

Just as loving-kindness has the far enemy of hatred, compassion also has a far enemy: cruelty. Cruelty is the diametric opposite of compassion. And just as loving-kindness has a proximate cause, seeing the lovable qualities in others, compassion's proximate cause is seeing others in suffering and incapable of relieving their distress.

The meditative cultivation of compassion succeeds when it causes cruelty to subside, and it fails when it produces merely sadness. Immeasurable compassion is limitless in the sense of being without barriers; it flows evenly in all directions. Immeasurable compassion is the great remedy to cruelty and is the foundation of spiritual maturation.

In the Mahayana Buddhist view, there is something even beyond immeasurable compassion, called "great compassion." Great compassion rises beyond the wish, "May you be free of suffering," to "May I make it so." Great compassion shoulders the responsibility for freeing others from suffering. If you shudder at this, you are getting the message. Consider all the conflict in the world. How can a single person take on the responsibility of freeing others from suffering? Recall over and over, deeper each time: compassion without wisdom is bondage. What "I" can take on the responsibility of alleviating the suffering of the world? I, as one finite individual, certainly don't have the ability. The Buddhist view is that "I" as a separate autonomous entity, as an ego, does not even exist. The Buddhist view is that my existence is one of interrelationship with all those around me. Furthermore, my existence is also in interrelationship with buddha-mind that is everywhere present. And this enlightened awareness has an inexhaustible capacity for serving the needs of the world. This is what is meant by great compassion. To cultivate and sustain great compassion you need deep insight into the fundamental nature of mind.

There are levels of compassion. There is "episodic compassion," when you feel sympathy for those whom you see are presently in distress. There is a deeper compassion that arises coupled with insight, in which you realize impermanence, the flux, or transient nature, of everything around you. Everything you grasp onto for dear life, the body, happiness, everything, is in a state of flux. Anything acquired will be lost. Realize impermanence deeply and recognize how sentient beings bet their lives and happiness on what is impermanent. Finally, the deepest form of compassion, great compassion, without boundaries and non-dual, arises wedded to the realization of emptiness and has no reified object at all.

The cultivation of loving-kindness and compassion is a primary practice for the hours of the waking day when we are not sitting in formal meditation. There is no better time for the cultivation of loving-kindness and compassion than while engaging with others. No special conditions are necessary.

There is no more powerful way to accumulate merit than through the cultivation of compassion. Merit is spiritual power and is the force empowering meditative practice for insight, purification, and spiritual transformation. The cultivation of loving-kindness and compassion is the basis of the practice described in the Mind-Training as "alternately practice giving and taking," known in Tibetan as *tonglen*, which is among the most highly cherished practices in the Tibetan tradition.

The Practice of Tonglen

The practice of giving and taking, *tonglen*, uses the power of imagination to engage with realities beyond immediate experience. The enactment of loving-kindness is the "giving" component of the practice of giving and taking, and the enactment of compassion is the "taking" component. The taking component begins by bringing to mind as vividly as you can a loved one or a community of people whom you care about deeply and who is suffering. The cause of the suffering may be physical, psychological, social, or environmental. For a moment, empathetically enter into the suffering of this person or group. Imagine experiencing the burden of their adversity. Now, in your mind's eye, stand back and bring forth the wish, "May you be relieved of this burden and may this adversity ripen upon me." Whatever the affliction or adversity, physical or mental, imagine taking from this person the despair, affliction, and pain. Imagine the suffering in the form of a black cloud being removed from the other person's body and mind and being drawn into your heart. Imagine that as the suffering is funneled into your heart, that person is gradually relieved. As soon as this dark cloud enters your heart, imagine that it meets with your own sense of self-centeredness, visualized as an orb of darkness, and that in an instant both that cloud of misery and your self-centeredness mutually extinguish each other, leaving not a trace of either behind. Now imagine all of your merit, prosperity, happiness, all the blessings in your life from the past, present and future, as a powerful wellspring of brilliant white light emanating from your heart in the reverse direction. Imagine these powerful rays of light reaching out and suffusing the person with the prayer, "All that is good in my life, my possessions, my happiness, my good health, my virtues, of the past, present and future, I offer to you. May you be well and happy. May your greatest yearnings and deepest aspirations be fulfilled." Imagine that the light of virtue and happiness begins to suffuse the people you have brought to mind and imagine their most meaningful desires and aspirations being fulfilled. Yet as this light from your heart flows forth unimpededly, it is not depleted from its inexhaustible source.

The next step is to focus on a person or group who is deluded and acts in ways harmful to themselves and others. Again, practice taking this burden upon yourself. Imagine their delusion or other mental afflictions, such as anger, resentment, and craving, and bring forth the yearning, "May you be relieved of the terrible burden of delusion and affliction." Imagine that the mental afflictions in the form of a black cloud are drawn from that person or group and taken into your heart, where once again it is annihilated, together with your own sense of self-centeredness. As before, imagine sending forth all of your virtue, your compassion, wisdom, and generosity, in the form of radiant, purifying white light suffusing this individual or group with the aspiration, "All that is good in my life, I offer to you. May your most meaningful aspirations be fulfilled." Vividly imagine this to be so.

Now expand the practice of *tonglen* to take in all suffering and mental afflictions and send forth all your virtue and goodness. Let your mind rove throughout your environment and throughout the world, alighting upon an individual, a community or a nation one after another. During each inhalation, imagine taking in the burden of suffering and the sources of suffering. With each exhalation imagine rays of white light emerging from your heart, a light of healing, grace, blessing, that illuminates wherever you attend.

Draw your awareness into your own body and imagine the radiant white light of virtue and joy emanating from your heart suffusing your body. Imagine your body so full of light that the light cannot be contained and rays are emitted from every pore of your body in all directions.

Complete the practice of *tonglen* with dedication of merit: "By the merit of this practice, may every sentient being gain liberation from suffering and the sources of suffering. May the deepest yearning of each be fulfilled."

This completes the practice of *tonglen*.

In the traditional Buddhist practice, *tonglen* begins by focusing on your mother. For example, a lama in a Tibetan Buddhist monastery would begin teaching *tonglen* by having the monks recall the kindnesses of their mothers from the time of being in the womb, through the trials of birth, the loving care given in infancy when one is totally helpless, being there every time for every need. Your mother cares for you as if you are the most precious of all beings.

Visualizing one's mother as the first step of *tonglen* practice presents a problem for many Westerners. Many Westerners think of parents in unflattering terms, even as the source of all their problems and hang-ups. Traditional Tibet was not free from familial difficulties, but the norm was to have very deep and loving ties with parents. In Buddhist cultures, children are encouraged to look upon parents with a deep sense of gratitude and respect. Parents are the source of this human life of leisure and opportunity, which, in the Buddhist perspective, is the basis for engaging in spiritual practice to find the happiness you have been looking for since time immemorial. Buddhists have many meditations focusing on the special kindness of parents.

In the contemporary West, children (and even "adult children") all too often focus on the defects of their parents. Tibetans find a lot to admire in Euro-American civilization, but they are amazed at the uncivilized way we regard and treat our parents. The intention of *tonglen* practice is to start with the easiest person, the person for whom you naturally feel the most love and affection. In Buddhist culture, this would be one's mother. In modern Western culture, an easier first subject can be substituted. In any case, start *tonglen* with an easy person, a loved one or dear friend. From there, progress toward unconditional love for your parents. Even if your parents were abusive or uncaring, it is possible to nurture a sense of gratitude for whatever good was given you and accept the rest with forgiveness. This is not easy, but we are all, parents included, defective sentient beings suffering from mental afflictions. Practicing *tonglen* for parents leads to great breakthroughs for many people. The goal here is opening our hearts unconditionally, especially to our parents.

Buddhist teachings recognize that the first victim of contemptible behavior is the person committing it. The challenge is to recognize that the only appropriate response to abusive behavior is compassion. If you have parents who have been less than ideal, bring them to mind with all their faults. Imagine taking their suffering into your heart and dissolving it there with the wish, "May you be free."

As in the traditional Tibetan Buddhist practice of *tonglen*, focus on your mother, recalling her kindness and open up the warmth in your heart. Tibetans focus more on the mother than the father because the mother generally spends more time with the children and is often more nurturing. Imagine taking all your mother's suffering and its causes into your heart, and imagine offering all your possessions, virtues, and happiness to her without reservation. Do this then for your father as well.

It is good to help people materially or with friendship or protection. These gifts are helpful during specific times of life. In the Buddhist tradition, the greatest gift of all is considered to be the gift of Dharma, because it is the means of alleviating suffering from its source and of finding genuine happiness. Imagine offering to your mother everything she needs on the material level. Then imagine offering her the gift of Dharma. If she is a Christian, offer her Christian Dharma. If she is Jewish, offer Jewish Dharma. Imagine offering your mother whatever Dharma is appropriate.

The practice of *tonglen* may actually alleviate the suffering of another person, but the true criterion of success in this meditation is the attenuation of our own self-centeredness and the growth of love and compassion in our own hearts.

There have been generations of Buddhists from the time of ancient India until today who have taken *tonglen* as their main practice for life. Geshe Ngawang Dhargyey, who knew I was very drawn to breath awareness, told me, "Breath awareness is a really good practice, but every breath conjoined with *tonglen* has immeasurably greater merit than simply attending to the tactile sensations of the respiration." Every breath becomes meaningful when you imagine taking in the suffering of others and offering them your joy.

Mount them both upon your breath.

The meaning of the next line of the text is to mount both the giving and taking aspects of the *tonglen* practice upon your breath. Specifically, on the in-breath imagine taking in suffering, on the out-breath imagine offering all your joy.

In his commentary on this Mind-Training, Dilgo Khyentse Rinpoche commented that in Tibet, when people gained some experience in the practice of *tonglen*, "their understanding would become clouded and they would feel that their obscurations had increased."[60] But he counseled that if this happens, one should not be dismayed, because this is an indication that the practice is working. This mental disturbance won't last. If you find that your mind actually takes on the suffering of others, simply be present with the suffering, without grasping onto it or identifying with it. Additionally, he said that although it is difficult, don't shrink from focusing on malevolent people with the wish that they may be free from the terrible afflictions that cause them to suffer and which cause them to make other people suffer. This is exactly what is called for in the practice of *tonglen*.

A principal source for this practice is, once again, Shantideva's classic, *A Guide to the Bodhisattva Way of Life*. After asking himself why one should add to the burden of one's own problems by taking on the miseries of others, he responds, "If the suffering of many disappears because of the suffering of one, then a compassionate person should induce that suffering for his own sake and for the sake of others."[61]

Three objects, three poisons, and three roots of virtue.

This line suggests a simple but very transformative practice for active life. "Three objects" refers to three categories of people: people you like, people you don't like, and people toward whom you feel neutral. In contact with these three types of people, "three poisons" are aroused in us: people we like arouse the poison of self-centered attachment; people we don't like arouse aversion; people toward whom we feel neutral arouse indifference. The "three roots of virtue" arise when we counteract the three poisons. This is a practice for engaging with all types of people by shifting the patterns of mind to become free from attachment, aversion, and the delusion of indifference, allowing virtue to arise.

For example, when you see reprehensible behavior and experience the knee-jerk response of aversion, instead of standing in judgment, immediately practice *tonglen*. "Mount the two on the breath" means with the in-breath send the wish, "May this affliction be drawn into me and may you be free" and with the out-breath send the wish, "May you experience all that is good in my life." The three roots of virtue lead to the growth of virtue. Through a kind of emotional alchemy, attachment is transmuted into loving-kindness; aversion is transmuted into compassion; and indifference is transmuted into warm-hearted equanimity.

In everything you do, practice with words.

While entering into all kinds of activity, you can engage in this practice by expressing the wish quietly under your breath, "May the suffering and sources of suffering of all sentient beings ripen upon me. May the causes of my well-being ripen upon all sentient beings." This is the final practice for the cultivation of relative bodhichitta and completes the Second Point of the Seven-Point Mind-Training concerning the cultivation of ultimate and relative bodhichitta, wisdom and compassion, the heart and essence of Buddhist practice.

It is not enough to train in the preliminaries, the First Point of the Mind-Training, and then train in the two bodhichittas, the Second Point. We have to be sure, again and again, that what we are practicing is genuine Dharma. How can spiritual practice be evaluated? The Buddha lived at a time of many teachers and teachings and a standard question from prospective students was why should anyone follow him and not another teacher. There were many choices then just as there are now. When a community known as the Kalamas reported to the Buddha their doubt and perplexity in the face of the diversity of teachers and teachings they had been exposed to, he responded,

> Yes, Kalamas, it is proper that you have doubt, that you have perplexity, for a doubt has arisen in a matter which is doubtful. Now look, you Kalamas, do not be led by reports, or tradition, or hearsay. Be not led by the authority of religious texts, nor by mere logic or inference, nor by considering appearances, nor by the delight in speculative opinions, nor by seeming possibilities, nor by the idea: "this is our teacher." But, O Kalamas, when you know for yourselves that certain things are unwholesome, and wrong, and bad, then give them up...And when you know for yourselves that certain things are wholesome and good, then accept them and follow them.[62]

There are two criteria on which to judge the efficacy of this path. One criterion relates to the powerful, deeply imbedded tendency to grasp onto a reified sense of "I." In Buddhist teachings, the reification of "I" is the fundamental delusion and the root of suffering. Practice is effective if reification of self is decreasing, if words of abuse don't find a target so easily, if the sense of "I am" is getting lighter.

The second main indicator of success in Buddhist practice relates to "self-centeredness," the sense that your own personal well-being is your number-one priority. This is the attitude that proclaims, "me and mine first." If you don't find that your practice diminishes self-centeredness, you need to find another practice.

The cultivation of ultimate bodhichitta is designed to counteract self-grasping through the realization of emptiness, the lack of inherent existence of phenomena, including yourself. The practice of relative bodhichitta is designed to counteract self-centeredness. That is enlightenment in a nutshell. Every Buddhist practice, including Dzogchen, Mahamudra, and Vajrayana, is aimed at just those two things: ultimate and relative bodhichitta. The effectiveness of practice is measured by the decrease of self-grasping and self-centeredness. The first two points of the Seven-Point Mind-Training cover the heart of Buddhist theory and practice. Why would you need anything more?

The remaining five points are practices for day-to-day living. These five points are designed to cultivate a way of engaging with day-to-day events that supports and nurtures progress gained through formal meditation. Instead of having spiritual practice deteriorate in the wear and tear of daily life or being maintained as a compartmentalized, separate entity, the aim of the next five points is to fully integrate spiritual practice within active life so that they are mutually supportive.

The remaining five points of the Mind-Training address the endemic problem of spiritually unraveling in the face of adversity. Shantideva, in *A Guide to the Bodhisattva Way of Life*, points out the mental impulse that is the great blowtorch for incinerating merit. That is anger. When anger grips the mind, it dissipates merit, the mind's repository of spiritual power. The Buddhist tradition says that virtue arises easily in a mind empowered with merit. If we want to mature spiritually, actually make some progress, and not be like rodents lapping the wheel of samsara, then we need to learn how to deal with anger. As the saying goes, "Even if you win the rat race, you're still a rat!" Dealing with anger means learning how to deal effectively with the adversities of everyday life.

Jigmé Tenpey Nyima, an early twentieth-century Tibetan Dzogchen master, offered this quintessential advice:

> In order not only to prevent all unfavorable circumstances and adversity from afflicting your mind, but to cause them to elicit a sense of good cheer, you should put a stop to experiences of aversion toward both inner and outer obstacles—illness as well as enemies, spirits, vicious gossip, etc. externally. Practice seeing everything solely in an agreeable way. For that to happen, you should stop seeing those harmful situations as something wrong, but give all your effort to seeing them as valuable. For it is the way our minds apprehend situations that makes them agreeable or disagreeable....
>
> By training in this way, you will become gentle-minded, easy-going, and courageous; there will be no obstacles to your spiritual practice; all unfavorable circumstances will arise as splendid and auspicious; and your mind will continually be content with the joy of serenity. To follow a spiritual path in a degenerate era, such armor as this is indispensable.[63]

If spiritual practice is put on hold every time adversity strikes, years of practice will produce no result except frustration and disappointment. This cannot be written off as bad luck or a defect in the practice one has been taught. The ability to transform adversity into the path is absolutely imperative for spiritual practice to flourish. Transforming adversity into the path is the subject of the Third Point of the Mind-Training.

Is it possible to attain enlightenment in our circumstances and in this lifetime? Enlightenment doesn't happen in a single flash. It is not an all-or-nothing proposition, for there are many stages of realization prior to the enlightenment of a buddha. Attaining meditative quiescence, ascertaining primordial awareness, cultivating the heart so that bodhichitta, the spirit of awakening, arises effortlessly— these stages are the central themes of Tibetan Buddhist practice.

The Seven-Point Mind-Training is a synthesis of practices aimed at the attainment of enlightenment, stage by stage. If spiritual awakening is the highest priority in life, the greatest passion, enlightenment is possible. What is required is a voracious appetite for Dharma that consumes every second of life, turning our whole lives into spiritual practice.

Dharma is not just sitting cross-legged following the breath, watching our minds, or engaging in visualization practices. Dharma also encompasses what we might ordinarily consider "down time," moments when a richness of understanding can develop. Dharma includes being ingenious—do what you *can* do in the midst of whatever obstacles arise. The more voracious we become, the more opportunities we see to transform all of life into Dharma. You do not have to be a monk or nun to attain enlightenment. It is not necessary to spend your life in retreat. What is necessary is voraciousness—transforming all of life, family, job, good and bad, everything, into Dharma.

The Third Point:
Transforming Adversity into an Aid to Spiritual Awakening

The goal of the Seven-Point Mind-Training is to integrate Dharma into life, all of life, not just the good parts. The goal of Dharma is to transform the mind so that, even during adversity, the mind is a good friend, so that joy and happiness arise in times of both felicity and adversity. We know the mind is malleable because it fluctuates; sometimes the mind is unbearable and sometimes it is a good friend. Sometimes joy and virtue arise easily and at other times you want to escape from your thoughts. The malleability of the mind indicates that the mind can be adjusted. The mind can be balanced.

Buddhism categorizes the mind's functions into conceptual and perceptual functions. The mind operates in a conceptual mode when we are thinking about the past and planning the future. In the conceptual mode, we become anxious about events that may or may not happen, we get angry with people who may or may not do something. In the conceptual mode, the mind is not dealing with present reality but its interpretation of reality. This conceptual mode, using the intelligence to plan and integrate, is appropriate most of the time.

The perceptual mode of the mind is generally over-whelmed by our concepts. When the stressed-out conceptual mind is tired, we can give it a little break by switching into the perceptual mode and following the breath. But when the conceptual mind is told to take a break, it's hard for it to break the habit of being a thought junky. The conceptual mind talks right through meditation. We need the conceptual mind to think, plan, coordinate, and remember. But a conceptual mind that turns on automatically in the morning, runs non-stop sixteen hours a day, taking only an eight-hour break to sleep, day in and day out, is not healthy.

What is healthy is exploring and developing the perceptual mode of awareness that quietly attends without ongoing commentary. To explore the perceptual mode, we have to outwit the conceptual mind. For example, when walking, you can slip into the perceptual mode by becoming aware of the breath, being present in your body or letting awareness be present in the environment. In this way, we can slowly begin to balance the mind by balancing its two functional modes, conceptual and perceptual.

When the whole world is enslaved by vices, transform adversities into the path of spiritual awakening.

First, train in the preliminaries. Second, cultivate the two bodhichittas. Third, transform adversity into the path of spiritual awakening. With the Third Point, the Mind-Training begins the integration of relative and ultimate bodhichittas, cultivated in the first two points, with the stuff of active life: felicity and adversity.

The first aphorism of the Third Point says, "When the whole world is enslaved by vices, transform adversities into the path of awakening." Since we seek happiness and wish to avoid suffering, we might assume that the most direct tactic in dealing with suffering would be to get rid of it, or at least be more effective in avoiding it. The advice of the

Mind-Training is radically different. Rather than try to get rid of or avoid suffering, *use* it. Transform adversity into the path of spiritual awakening. Transform adversity into bodhichitta. The straight path takes no detours around suffering; instead it incorporates suffering and transforms it into the path itself.

We begin our day with meditation. We may practice Dharma while having breakfast and driving to work. But at some point, Dharma practice tends to fall apart. Something derails us. Life is full of apparent obstacles to practice—children, co-workers, a loved one in a bad mood. The meaning behind the phrase "the whole world enslaved by vices" is that our lives are saturated with things that can be regarded as adversity. We are dealing with other people who, like ourselves, suffer from mental afflictions—attachment, anger, jealousy, pride, arrogance, competitiveness, and thoughtlessness. The more we learn to identify the afflictions in our own mind, the more we can identify them everywhere in the world, within and without. The whole world can appear afflicted or "enslaved by vices."

The Mind-Training says, "transform adversity into the spiritual path of awakening." If you can take things that appear as obstacles and transform them into spiritual practice, you are en route to attaining enlightenment. In Buddhist understanding, obstacles are related to karma: what we experience as adversity consists of repercussions of deeds done in the past. If you believe in the ethical coherence of actions and their consequences and the continuity of consciousness from lifetime to lifetime, the Third Point is where these working hypotheses integrate into daily life—engage with adversity as the fruit of past actions.

The practice of transforming adversity into the path is exemplified by the Tibetans themselves, who have suffered greatly during the past fifty years of the Chinese Communist occupation of their homeland. Tibetans view the Chinese invasion as the ripening of past deeds; at some time in the past, deeds were committed that are now coming to fruition. One great benefit of this view is that it arrests self-pity. Tibetans don't just bemoan their misfortune. The karmic hypothesis that previous actions come to fruition in future lifetimes implies that self-pity is a total waste of time.

Consider the nature of adversity. At first glance, adversity appears to be something that we perceive objectively. If our fundamental motivation, our central desire, is to have a comfortable life, then we will try to structure our circumstances to make sure this happens. But the task of modifying the environment, including all the people in it, into a constant stream of pleasant experiences so that adversity never arises, will lead to almost constant frustration.

On the other hand, if our highest priority is spiritual awakening, transforming the mind so that it becomes its own source of well-being, then our orientation to the people and environment around us will be quite different. With this motivation, adversity appears malleable, not fixed. When the top priority is pleasure, adversity will always appear as bad. If the top priority is to attain spiritual awakening, adversity becomes an important element of practice.

How can adversity be transformed "into the path" to cultivate the two bodhichittas, ultimate and relative? Geshe Ngawang Dhargyey commented to me once, "No one has ever attained enlightenment during the course of an easy, comfortable life." This statement means that no one attains enlightenment gliding along from one pleasant circumstance to another. It never happens in this universe. All of us experience adversity. No one attains enlightenment easily. Enlightenment is accomplished by being voracious, by transforming all of life, the good, the bad, and the weird, into the path.

It is impossible to mature spiritually without developing fortitude, patience, forbearance, and equanimity. Before Buddhism was brought to Tibet, Tibetans were known throughout Central Asia as a warrior race, so they could easily relate to the many warfare analogies for spiritual practice in Buddhist writings. Shantideva noted that a warrior kills people who are going to die anyway. Just wait, enemies die. His advice regarding spiritual practice was to use the stance of the warrior appropriately against the *real* enemy, our own mental afflictions. He continued on this theme, "Some, seeing their own blood, show extraordinary valor, while some faint even at the sight of others' blood. That comes from mental fortitude or from timidity. Therefore, one should be dismissive of pain and not be overcome by suffering."[64]

The first difficulty in this battle is recognizing the true enemy, self-centeredness, and the true ally, the sense of cherishing others. The Buddhist definition of "enemy" is a person who maliciously makes you suffer. An enemy is not just someone you don't like. Whether at war or at work, we identify enemies and try to protect ourselves from them. Shantideva raises a very deep issue in his definition of the "true enemy." Is there an enemy that harms us again and again, in a thousand ways, from every angle, at every opportunity, robbing us of happiness and giving us misery? Shantideva says yes, and this true enemy is self-centeredness. Self-centeredness is the attitude of thinking, "My well-being is most important." With self-centeredness we demand everything good for ourselves—the good house, the good income and job, the good friends, the good family. Everyone else can have what is left over.

From the Buddhist perspective, self-centeredness has dominated our minds since time immemorial, throughout all previous lifetimes. Self-centeredness promises to look after us as our servant, just as we take care of it.

Self-centeredness presents itself as our indispensable, number-one ally and advises us that if we don't cooperate, we will lose all the good stuff, everything. We will never get anywhere because if we don't take care of ourselves first, other people will get everything we want.

Self-centeredness presents itself as being our loyal ally in the search for happiness. The Buddhist tradition tells us just the opposite—seeking happiness with an attitude of self-centeredness is in reality the greatest source of suffering. Self-centeredness is like a spy who has infiltrated the society of our minds, our worst enemy posing as a trusted personal counselor. Shantideva says other enemies come and go but our greatest enemy, the true enemy, destroys our well-being every day. Its name is self-centeredness.

There is a simple reason why self-centeredness damages us again and again. Self-centeredness puts us at odds with virtually everyone else on the planet, who are also, just as we are, acting out of self-centeredness. Shantideva makes the radical suggestion that we suspect this apparent ally, who is in reality our worst enemy, and examine it closely. Does self-centeredness bring happiness or suffering? If adversity is examined carefully, it is found to have no inherent existence. Adversity appears as adversity because of self-centeredness. Self-centeredness is what makes our problems large and other people's problems seem insignificant.

Blame everything on one culprit.

When adversity strikes, trace it to its root, the one culprit. When somebody irritates you, when you become angry or disappointed, find the culprit. The mind does not get disturbed because of other people's behavior. Frustration and unhappiness occur because self-centeredness makes us unable to bear other people's behavior. Self-centeredness has us in its power and can make us very unhappy. When the Mind-Training says, "Blame everything on one culprit," the one culprit is self-centeredness. During the course of the day, identify moments of self-centeredness. Identifying self-centeredness in other people is easy but benefits no one. Only identifying our own self-centeredness brings about spiritual growth for ourselves. It is my self-centeredness, not yours, that gives me grief.

Atisha encourages us to recognize self-centeredness, our dearly beloved malevolent enemy that harms us day after day and will do so forever until it is counteracted. This advice, central to Dharma, seems to run counter to some of our favorite modern ideas about the route to happiness, such as "Embrace every aspect of yourself" and "Don't judge or reject any part of yourself. Accept yourself wholly." Shantideva's advice is to check within your mind, recognize that some of the impulses that arise there are poison and need to be absolutely annihilated. Which approach should we choose?

Bear in mind the metaphor of the warrior. The Buddhist tradition describes the spiritual path as war. Military analogies abound Shantideva's *Guide to the Bodhisattva Way of Life*. Our real enemies are not human beings, they are the mental afflictions of anger, jealousy, arrogance, and delusion, with the top general-in-command being self-centeredness. Shantideva says identify your number-one enemy, self-centeredness, and vanquish it.

From a modern psychological point of view, destroying the enemy of self-centeredness might appear to be a radical fragmentation of individuality. The notion that some mental processes, such as generosity, openness, cheerfulness, are acceptable, but others, the chief being the "great demon," self-centeredness, are to be exterminated, seems the antithesis of the modern psychological viewpoint of self-acceptance and integration. However, the modern psychological theme of global self-acceptance and the Tibetan

Buddhist warrior stance of complete annihilation of the enemy of self-centeredness may not be as different as they first appear. For example, when you get the flu, you never think, "Oh, this flu is a part of me. I must embrace it!" The flu virus is not you, it is a foreign element that has invaded your body and is doing it harm. Similarly, mental afflictions, all of them, are not innate constituents of your mind. Self-centeredness is not an innate element of your mind. Habitual, yes. Innate, no. You can accept yourself and yet recognize that there are invaders of the mind just as there are viruses that invade the body. As you ponder this, consider: Who are you really? Apart from your mental afflictions, the personal history, virtues, and talents you have acquired, your body and behavior—none of which are you—what "you" is left over? Before you wholeheartedly embrace the ideal of accepting yourself as you are, it might be a good idea to discover who this "you" is.

Shantideva writes, "If all the harm, fear, and suffering in the world occurs due to grasping onto the self, what use is that great demon to me?"[65] The challenge here is to *identify* self-centeredness, but not to identify *with* it. Self-centeredness is an affliction, metaphorically a demon, that possesses the mind. Shantideva continues, "How can I take delight in the cycle of existence when constant, long-lasting enemies, who are the sole cause of the perpetuation of a mass of adversities, fearlessly dwell in my heart?"[66] As long as the mind is encumbered with self-centeredness and its attendant mental afflictions of anger, attachment, jealousy, arrogance and the rest, no matter how hard you strive to have the ideal environment, the ideal family, the ideal job, happiness will remain elusive. Shantideva concludes, "Note the difference between the fool who seeks his own benefit and the sage who works for the benefit of others."[67] Without exception, spiritually enlightened beings haven't take the path of "me first," craving and latching onto their own well-being at the expense of others, but instead have sought to be of service to others. Only by cherishing others more than ourselves can we find genuine, lasting happiness.

By identifying with "I am angry, belligerent, offended, indignant," the ramparts of the mind are stormed and the mind succumbs to afflictions. Using the warrior metaphor from Tibetan Buddhism, the remedy is to "stand at the gateway of the mind and watch." When afflictions attack, counterattack. The strategy here is to draw upon the arsenal of Dharma practice whenever mental afflictions arrive at the entrance of the mind. When afflictions retreat and the mind is calm, with wholesome thoughts and emotions arising easily, be at ease.

Dharma is similar to guerrilla warfare. When your opponent is stronger than you are and you enter battle head-on, you lose. Assess the power of your mind for effortless virtue, loving-kindness, and wisdom. Then measure yourself against the enemy of the habitual propensities of selfishness, egotism, jealousy, arrogance, anger, and attachment. Relative to the power of habituation of mental afflictions, the power of virtue and compassion may look pretty puny. If so, we have to be smarter and quicker. The strategy is to apply the remedy *before* ego-grasping and self-centeredness gather strength. If we wait until the afflictions have mustered their forces and dominated our minds, our options are narrowed. The tactic used to outwit and arrest mental afflictions in their tracks is vigilantly standing guard at the gateway of the mind. When ego-grasping, selfishness, attachment, or anger first make their move, we have a fighting chance. As in guerrilla warfare, when the enemy advances, retreat—don't identify with them and lend your strength to theirs; when the enemy retreats, advance. The signs that we are winning the war are a weakening of the mental afflictions and a resultant sense of increasing well-being.

It would be wonderful to achieve meditative quiescence in this lifetime. It would be wonderful to realize our buddha-nature. But these attainments are not the most important goal of Buddhism, because whether or not we have achieved quiescence or realized our buddha-nature, we may die at any time. Therefore, the most important goal is establishing ourselves on the path, integrating Dharma into life so that there is a continuity and momentum that will carry over into the next lifetime. If there is continuity of consciousness beyond this lifetime, then the quality of mind that we cultivate in life will carry on, too. What is necessary to establish a path of continuity to carry on from this lifetime to the next is a voracious appetite for Dharma. To help establish such continuity, you may offer the following prayer each day:

> Wherever this precious, supreme spirit of awakening,
>   bodhichitta,
> Has not arisen, may it arise,
> And where it has arisen, may it never decline
> But grow stronger and stronger.

Dharma can be difficult, but is never impossible. If you believe the aim of Dharma is to practice everything taught in Buddhism, then when you think about the richness and diversity of Dharma practice, it will seem overwhelming. But the purpose of Dharma is cultivating a good heart, and the aim of Dharma is to establish continuity of practice throughout this lifetime and beyond.

In Buddhism, self-grasping is understood as a form of ignorance and self-centeredness is ignorance in action. When the root of self-grasping is severed by insight, then even when adversity strikes, self-grasping won't afflict us. There is no target. Gyatrul Rinpoche commented about the suffering endured by Tibetans in Chinese Communist concentration camps, "As long as you have self-grasping, don't imagine you can be courageous." As long as there is grasping onto "my body" and "my feelings," pain can overwhelm you.

The deeper the insight into the nature of reality, the more powerful the passion for Dharma becomes. By nurturing a desire for freedom, your whole life becomes polarized toward Dharma. This is it. This is all there is to do. Shantideva asks of himself, "How can I take delight in the cycle of existence when constant, long-lasting enemies, who are the sole cause of the currents and floods of adversities, fearlessly dwell in my heart?"[65] It is not possible to have a nice time in samsara with a mind saturated with mental afflictions. The only solution is to purify the mind so that mental afflictions no longer torture us.

Reflect on the kindness of all those around you.

What this aphorism encourages us to do is to focus on the kindness of others, but in a way that does not deny the evil in the world or the fact that many people act in unkind ways. Recall that in the Buddhist context, an "enemy" is someone who wishes you harm, regardless of your reciprocal feelings. In this practice, when we reflect on the kindness of others, "kindness" doesn't mean kind intentions. Rather, it refers to *benefit*, regardless of intentions. If another person brings you benefit, then that person is said to have shown you kindness, *regardless of motivation.*

We determine our experienced reality by *what* we choose to attend to and *how* we attend to it. We create a problem when we focus on how much we have done for other people and how much they are indebted to us. Cataloguing all the nice things we do for others and how much they owe us dooms us to a sense of entitlement that is never satisfied. The challenge here is to focus on ways we are the recipients of others' kindness.

How are we the recipients of the kindness of others? Geshe Rabten told me that after meditating on the kindness of others in retreat day after day, week after week, he felt like a baby in the cradle of humanity—every experience he had arose in dependence upon the kindness of others. Consider your breakfast this morning. Did you raise the wheat, grow the oranges or milk the cow? Every stitch on our backs is due to the kindness of others. We could not make it through the day without the overwhelming support from the sentient beings around us. Therefore, attending to the kindness of others, all the ways they have helped us, is more than a beneficent attitude, it is a step toward the bodhisattva ideal, because it is appreciating the dependently related nature of our own existence.

The practice of meditating on the kindness of others becomes more specific when it is divided into two categories: people we like and people we don't like. Meditating on the kindness of others is not difficult for the people we like. But the affection we feel for people we like becomes problematic when it slips over into attachment: "You have been so kind. What more can you do for me?"

Meditating on the kindness of people we don't like is more difficult. These people are easy to criticize, for we find their behavior and ways of talking unpleasant. What kindness has a person we don't like shown us? The aphorism points out the opportunity for compassion. Chances are that you are not the only person who finds this person disagreeable. In the Buddhist view, we carry within us the sources of our own suffering. The person who is arrogant, domineering, thoughtless or manipulative will be the first to suffer from these afflictions. A person with unpleasant behavior, whose buddha-nature is obscured by disagreeable qualities, is an excellent subject for *tonglen*. While you are engaging with a disagreeable person, imagine the person being free from afflictions, with his natural virtues shining forth. Disagreeable people are kind because they provide us—whether they intend to or not—with the opportunity to cultivate patience and compassion, two of the most indispensable virtues on the path to enlightenment.

In Buddhist cosmology, among the countless life forms in the universe, human life is the most fertile because we can use our intelligence to transmute a wide range of experience, to purify our minds, and to cultivate virtue. According to Buddhist cosmology, humans have a spectrum of experience no other sentient beings have. From joy to misery, it is all in the human realm. The gods may have greater joy and greater powers, but they are locked into experiences of happiness and pleasure, which limits their potential for spiritual maturation. Beings in miserable states of existence are locked into experiences too narrow to be very fruitful. Humans have the whole range—from facsimiles of hell, such as concentration camps, to earthly facsimiles of heaven, and everything in between. The practice of looking upon all sentient beings with gratitude is a crucial key for deriving benefit from our wide range of experience. Otherwise, we tend to simply live life trying to maneuver from one pleasant experience to the next, while avoiding unpleasant ones.

Meditating on the kindness of everyone is instrumental in cultivating relative bodhichitta in any circumstance. Consciously bringing this practice to mind when dealing with others is the key to transforming daily life. At the bank, instead of thinking, "You are a bank teller getting paid to do your job," meditate on this person's kindness for making it possible for you to write checks.

The practice of meditating on the kindness of everyone is applicable at all times. The greatest opportunity for developing compassion is the gift that disagreeable people give us to deepen understanding, to open our hearts and embrace all sentient beings. This aphorism has a parallel in Christianity. Meister Eckhart, a thirteenth-century German Christian mystic, declared that if the only prayer you say in your life is "Thank you," that will suffice. This is exactly the point the Mind-Training is making. If you move through life with a sense of gratitude toward everyone, including people you find disagreeable, that will suffice.

The focus of the Third Point of the Mind-Training is to transform adversity into the spiritual path. All of life is to be transformed. This requires changing our perception of adversity so that we view it as an opportunity for practice. For example, Dharma practice entails arousing relative bodhichitta, the aspiration for enlightenment for the benefit of all beings, including disagreeable persons. When dealing with disagreeable people, we can be thankful to them for providing special opportunities for the cultivation of bodhichitta.

One of the subtle points in spiritual practice is to be aware of how you are doing. Is your Dharma practice working? When things are pleasant, it is easy to relax into thinking of yourself as a blossoming bodhisattva. Your wake-up call will come from people who are rude, thoughtless, spiteful, people who do you harm. How you deal with harmful people is a litmus test of practice. From month to month, if your practice is effective, you should see some change. It won't be black and white. Afflictions don't just abruptly stop one day, but there should be gradual transformation. Apparent enemies can be our greatest spiritual allies by spurring us on to practice and providing benchmarks of progress.

Milarepa's uncle was an example of an enemy. Milarepa's father died when he was a child and his paternal uncle robbed Milarepa's family of everything and reduced them to servitude. Milarepa's mother was resentful and encouraged her son to retaliate. By traditional accounts, he then used black magic to kill his uncle and his uncle's family. When he realized what he had done, he had an enormous shift of awareness. Anticipating the terrible karmic repercussions of his deed, he transformed his remorse into spiritual practice and became one of the greatest and most beloved yogis of Tibet.

Who was Milarepa's greatest friend? Where did he get his passion for spiritual practice? The easy answer would be Marpa, his lama. In another sense, Milarepa's uncle who caused him great harm was his greatest friend. Milarepa might not have accomplished what he did without the "kindness" of his uncle.

His Holiness the Dalai Lama has shocked many people over the past few decades by speaking about the "kindness" of the Chinese Communists. Because of the Chinese invasion, a million Tibetans died and nearly all of the 6,000 monasteries in Tibet were destroyed. The Chinese invasion was a tremendous tragedy. Yet, the Dalai Lama speaks of the "kindness" of the Chinese Communists, adding, "for me personally." His Holiness doesn't think that Chairman Mao was trying to do him a favor. He is considering the benefit he derived. His Holiness says that in Tibet he lived an isolated life because of the inertia of culture and tradition. The Dalai Lamas lived in a golden cage, always separate. The public never raised their eyes to the Dalai Lama. He could see his people only at a distance. Thanks to the invasion of the Chinese Communists and his forced exile, he has come into intimate contact with his people. He meets many thousands of Tibetans on a personal basis and the horizons of his own world have expanded to embrace the entire planet, other cultures, modern history, science, all thanks to the Chinese Communists. What is most miraculous about this is that His Holiness actually means it. He is grateful and bears no ill will.

By meditating on delusive appearances as the four embodiments, emptiness becomes the best protection.

Meditating on delusive appearance as the four embodiments" entails engaging with all circumstances to cultivate wisdom. "Delusive appearances" include all appearances of the environment, sentient beings, and our own body and mind. Mahayana Buddhism identifies the central element of spiritual practice to be the development of bodhichitta, and a person in whom this motivation arises effortlessly is called a bodhisattva. There is a caveat, an important and subtle one, concerning the happiness of a bodhisattva. Recall that a bodhisattva empathizes with the suffering of others but doesn't become overwhelmed by it. Instead, the suffering of others acts as a catalyst for genuine compassion. When all of life is brought into Dharma practice, this includes unhappy circumstances, and it is exactly these unhappy circumstances that serve as platforms from which to cultivate the Six Perfections—generosity, ethical discipline, patience, zeal, meditation, and wisdom—that provide the structure of the bodhisattva way of life. The bodhisattva embraces adversity with the aim of attaining enlightenment by transmuting everything, felicity and adversity, into spiritual practice. In the bodhisattva way of life, it is the cultivation of relative bodhichitta that serves as protection from mental suffering, by empowering spiritual practice with the momentum to move beyond empathy to genuine compassion.

Relative bodhichitta provides protection from mental suffering, but there can still be physical suffering. The "best protection" against physical suffering, Atisha tells us, is the realization of emptiness, ultimate bodhichitta. The challenge here is to ascertain that all phenomena, including those that inflict harm, are solely delusive appearances to our own minds. Ultimately, no phenomenon has its own inherent existence; all are like apparitions emerging from space. The ascertainment of emptiness counteracts the reification of subject/object, even for those objects that inflict harm. By realizing the lack of inherent existence of both that which inflicts suffering and an "I" who suffers, phenomena appear to arise out of space and dissolve back into space.

If meditative quiescence is weak, the mind is not stable enough for the realization of emptiness to have a deep and lasting impact. There are many examples of Hindu and Buddhist yogis who were able to withdraw their attention, by the power of meditative concentration, from what would otherwise be great physical pain. The ability to withdraw and stabilize attention at will through the practice of meditative stabilization is a very valuable skill. But insight goes deeper. With the realization of emptiness, there is no need to withdraw awareness from pain. The pain is experienced, but with insight into emptiness, you are not captured by it.

The aphorism of the Mind-Training refers to "delusive appearances as the four embodiments." In his commentary to this training, Dilgo Khyentse explains that the first embodiment, the *dharmakaya*, or embodiment of reality, is the absence of inherent existence of everything, all objects and all subjects, including our own mental afflictions. None of these phenomena truly come into existence by their own nature, so they are in reality "unborn." That which is unborn never ceases, and the unceasing nature of pure awareness is the *sambhogakaya*, or embodiment of perfect enjoyment. While the mind and all objects apprehended by the mind are by nature empty, this emptiness is not merely a kind of vacuity like empty space. Rather, all experienced phenomena arise like reflected images in the mind, and that reflection-like nature is called the *nirmanakaya*, or embodiment of emanations. The inseparability of the unborn, unceasing, and all-manifesting nature of awareness is called the *svabhavakaya*, or natural embodiment. By viewing all phenomena, especially our mental afflictions, as delusive appearances of these four embodiments, we see that in reality there is nothing to purify, nothing to reject. All is seen as perfect displays of pure awareness, which by nature is empty, luminous, and infinitely creative.

The best strategy is to have four practices.

The four practices referred to here are accumulating merit, purifying vices, making offerings to spirits, and making offerings to the Dharma Protectors.

"Accumulating merit" can be approached from a psychological perspective that lends itself to experiential verification or from a spiritual dimension that requires some faith. "Merit" can be understood as "spiritual power" that manifests in day-to-day experience. When merit, or spiritual power, is strong, there is little resistance to practicing Dharma and practice itself is empowered. Tibetans explain that people who make rapid progress in Dharma, gaining one insight after another, enter practice already having a lot of merit. By the same theory, it is possible to strive diligently and make little progress. Tibetans explain this problem as being due to too little merit. Merit is the fuel that empowers spiritual practice.

How do you accumulate merit? Engaging in virtue of any sort, with your mind, your speech, or your body results in merit. Just as merit can be accumulated, it can also be dissipated by doing harm. In general, mental afflictions dissipate merit. The mental affliction that is like a black hole sucking up merit, worse than all the others, is anger. Attachment or sensual craving can get you in a lot of trouble, but it doesn't have the debilitating impact upon spiritual practice that anger does. Remember the warrior metaphor—standing at the gateway of the mind, vigilant, spear ready. The spear is for mental afflictions, especially anger. Nip anger in the bud.

The superficial cause of anger is adversity. The remedy is strength of the heart, a courageous attitude so that when adversity strikes we respond, "May I have the courage to transform adversity into spiritual practice. May adversity empower the cultivation of compassion." This doesn't mean we should respond to adversity or injustice with apathy. It means not responding to adversity with hatred. When you encounter wrong behavior, respond with the wish, "May this person be free." Compassion doesn't mean acquiescence or apathy. Whenever we are really angry at somebody, we are locking onto a target, and this reification provides an excellent opportunity to look at delusion. Try to find the "me" that is standing in judgment. To look at it, recognize the delusion, and by recognizing it, undermine it, and allow wisdom to come forward: ultimate bodhichitta. Adversities are prime opportunities, the most stimulating and challenging opportunities for developing relative and ultimate bodhichitta.

The second of the four practices is purifying vices by means of the four remedial powers, which were discussed earlier. This addresses the inevitable problem of making mistakes. Our minds become dominated by delusion, lust, hatred, jealousy, arrogance, or just plain bad judgment, and we sometimes do things we later regret. No matter how vigilant we are, we still make mistakes. But the four remedial powers provide us with methods for dispelling the karmic impacts of misdeeds.

The four remedial powers—the power of remorse, of reliance, of resolve, and of engaging in purificatory behavior to counteract our misdeeds—point to a crucial Buddhist teaching: there is no deed so evil it can't be purified.

The four remedial powers have clear psychological benefits. You can tell purification has been effective when you are no longer prone to the behavior. If adultery was the behavior, it has been purified when there is no longer any tendency toward adultery, just as a tiger will decline a bale of hay for dinner. By practicing the four remedial powers, we lose the appetite for our vices.

The third of the four practices is: "Make offerings to spirits." Due to advances in scientific knowledge, we now know the physical causes for many phenomena formerly attributed to "spirits," such as schizophrenia, plague, and inclement weather. However, belief in spirits is not limited to "primitive" cultures. In fact, most people in all other societies and in all other civilizations have believed in spirits. Scientific materialists are virtually unique in their disbelief in spirits.

"Make offerings to spirits" refers to spirits and not deities. I lived closely with Tibetans for many years and many times witnessed them making offerings to spirits. When Tibetans start a meditation retreat, for example, the first thing before starting out is to make offerings to the spirits with the thought, "All spirits of the earth, water, trees and air, all invisible beings around me, I am in your domain. I have come to practice benevolently and do no harm, so please do not harass me in my practice or create obstacles." Tibetans take this very seriously. It is similar to the old custom of going out to meet everyone when you move into a new neighborhood. Tibetans believe in making a friendly gesture to the spirits present in any location, because if you get on the bad side of spirits, they can create a lot of trouble.

On every mountain pass in Tibet there is a mound of stones. When going over a mountain pass, the tradition is to take a stone and toss it onto the mound saying, "May the gods be victorious." This is a polite gesture, like tipping your hat, to any mountain spirits who might be dwelling in that area. Tibetans traditionally believe that if you neglect to pay respect, when you head down the backside of the pass, the mountain spirits may be offended and cause you to fall off your horse and break a leg or experience some other mishap. When the Chinese invaded Tibet, they found spirit mounds everywhere and blew them up. Tibetans watched to see that would happen to the Chinese. When nothing happened, the Tibetans concluded the Chinese must have even bigger spirits on their side.

But do spirits really exist? Many modern Westerners don't take spirits seriously. But science has not proven that spirits don't exist. If you examine the issue of spirits and demons in the West during the witch-hunting era of 1450-1650, an interesting picture emerges. Many of the thousands of so-called witches killed by Europeans and colonial Americans were vulnerable widows. The witch hunts were fueled by belief in demons, and in particular, the belief that humans could be possessed by or married to a demonic spirit.

The witch hunting of Euro-American history traumatized Western civilization during the same era that gave rise to modern science. Isaac Newton, who is better known for his innovations in physics than his avid interest in theology, declared that evil spirits are in reality nothing more than mental disorders. Thomas Sprat, a less prominent scientist who was a contemporary of Newton, similarly maintained that spirits and demons are illusions, the non-existence of which had been demonstrated by *experiments*, though he didn't say exactly which experiments he had in mind.[69] Three hundred years later, there are still many intelligent people in the West who believe in the existence of spirits and the efficacy of exorcism. In the meantime, scientific materialists continue to insist that suitably controlled experiments would quickly demonstrate that exorcism does not affect devil-possession type behavior, and that certain other therapies do.[70] But many experiments have been run, and intelligent people continue to draw different conclusions from the evidence presented to them.

While it is certainly debatable whether spirits exist, when belief in spirits is condemned as superstition on the grounds that only matter and its properties exist, I find this ludicrous. Should we really take seriously the idea that nothing exists but matter and its emergent properties? What exactly is the atomic mass of justice, love, consciousness, dream imagery, information, numbers, geometrical forms, the mathematical laws of nature, space, and time? The list of immaterial phenomena goes on and on, and it takes an enormous leap of faith to believe that somehow these all exist as configurations of matter. Why would anyone believe in this great superstition of our times? Perhaps the grounds of this faith are simply that natural science is only good at measuring matter and its properties, and if we think the methods of physical science are our only avenues to knowledge, then we're stuck with the weird notion that only matter exists.

If our sole avenue to knowledge were the methodology of science, its instruments and techniques, we could state with confidence that there is no such a thing as consciousness, because there is no objective, scientific evidence for its existence. Science has not shed light on how or why consciousness originates, what the role of consciousness is in nature, or what happens to consciousness at death. If we had no mode of knowledge other than science, we would not know that consciousness exists in the universe at all. We would know about physical events (by means of our scientifically undemonstrated consciousness), but the realm of mental phenomena would be unknown.

There is no scientific evidence that amoebae or squirrels are conscious. We can measure their behavior and see how fast they move when they get too hot, but we can't measure their consciousness. Because science can't measure consciousness, does that mean it doesn't exist? Because science can't detect spirits, does that mean they don't exist?

Other solar systems have recently been discovered. Statistically, there are probably other planets that have oxygen and water. If conscious life forms exist in other world systems, they would not necessarily look like us because they would have evolved in different ways since they are on different worlds. It would be logical to conclude that there could be sentient beings in other world systems that are so dissimilar from us that we could neither see nor touch them even if they were right in front of us. If life forms like that could exist on other worlds, why not right here? If they did exist here, we could call them "spirits."

Tibetan medicine takes a very interesting and practical stance regarding spirits. This ancient medical system looks at the etiology of illness in terms of behavior, environment, and diet. It also acknowledges the existence of tiny sentient beings in the body, too small to be seen with the naked eye, some benign, some malignant. This seems like a description of microbes. Tibetan medicine also describes a class of illness caused by spirits that cannot be cured with medicine. These illnesses are treated by having a lama do spiritual practice or by making offerings. Tibetans take spirits seriously.

The late nineteenth-century Dzogchen master Düdjom Lingpa wrote:

> In general, living creatures experience what they have brought upon themselves, like a spider that catches itself in its own web. Fear of demons fabricated by old superstitions is like a bird frightened by the sound of its own wings, and like a deer terrified at the sound of its own footsteps. Know that there are no demons other than those you create.[71]

He elaborated on this point, stating that the wide range of malevolent spirits and demons known to Buddhism are in reality apparitions of delusion, hatred, and attachment, which actually exist nowhere outside one's own being.[72] This statement appears, at least at first glance, to be remarkably similar to that of Newton. But the context for Düdjom Lingpa's statement is that not only spirits, but all mental and physical phenomena, are brought into our experienced reality by the power of conceptual designation. Nothing exists apart from appearances to awareness, and awareness itself is empty of any inherent existence of its own.

Of course we are free to adopt a psychological interpretation of the advice to "make offerings to spirits." For example, when a person acting out of a "spirit" of resentment harms us, we can express thanks for the adversity that fuels our spiritual practice. Even if we can't express thanks for adversity, we can still offer gifts of loving-kindness and compassion for the person who has been possessed by that demonic spirit.

The fourth of these four practices is making offerings to the Dharma Protectors. Tibetans recognize many kinds of Dharma Protectors, or *dharmapalas*. There are protectors for the various orders of Tibetan Buddhism and for specific monasteries, as well as dharmapalas upon whom one can call for personal help. The latter are like personal guardian angels. Some dharmapalas are fully enlightened beings, while others are unenlightened beings who may be called upon for assistance.

The most powerful dharmapala, the best protector of Dharma practice, is bodhichitta. The motivation of relative bodhichitta transforms all of life, including adversity, into the path of spiritual awakening. Ultimate bodhichitta cuts right through obstacles by insight into their ultimate nature, emptiness. Therefore, take refuge in the greatest Dharma Protector of all, the heart of Dharma itself, bodhichitta.

Whatever you encounter, immediately apply it to meditation.

This aphorism is a post-meditative yoga for the hours in a day not spent in formal meditation. "Whatever you encounter, immediately apply it to meditation." As long as there are sentient beings in the world with mental afflictions, problems will arise. If your deepest aspiration in life is to have no problems, Dharma practice won't fulfill that aspiration. If your deepest aspiration is for spiritual maturation, then all of the adversity possible in life, without exception, can give rise to deeper insight, deeper compassion. This aphorism refers to the First Noble Truth, the reality of suffering. The essential nature of our awareness is pure, but in terms of habituation, our minds are deluded. By recognizing that sentient beings are troubled by mental afflictions, we won't be surprised when difficulties manifest and provide us the opportunity to respond in a meaningful way.

The fundamental issue here entails an incremental shift of awareness, moving beyond mundane hopes and fears. As long as life is dominated by hopes and fears, Dharma practices go by the wayside because when adversity arises, the knee-jerk reactions of fear, aversion, and hostility get the better of us. If happiness arises, we hold on to it with anxiety that it will slip away. The Buddhist hypothesis is that it is possible to live without mundane hope and fear by finding a source of well-being within that leads to an increasing fearlessness and broadens the scope of imagination.

In this practice, we nurture the few desires that are of greatest value. Dilgo Khyentse Rinpoche commented that as the spirit of awakening matures, we even become free of the hope of accomplishing spiritual awakening and the fear of not accomplishing it. As we draw closer to spiritual awakening, stabilizing in the center, hope and fear fall away. As

Langri Tangpa, one of the beloved teachers of ancient Tibet, said, by training in this way with regard to friends and enemies, the crooked tree of the mind is made straight.

This concludes the Third Point of the Seven-Point Mind-Training: transforming adversity into an aid for spiritual awakening.

The Fourth Point:
A Synthesis of Practice for One Life

The next two lines take a bird's eye view of the entire Seven-Point Mind-Training by synthesizing many practices into a practice for the whole of life. This is not a scholar's view, not an encyclopedia of Buddhism to be pulled out whenever we want to know something specific. This is a short, simple, practical synthesis, aimed at the goal of sustaining daily practice. The entire text of the Seven-Point Mind-Training presents a four-page quintessential practice for living and dying. If you would really like to integrate this training with your life, you might try memorizing it.

To synthesize the essence of this practical guidance, apply yourself to the five powers.

The five powers are the power of (1) resolution, (2) familiarization, (3) positive seeds, (4) abhorrence, and (5) prayer.

The power of resolution is resolving never to be separated from the two bodhichittas. Resolution is a forward-looking stance firmly grounded in the present. Resolution is not the thought, "I hope one day I will have deep insight." You are in the present, anticipating the future with the resolve, "From this time forward, may my mind never be separated from the two bodhichittas." Never to be separated from the two bodhichittas means never to be separated from wisdom and compassion. Why is it so important never to be separated from bodhichitta?

This bodhisattva ideal identifies self-centeredness as the root of suffering. Self-centeredness, the closely held belief that other people are less important than ourselves, directly undermines the happiness of both ourselves and others. Self-centeredness, seeming to be our dearest ally in the pursuit of genuine happiness, is, in reality, our greatest enemy. Experientially ascertaining this to be true generates a powerful incentive never to be separated from the direct remedy to self-centeredness, relative bodhichitta. Bodhichitta is the well-spring of happiness in the face of adversity, even in what might be considered the greatest adversity of all—death.

Likewise, resolve never to be separated from ultimate bodhichitta, the wisdom which cuts through the deep habit of reification, decontextualizing events so that they appear as independent entities. The Buddhist path is to examine closely the sense of "I am." Is this "I" real, separate, important, in charge of my body, and more important than everyone else? With examination, we find that we view other people out of the contexts of their history, environment, and all other conditions that have been influencing them throughout life. The Buddha's insight, corroborated by generations of contemplatives, is that grasping onto "me" and "you" as independent entities seems natural only because it is habitual. The absolute dichotomy of self and other is in reality a profound delusion and the source of suffering. Before we have experiential confirmation of this insight for ourselves, we can intuitively affirm it as a working hypothesis.

The Buddhist hypothesis is radical. Most of us don't believe that the root of suffering is within us. We believe the root cause of our problems is external. We point "out there" and believe we can't be happy until all those irritating things change. This is truly and logically a hopeless situation. Buddhism presents the radical hypothesis that our situation is not hopeless. It is possible not to be upset every time you encounter a malicious person. Resolving never to be separated from the two bodhichittas entails a radical attitudinal adjustment to respond to adverse situations in ways that give rise to happiness.

The second power is the power of familiarization. Familiarization is a strategy. Shantideva declared, "With familiarization, there is nothing whatsoever that does not become easier."[73] There are many things in the course of life that will blindside us. Without preparation, we can be devastated by tragedy, loss, and fear. In the meantime, when health is good and disaster has not yet struck, we have the opportunity to practice. We have leisure and opportunity, the two defining characteristics of a precious human life. We can develop courage of mind and heart, and draw adversity into practice. By transforming small adversity, practice becomes stronger and we will be able to handle greater adversity. The power of familiarization is applying practice to fill all of life.

The third power is the power of positive seeds, constant devotion to spiritual practice in all its diversity and richness. Imagine your present situation to be a seed that will eventually mature into the tree of awakening. Cultivate this seed by welcoming any circumstance, adversity or felicity, as an opportunity for spiritual practice.

The next power is the power of abhorrence. This refers to abhorrence for self-grasping and self-centeredness, both of which inevitably result in suffering. If you respond to disgusting things crawling round in your mind by identifying with them and acting on them, this is like eating rotten food. The first meal I had in Dharamsala in 1971 consisted of noodles, vegetables cooked in rancid oil, and meat taken off a nail on the wall, all stirred together and fried to smithereens. I spent the next three days throwing up. That led to abhorrence for that particular dish, which made me miserable for just a few days. The power of revulsion mentioned here helps us turn away from mental habits that have made us miserable for lifetimes.

Tendencies of self-grasping, self-centeredness, the various shades of malice, resentment, and contempt damage our hearts and minds. The power of abhorrence helps us recognize self-centeredness as the source of suffering. When we notice the subtle and not-so-subtle "I" that says, "How dare you speak to me that way! Don't you know who I am?" when we are hurt or insulted, we are encountering the reification of self that is the source of suffering. Abhorrence is an excellent response.

There is an old Tibetan aphorism Dilgo Khyentse Rinpoche used, "Hit the pig on the nose. Clean the lamp while still warm." This wisdom stems from rural Tibet, where the animals make themselves at home on the bottom floor of the house. Sometimes the animals climb upstairs into the bedrooms and kitchen. What do you do when a pig pokes his snout through the kitchen door looking for stuff to munch? Hit him on the nose before he gets the other 200 pounds through the door! Hit the pig on the nose quick enough and he turns tail. But a pig that is already feeding at the trough is hard to get rid of. The same goes for kerosene lamps. Cleaning a lamp when it is warm is easy. Wait until it is cold and you have a gritty problem.

As soon as you identify afflictive tendencies of the mind, as soon as their snouts poke through the door of your mind, hit them on the nose. And clean the lamp of your mind while it is still warm with afflictions. These are not abstract philosophical concepts.

The fifth power is praying never to be separated from the two bodhichittas. Pray never to be separated from genuine mentors, spiritual friends, the Dharma, and all circumstances conducive to following the spiritual path. The power of prayer is an aspiration, a marshaling of desire. We desire a lot of things. Here we focus on the desire: "May I never be separated in all my lives from the two bodhichittas, the heart of the path to spiritual awakening."

There is an old set of Tibetan aphorisms that can save a lot of unnecessary trouble as practice is integrated into a synthesis with active life. These guidelines have served generations of Tibetans well in establishing a firm foundation for practice.

> Rely not on individuals, but on the Dharma.
> Rely not on the words, but on the meaning.
> Rely not on the provisional meaning, but on the definitive meaning.
> Rely not on conventional consciousness, but on intuitive wisdom.

Rely not on individuals, but on the Dharma. It is easy to be enchanted by the charisma, knowledge, or humor of a teacher. Why practice Buddhism? "Because my teacher is so amazing" is not a good answer. What if your teacher does something unethical? Personality cults are only harmful, and our own spiritual practice should not hinge vulnerably on someone else's behavior. Teachers will pass away, you will be parted from your spiritual friends, and eventually you will be parted from your own body. Therefore, rely principally on the Dharma.

What is Dharma? *Rely not on the words, but on the meaning.* Dharma is the reality that the words point to. Loving-kindness, wisdom, quiescence, generosity, virtue are Dharma. Scholars often believe that the bigger their library, the more the Buddhism they have acquired, but Dharma is the reality, not the words on a page. Therefore, do not rely on the words, rely on the meaning.

Rely not on the provisional meaning, but on the definitive meaning. Sometimes the literal meaning of a word has a truer meaning underneath. There are many miracle stories from Tibet. One is a story about Tara, the feminine embodiment of compassion, emerging from a tear of Avalokiteshvara, the male embodiment of compassion. Getting hung-up on literal meaning can easily miss the point of this profound myth. Penetrate through words to the definitive meaning.

Rely not on conventional consciousness, but on intuitive wisdom. Conventional consciousness consists of the physical senses and our powers of reasoning. Beyond this domain of the mind is a fathomless source of intuitive wisdom that is neither acquired nor conditioned by external stimuli. Therefore, rely on the intuitive wisdom that is unveiled from within.

Those are the teachings for life. But death could come tomorrow. So there are also teachings for death.

The Mahayana teaching on transferring consciousness is precisely these five powers, so your conduct is crucial.

These five practices are the same five powers of the preceding aphorism specifically applied to the dying process. The first practice is the power of positive seeds. Fear is a big hindrance in the transitional process of dying, so it is very important to die without fear. Fear is useful in life when a truck is about to run you down, but in the face of death, fear is useless because death will run you down no matter what you do. For the Dharma practitioner, death presents the perfect opportunity for meditation—unimpeded by distractions from the senses and the body.

Facing death without fear is not simple. What are you afraid of? If you are afraid of leaving your loved ones, your possessions, and body, get used to the idea because it will happen. Everything you are attached to you will lose. Give up your material goods and all your honors with a sense of fearlessness regarding the hereafter. If you have objects of refuge, bring them to mind and offer everything up, even your body. Just as a car with 200,000 miles may cost more to fix than to replace, discard the body and prepare to get a new one. Fearlessly, give it all up without reservation. This is what is meant by the power of positive seeds applied to death.

The power of prayer applied to death refers to regret. The longer we live the more opportunity we have for doing things we regret. Milarepa said the aim of his practice was to die without regret. The power of prayer entails disclosing all misdeeds and taking refuge. In your mind's eye, make offerings and ask for blessings to sustain the two bodhichittas. Pray to meet spiritual mentors who can guide you on a path that leads to your continuing spiritual maturation both during the intermediate state after death, the *bardo*, and in future lives.

In Buddhism, as in other spiritual traditions, there is a difference between praying and marshaling desire. In Buddhism, one calls upon a power greater than the conscious mind to become infused with the transformative power of grace and blessings. This power may be conceived as being external or it may be recognized as internal. Both conceptions can be useful. Breaking down the distinction of inside and outside is even more useful. What is important, however it may be conceptualized, is the efficacy of prayer.

The power of abhorrence is recognizing self-grasping as the source of misery. The Buddhist view is that the force of grasping onto one's body perpetuates the cycle of birth, aging, sickness and death. If, by the power of abhorrence, you release all grasping onto your body and personal identity, you will experience death as liberation.

What would it be like to have no body, nothing physical to grasp onto? By the power of habitual attachment to this body, as we disengage from this life, we will experience intense craving for another embodiment. Samsara, vulnerability to suffering, is perpetuated by grasping. By craving another embodiment, we perpetuate our vulnerability to suffering, our own delusion. The power of abhorrence during the dying process is identifying the thought, "What will happen to me?" as grasping onto form, then releasing it completely and letting awareness simply be present in space.

The power of resolve applied to death refers to training in the two bodhichittas while in the bardo. Imagine that your heart and breath have stopped, and you are experiencing awareness similar to a dream. In the dreamlike awareness of the bardo, your body and the environment are unstable. The environment is altered just by a thought. Tibetans have many accounts of remembered experiences in the bardo, reporting that many confusing and frightening appearances can arise.

For the unprepared, death is very confusing. For several days after bodily death, the unprepared person is not convinced he is dead. After death, an unprepared person takes on a mental form, similar to being in a dream, and thinks, "Here I am!" In a mental body, the dead person is aware of everyone around him and gets upset that no one responds to him. Finally, the realization of death dawns and the craving arises, "I don't want to be dead! I want a body!" The power of resolve applied to death is cultivating compassion and insight in the dreamlike state of the bardo. Instead of confusion, anger, and craving, practice the two bodhichittas—penetrate into the nature of reality-itself, explore the nature of mind in the bardo, and cultivate compassion.

While you are dying resolve, "Soon I will be in the bardo and I will cultivate the two bodhichittas."

The fifth practice while dying is the power of familiarization. Familiarization means maintaining the continuity of the practice of the two bodhichittas through life and through death.

If possible, it is generally advised in the Buddhist tradition that one die while adopting the "sleeping lion's posture," lying on the right side with the right palm supporting the right cheek. This posture lines up the subtle channels in the body, facilitating conscious death. Optimally one dies gradually, without great pain, so that one can apprehend fully each stage of dying. A sudden death makes it more difficult to pass through this great transition consciously while deepening one's insight into the nature of awareness.

It is most important when dying to let go of all attachments and face the future without fear. Grieving loved ones not only cannot help you when you're dying, their lamentations can be very distracting. Politely ask them to leave. If you have a trusted companion, a Dharma friend or spiritual mentor, who is not going to be freaking out that you are dying, that person can be helpful.

As you practice a dress rehearsal for death, imagine that your final energies are waning. Imagine being lucid during that time, letting go completely everything familiar, releasing everything without a second thought. What is here and now? The two bodhichittas. Cultivate compassion as you die. Imagine that while you still have breath, you practice *tonglen.* Imagine taking in the suffering of the world on the in-breath and offering all your happiness on the out-breath. Move to the practice of ultimate bodhichitta. Releasing, move right into the nature of awareness. If awareness becomes vague, go back to *tonglen.* Move back and forth between the practice of ultimate and relative bodhichitta. Practicing the two bodhichittas while dying is dying perfectly.

Who dies? The body gets old, stops functioning as a living organism, and decays. That is straightforward. But who is the "I" that dies? Is the sense of "I" that has been cultivated in life anything more than a fiction based upon this body, this brain, this personal history? At death, the body no longer supports any kind of ego because the brain shuts down. Personal history ends at death.

Unborn awareness continues beyond the death of the physical body and the dissolution of the personal ego. Unborn awareness does not die because it was never born. It is unborn during life and it is unceasing after life. If the self-created fictions of "I" and "mine" are released before or during the dying process, it is possible to realize the deathless state. No one dies when the fiction of the "I" has been released and the unborn state is realized. If you are able to rest in the nature of your own awareness, the unborn, as you are dying, spiritual awakening is very close. If you ascertain unborn awareness in life, you attain the deathless state here and now before physical death.

In two lines Atisha synthesizes the essence of practice for life and death: apply the five powers, cultivate the two bodhichittas. These are quintessential practices to live for and to die for. Training in dream yoga is excellent preparation for dying. Cultivating the ability to apprehend the dream-state during a dream prepares for the state just after death when the bardo is entered. If you are able to recognize the bardo for what it is, you can choose your next rebirth with wisdom, rather than being propelled through simply by the force of your own habituations. However, the bardo, just like dreams, cannot be recognized for what it is without preparation. Without training in apprehending the dream, we mistake everything as real and habitual responses propel us from one life to the next. The Tibetan Buddhist view of dying as the final opportunity for meditation in this life is counter to the view of most modern scientists and philosophers that consciousness is an emergent property of the brain. The materialistic view that when the brain dies, consciousness vanishes, and the Buddhist view of continuity of consciousness from one lifetime to another are mutually exclusive. The Buddhist belief is that you, your history, abilities, and intelligence, will withdraw into a deeper level of your own awareness at death. Passing through the dying process is similar to passing through a corridor with doors closing on either side. The dying person enters into a blackout state that is like deep unconsciousness and subsequently emerges into the clear light of death, a luminous state in which there is no sense of personal identity. Without personal identity, who emerges in the bardo? You. Your brain will decay, but characteristics and memories emerge following death out of a deep level of consciousness just as you remember who you are in the morning after awakening from a night of dreaming. Imprints, habitual tendencies, knowledge, conceptualizations, emotions, all the stuff of ego, are stored in your mind-stream and will manifest in the bardo. Unlike cognitive scientists, Buddhists do not consider the brain to be primary. Consciousness is primary, and it carries on without support or influence by the brain. Therefore, the dying process is very important because death is not an end; it is a transition.

The Fifth Point:
The Criterion of Proficiency in the Mind-Training

Whatever path we take in life, one thread is common to us all: we are seeking genuine happiness and fulfillment. If one is not following a spiritual path, then the sources of satisfaction are typically related to the eight mundane concerns, not bad in themselves, but culminating in transient pleasures at best. The path of Dharma leads to a deeper, permanent source of well-being independent of environment and other people. In the shift of mind in which virtue begins to arise spontaneously and the mind is increasingly free of afflictions, happiness arises right along with virtue. When virtue emanates from within one's own mind, this produces a sense of well-being. However, this is not a stable state. Tara Rinpoche emphasized to me the importance of cultivating wholesome thoughts before trying to still all thoughts in deep meditation. As long as the mind is still highly prone to irritation, anxiety, and craving, even if you make a little progress in cultivating meditative quiescence, it will be eroded as soon as these old, unwholesome habits reappear. While wholesome thoughts provide an excellent platform, meditative quiescence goes deeper. In quiescence, serenity becomes incrementally less contingent on external circumstances. Just as virtue is a platform for the cultivation of meditative quiescence, once the mind becomes stable through training, quiescence itself becomes a platform for penetrating deeper into the nature of awareness, into stages of insight that ultimately eradicate the sources of suffering. With practice, joy and confidence in the practice increase, Dharma becomes self-nourishing and practice is spontaneous. But first you have to get your foot in the door. The Fifth Point of the Mind-Training tells us what the criteria are for assessing how we are progressing in our spiritual practice.

The whole of Dharma is synthesized in one aim.

The criterion of having gained proficiency in this Mind-Training is summed up as one aim: the challenge of subduing self-grasping. Once you recognize self-grasping as the fundamental source of your problems, then, no matter what path or faith you adopt, your objective will be to eradicate self-grasping. So the principal sign of how well you are doing in your practice is the extent to which your tendency of self-grasping is diminishing. I had my first personal meeting with the Dalai Lama when I was twenty-one. I had been living and studying in Dharamsala for several months by then, and I had been told that it would be possible for me to have a private audience with him. I didn't want to waste his time, so I felt I should have a really meaningful question to pose to him. By this time, other Western Dharma students had settled in Dharamsala after my arrival, and some of them would occasionally come to me with questions about Dharma. Even with the few months of training I had had at that point, I found I was often able to answer their questions, and I began to feel that I was a bit special. I knew more than they did! But I thought about this budding sense of personal superiority, and I foresaw that if I continued on that track, this would not bode well as I progressed along the path. The more understanding, experience, and insight I gained, the more superior I would feel. But I knew that true spiritual maturation results in increasing humility, not arrogance, so I found myself facing a dilemma: as you develop better and better qualities, how can you avoid feeling more and more superior to others? This was the question I decided to pose to the Dalai Lama in my first conversation with him. His Holiness gave me a response that has nourished me ever since. He said, imagine that you are very hungry and you knock on someone's door asking for food. You are welcomed in, your host gives you a delicious, nourishing meal and you eat. The Dalai Lama asked me, "In this situation, would you then feel proud or superior?" "No, of course not," I replied, "I would feel satisfied, but not proud." Then he explained, "You have come here out of hunger for spiritual teaching and wisdom. Teachers here offer you a balanced meal of spiritual teachings and you have been freely helping yourself to them. If you become satisfied in the process, be happy. There's no reason to be proud."

His Holiness continued by pointing to a fly, "Suppose I set out a saucer with a drop of honey on it. The fly comes to the honey and then another fly arrives. What will the first fly do? It will try to keep all the honey for itself by aggressively chasing off the second fly. We might look down upon this fly, but the fly doesn't have many options other than to act out of self-centeredness and self-grasping." Flies are driven by the same instinctive forces that humans are, self-grasping and self-centeredness, but they don't have the intelligence or opportunity to learn about the disadvantages of these tendencies. The Dalai Lama said, "We can't really blame the fly. A fly knows so little Dharma that there is not much else it can do." Then His Holiness pointed to himself, "I am a Buddhist monk. I have studied Dharma and taken monastic precepts. With all my understanding and intelligence as a human being and Buddhist follower, if I act like a fly and grasp onto good things for myself alone, this is a disgrace. The more understanding and intelligence you have, the greater the responsibility." The more understanding, experience, and insight we gain through our spiritual practice, His Holiness was pointing out, the more responsibility we have; and that awareness by itself should override any sense of specialness or superiority that may arise. The central theme of this Mind-Training is to direct our entire practice to the elimination of self-grasping. When we examine all our physical, verbal, and mental activities, if we find our sense of ego is inflated by our spiritual practice, then our efforts have been subverted into the pursuit of the eight mundane concerns. When Dharma is misused for the sake of mundane concerns, such as the pursuit of fame, power, wealth, and reputation, it's no longer being used in the pursuit of genuine happiness. If you still think it's possible to perfect samsara, to engineer the outside world to suit your aims and bring you real satisfaction, go for it. You don't need Dharma. You can try everything else. But when you figure out that samsara can't be perfected and that the eight mundane concerns are a hopeless venture, then turn to the one thing that holds any real promise of bringing you the fulfillment you seek. You are ready for Dharma when you see that nothing else works.

Attend to the chief of two witnesses.

Who can be trusted to judge the progress of our spiritual practice? We might appear impressively spiritual to other people, but they are not necessarily the best judges of our progress. The Mind-Training says the best judge of our progress is "the chief of two witnesses." Who are these two? One witness is other people who observe us from outside, but they are limited by their inability to observe what happens in our minds. This requires the second witness: ourselves. We alone can observe our motivation and the quality of our minds from moment to moment. Of the two witnesses, yourself and others, the chief witness is yourself. Rely on yourself honestly to monitor the quality and progress of your practice. This is not simple because there is no question that we can delude ourselves, so this is why we also consult spiritual friends and teachers. In short, we need to attend to both witnesses, but rely primarily upon the chief witness, ourselves, to monitor and observe the quality and results of our practice.

There is an important distinction to be made here regarding our concern for the opinions of others. One of the eight mundane concerns that Buddhists constantly warn about is reputation, which bears on the opinions of others. If I am worried that the neighbors think that I am not a good person, this can be a simple fixation on my reputation. Yet Buddhist psychology also refers to concern for the opinions of others as a virtue. This virtue is a type of social conscience that restrains us from doing things we know are wrong, because if others knew of our misdeed, they would think poorly of us. The distinction between the two types of concern for others' opinions hinges on motivation. If you are focused on virtue, doing your best, remedying mistakes and moving on, then you're doing all you can. If other people still think ill of you, that's their problem. You can never be so perfect, compassionate, wise, and virtuous that you will be above everyone's criticism. Buddha's cousin slandered him and tried to kill him, and Jesus died at the hands of his enemies. Since we can't control other people's minds, no matter what we do, we are still prone to others' criticism, slander, and abuse. However, our happiness need not be contingent on the opinions of others. The chief witness, our primary judge, is ourselves. The chief witness can carefully assess whether criticism is valid or not. If criticism is valid, deal with it. If it is not, forget it.

Constantly resort to a sense of good cheer.

Imagine a constant sense of good cheer. Imagine a mental disposition more desirable than a continuum of pleasant circumstances filled with lovely people and appliances that never fail. Imagine constant good cheer. If good cheer can arise only within happy and pleasant circumstances, it will constantly be interrupted. However, we can choose to shift priorities so that we constantly resort to a sense of good cheer. We can choose what we want above all else, more than possessions, praise, reputation, and even health. If more than anything else we desire a compassionate heart and a mind of wisdom, if our highest priority is the cultivation of the two bodhichittas, then this focus is the key that makes it possible to cultivate and accomplish a constant sense of good cheer in the midst of all the vicissitudes of life.

When bodhichitta is the highest priority, any circumstance is an opportunity for insight and compassion. With bodhichitta as the highest priority, when we are with a disagreeable person, we can appreciate the circumstances that gave rise to his behavior, transforming judgmental thoughts to, "May this person be free of this circumstance and find happiness." When the heart softens, harsh judgments evaporate. Recall that sadness is the near enemy of compassion, a transitional state and precursor to genuine compassion. When sadness arises, imagine "How can I be of benefit?" and constantly resort to a sense of good cheer.

Mundane concerns are little things that can seem enormous. The mind is like a balloon—sometimes it shrivels and sometimes it expands, depending on the volume of its perspective. Keep the mind big and balanced. There are colossal issues. In the midst of being aware that millions of people are suffering from abject poverty, maintain a sense of good cheer, not succumbing to compassion's near enemy, sadness, and not succumbing to a sense of futility and apathy. Practice *tonglen*, giving and taking, together with your respiration.

Resorting to a sense of good cheer is indispensable. By and large, I find that if I start the day with happiness that wells up from the heart, this sets the tone for the rest of the day. Starting from a sense of balance, as your day progresses, vigilantly watch for any source of unhappiness and apply Dharma. See if your sense of good cheer can survive until 9:00 a.m. Gradually, see if you can get through the whole day in a state of good cheer. In the meantime, watch what circumstances impede your well-being, and respond to them with Dharma.

Shantideva makes this simple point: "If there is a remedy, then what is the use of frustration? If there is no remedy, then what is the use of frustration?"[74] When a problem arises, either you can do something about it or you can't. If you can do something, do it. If there is nothing you can do, being miserable doesn't help. This attitude cultivates the warrior mentality for spiritual practice. Meet adversity, hassles, and disagreeable people like a boxer in the ring, prepared to subdue all adversity with good cheer. Take a wimpy stance to adversity and you are toast. Maintaining courage in adversity becomes an aid to practice, enhancing the cultivation of the two bodhichittas. This is the choice we have. When adversity becomes an ally in the fulfillment of our deepest aim, the cultivation of wisdom and compassion, it is no longer adversity. When adversity is no longer experienced as adversity, this is a sign of success in spiritual practice.

The Sixth Point:
The Pledges of the Mind-Training

The Sixth Point of the Seven-Point Mind-Training is a list of pledges that look like a bunch of "thou-shalt-nots." In Buddhist practice a "pledge" is a commitment, or a resolve, to refrain from certain types of behavior that harm ourselves and others. Almost all the pledges of the Sixth Point are stated in the negative, making the list tedious from one perspective, but encouraging from another. It can be seen as encouraging in the sense that if we merely *refrain* from engaging in certain harmful ways of conduct, our bodhichitta will grow effortlessly, like the river that vitalizes itself once pollutants are no longer fed into it. The purpose of this list is to keep us on track. The overall idea of the Sixth Point is that if you want to cultivate inner well-being throughout states of adversity and felicity, if you want to cultivate ultimate and relative bodhichitta, then save yourself lots of valuable time by stopping certain habitual behaviors that cause suffering. There is a lot to do in transforming all circumstances into the path of spiritual awakening. There is also a lot not to do. The Sixth Point comprises a list of behaviors to stop. This is a list of the things we do that cause unnecessary trouble and suffering. While some suffering is unavoidable, there is also suffering that we can prevent.

Recall Shantideva's compassionate observation, "Those desiring to escape from suffering hasten right toward suffering. With the very desire for happiness, out of delusion they destroy their own happiness as if it were an enemy."[75] The Sixth Point lists behaviors that can be changed by acts of will. An act of will won't be effective for achieving ultimate bodhichitta overnight, any more than you can make flowers grow overnight by sheer will power. However, just like a garden, bodhichitta will flourish if you attend to it and nurture it, and this can be accomplished with volition exercised in the right way.

If the list arouses resistance, take the pressure off by evaluating its efficacy. Is it beneficial or not? The goal of these pledges is to avoid pitfalls that undermine practice. If you cherish the cultivation of bodhichitta, then this is the list of things to avoid to ensure that your style of life doesn't tear down what you strive to build up through spiritual practice.

Always abide by three principles.

The three principles are: (1) do not contravene your commitments to training the mind, (2) do not have a sense of bravado in the Mind-Training, and (3) do not have an uneven Mind-Training.

1. *Do not contravene your commitments to training the mind.* This means do not be dismissive of vows. Paradoxically, when some people begin to feel progress in meditation, they feel that their spiritual realization overrides the importance of ethics. When you begin to experience a spacious quality of awareness, you may begin to think that you are so advanced on the path that you are above the ethical rules that apply to ordinary people. Padmasambhava commented in this regard that even though his view was as vast as space, his conduct was as fine as grains of barley flour. There is no point so advanced that we can be dismissive of ethics.

A second aspect of the commitment to training the mind is not being dismissive of other teachings. When I was studying Buddhism in my twenties, I wanted "the system" that would answer all questions. For me at that time, the system was the collected works of Tsongkhapa. There was security in the belief that all I had to do was study Tsongkhapa's eighteen volumes of truth, and everything I needed to know would be contained in them. The system had borders and I didn't have to look at anything else, not even commentaries, just the real stuff. Slowly, I emerged from this fundamentalist belief in the One True Path.

The Dalai Lama is a shining example of someone who refrains from the fundamentalist stance of being dismissive of the teachings of other traditions. Especially in our fast-paced, efficiency-oriented society, it is natural for us to want the best and fastest practices leading to enlightenment. This attitude incites many people to look for shortcuts, or ways to speed up the process and make it easier. The reality is that practice is situated in life. For some people, an uncomplicated practice such as mindfulness of breathing might be the fastest and most effective path for some period. There are other people for whom engaging in prayer, or cultivating a heart of loving-kindness, may be the fastest, deepest, and most effective path. Other people find optimal benefit reading Buddhist sutras, developing meditative quiescence, and cultivating ultimate and relative bodhichitta. Spiritual practice is embedded in life. Questions of "best" and "fastest" are relative. During a lecture series in Los Angeles, when the Dalai Lama was asked to reveal a fast and easy way to enlightenment, his immediate response was to hold up his hand with his index finger touching his thumb: "Zero."

The issue of speed is linked with the feeling that we just don't have time for spiritual practice. "Lack of time" is a problem addressed at the very beginning of the Mind-Training with the "four thoughts that turn the mind." What is time for? The purpose of these discursive meditations is to shift priorities so that you have more time for spiritual practice, ultimately recognizing every moment as an opportunity for practice. The fast track to spiritual maturity is through total commitment, intelligent practice, and perseverance. Any shortcut that bypasses these elements is bogus.

2. *Do not have a sense of bravado in the Mind-Training.* Imagine your practice is going well. You feel that you are rising above the vicissitudes of life and are filled with loving-kindness, wisdom, and courage. The urge may arise to test out the strength of your spiritual fortitude by finding some thugs in a dark alley and overwhelming them with loving-kindness. The advice here is, "Don't." Don't seek out dangerous situations to practice Mind-Training. Adverse situations will find you in their own time.

3. *Do not have an uneven Mind-Training.* An "uneven" Mind-Training means practicing only when things are going well, practicing only in some types of adversity but not in others, or with certain people but not with others. Practice evenly, in all circumstances.

Shift your priorities but stay as you are.

This aphorism tells us that we should transform our minds, but externally not radically alter our behavior to show how "spiritual" we have become. We strive to attenuate mental afflictions, improve the quality of attention, and cultivate equanimity, loving-kindness, and compassion. When a little bit of progress happens, along comes the natural inclination to show off, "I used to be stingy, but now look how generous I am! I used to be impatient, but now look how laid back I am!" We want to air our clean laundry, to externalize the good transformations that have taken place within. The pledge says to resist the temptation to externalize spiritual progress. Maintain these deep practices, bring about great changes in your mind, but let your conduct remain as it is.

This aphorism highlights a big cultural difference between Tibet and the West. In the fourteen years I lived with Tibetan monks, yogis, and lamas, I never heard any Tibetan say, "I just have to tell you about the insights I had in my morning meditation!" This is very different from the West, where so many of us are eager to share, or even broadcast, our spiritual experiences and insights. We meditate a little bit and then we have to tell somebody how well we did. One old Tibetan aphorism says, "If you shake a pot with a little water in it, it makes a loud noise. But if you shake a pot filled with water, it remains silent." Those filled with spiritual insight feel no need to draw attention to themselves about it. Avoid broadcasting your inner revelations, and also don't change external behavior to display new virtue. Of course, you stop previous negative behavior, but let your inner transformation remain quietly within.

The rationale for this advice is very practical. When we show off our accomplishments, this is a call for respect that says, "I am special." The external display of new virtue is an indication that Dharma practice is being put into the service of the eight mundane concerns— "Respect me. Praise me. I'm someone special." In which case we have blown it. Letting transformation take place inside, without such outer displays makes it less likely spiritual practice will be co-opted as just one more means for getting respect, admiration, wealth, and so on.

I once heard the Dalai Lama being asked by a Westerner what his degree of realization is, something no Tibetan would dream of asking, and he answered, "That's my business." This is not to say that Tibetan lamas never talk about their inner experiences, but they usually do it on a "need-to-know" basis, with the motivation to inspire others in their practice, not to arouse admiration for themselves.

Do not speak of others' limitations.

We tend to indulge the habitual urge to discuss in great detail other people's faults. This aphorism reiterates the old adage, "If you can't say something nice, don't say anything at all." Usually, discussing someone else's faults is a way to vent frustration, show contempt, and affirm one's own superiority. The more passion one has about the faults of others, the more agitated the mind becomes. Life is too short and too important to waste discussing the faults of others. This behavior has no benefit, undermines the cultivation of bodhichitta, and ultimately hurts ourselves.

There are a few exceptions. For example, a doctor may tell a patient his diagnosis out of benevolence and with the intention of curing him. Likewise, parents speak to their children about the children's problems. Among friends, there is also a responsibility to discuss shortcomings out of a spirit of altruism. When we notice a friend doing something that is harmful, something he may not even be aware of, out of affection and concern we have the responsibility to draw his attention to the behavior. That is being a good friend. When the motivation is to be of benefit, there are appropriate occasions and ways to discuss the faults of others. If the motivation is for anything other than benefit, it's best to keep silent.

Do not stand in judgment of others.

I have lived in close-knit Buddhist monasteries in India and Switzerland where everyone was practicing hard and trying to recognize their own mental afflictions and eradicate them. With attention concentrated on mental afflictions, it is easy to grow more and more sensitive to other people's shortcomings. But we have to ask ourselves: are the faults we observe really "out there" or might they be projections of our own defects? In the final analysis, all that appears to us consists simply of appearances to our own minds. We have no access to any absolutely objective realities. A pure mind sees with pure perception, and a polluted mind sees a world filled with pollution. Do other people have faults? From a conventional point of view, certainly, but no person is inherently evil; and even the mental afflictions themselves, the root of all evil, have no inherent existence of their own. What we attend to becomes our experienced reality, so if we make a point of attending to other people's faults, we will dwell in a world filled with disagreeable people. In the same way, it's not really useful to dwell on our own faults, for then we'll most likely learn to define ourselves in terms of those faults. Clear, precise awareness of our mental states and behavior is helpful. But dwelling on our own faults is debilitating.

There is a deeper issue here, called the "black box" problem in science. We can't perceive what is in people's minds, we can only try to make inferences based on their outer behavior. The input and output can be known, but what is inside producing output from input is a matter of conjecture. Scientists ranging from psychologists to physicists want to know what is inside various kinds of "black boxes" in nature—any system for which you can detect only what goes in and what comes out, but not what's inside. The scientific method is to introduce something into a system— be it another person's mind or the realm of subatomic particles—observe what comes out, and then hypothesize about how the system works internally. The deepest "black box" problem is another person's mind. We only have direct access to our own conscious minds, and even here there are problems and limitations. When we speculate about other people's motives, with what do we fill the "black box" of their minds? Most likely, our own possible motives, or at least those we find most easily imaginable. This doesn't mean we can't evaluate other people at all, but it is helpful to recognize the limitations of our own ego-based inferences.

The philosophical problem pertaining to any black box situation is called "underdetermination." This problem, simply put, is that no matter how much objective data you draw out of a black box, that information can always be interpreted in multiple, mutually incompatible, ways. The range of interpretations is simply a matter of the extent of one's imagination, and the objective data themselves can never narrow down your options to one and only one possible interpretation. The objective data by themselves are always insufficient to determine the unique validity of any one interpretation.

The simplistic view of science is that the scientific method tests hypotheses and thereby simply determines the nature of reality. Evidence that agrees with a hypothesis is naively thought to prove the corresponding theory. In physics, however, experiments might confirm a hypothesis, but another hypothesis, incompatible with the first, might also predict the same results. A group of imaginative physicists may come up with several theories, all interpreting the same body of data in mutually incompatible ways. Which hypothesis is the "truth?" The scientific method produces data, but that data doesn't necessarily determine only one theory that is both intelligible and predictive. That's the problem of underdetermination.

Let's get back to daily practice. We try to make sense of other people's behavior, but unless we can read minds and see emotions and motivations, their behavior is open to multiple interpretations. We might come up with one highly plausible (to us) explanation for their behavior, and that explanation might even enable us to predict some of their conduct in the future. If our prediction comes true, we might think, "I now have understood this person through and through." But someone else using a completely different theory may have also made the same prediction about that person's conduct and also have been correct. Only the limits of imagination determine how many intelligible theories with predictive power there are for human behavior—a truth that has become obvious to many in the field of psychology. Where does that leave us? I think it leaves us justified in being very cautious about thinking we have other people figured out.

There is a profound connection here between attention, reality, and *pure perception*. In cultivating pure perception, when one looks beyond the superficial faults of a person, the knee-jerk conclusions about behavior are averted. In cultivating pure perception, we move beyond habitual superimpositions and interpretations to engaging with the buddha-nature of ourselves and others. If we can intuitively affirm that there is more to people than personality traits, that their deepest identity is their buddha-nature, or primordial wisdom, we have a choice about what to attend to. We can choose to be in dialogue with the person's buddha-nature, or we can limit ourselves to engaging simply with their conventional nature. This is a legitimate choice, and we have the freedom to make it if we wish.

Abandon all hope of reward.

This aphorism can be understood in different ways (one more case of underdetermination!). For starters, it advises us to abandon all hopes of gaining status, respect, fame, magical powers, and other mundane rewards in this life. From the highest perspective, it means we are finally to abandon even the hope of enlightenment. As long as we are still caught in the dualistic mind-set of viewing ourselves as deluded sentient beings struggling to achieve something we don't have, that very mentality, together with its hopes for enlightenment and fear of failure, obstructs our realization of our own buddha-nature, which is already present.

The underlying context of this line is that the hopes and aspirations important at the beginning of spiritual practice become more of a present reality and less an abstract objective as one progresses in practice. As practice takes root and begins to nourish us from within, giving us fulfillment, well-being, and happiness in the present, practice becomes its own reward. When is your practice getting off the ground? When you start to enjoy it. As you find satisfaction and joy arising from practice itself, then it is time to release the hope for rewards or accomplishment. As Dharma practice progresses, hope of reward is unnecessary, even detrimental. Therefore, let go of hope itself. This does not mean we should be hopeless; it means we can move beyond the dichotomy of hope and anxiety.

Avoid poisonous food.

One can gain intellectual understanding of Dharma by reading and receiving teachings, and one can begin to gain some experience by putting the teachings into practice. But as a result, we may begin to feel we are superior to others, a theme I've mentioned before. This feeling of "I am special" is the poisonous food mentioned in this aphorism.

The reason Tibetan contemplatives rarely brag or promote themselves is that very early in life Tibetans are taught that "I am special" is poisonous food. In our society, on the contrary, self-promotion is widely considered the only way, and the right way, to get ahead. For those of us who are teaching Dharma in the West, we may feel a temptation to call attention to ourselves, our many years spent in meditation, our decades of practice and teaching, the number of books we have published. And we may justify this on the grounds that it's all for the sake of Dharma, or that this is the way that our society works. How different this approach is, though, from the model that Tibetans have practiced for centuries. As the Dalai Lama commented recently, a follower of Dharma, whether a student or a teacher, should seek a low profile, like a wounded deer seeking solitude. There is outer solitude, in which we actually withdraw from society, and there is inner solitude, in which we withdraw from the eight mundane concerns. While outer solitude is not always appropriate, inner solitude is.

The goal of spiritual practice is to overcome self-grasping and self-centeredness. If our goal is actually to feel more important than anyone else in the world, we can achieve this without any Dharma practice whatsoever!

Do not indulge in self-righteousness.

When we detect inappropriate behavior on the part of others, we may experience a knee-jerk reaction of flaring up in righteous indignation and resentment. But this aphorism encourages us to attend closely to the circumstances under which others' vices emerge, and the influences that have led to our own virtues, such as they may be. When you witness behavior that you think is wrong, put the righteous indignation on hold, and consider that person's circumstances and history. Then consider your own history, particularly related to Dharma, and consider that whatever virtue you have cultivated has been cultivated in dependence on the kindness, guidance, and inspiration of others. A sense of gratitude takes the wind out of the sails of self-righteousness. Instead of standing in judgment, consider what circumstances might have given rise to bad behavior and cultivate the beneficial attitude of seeking to help that person.

Keeping these pledges helps us check the relation between our deepest motivation and our behavior. The need to periodically check motivation is exemplified by stories of enlightenment enthusiasts who make some progress in meditation, only to be disappointed to discover that a good twenty-minute meditation produces a high that quickly wears off. Why meditate when you can more easily get a temporary high by taking a pill or smoking a joint? The goal of Dharma is not a temporary high but a lasting state of well-being realized by tapping into our own primordial wisdom. It is motivation that links behavior to this deep transformation far beyond temporary state-effects of meditation.

The distinction here is huge. Both meditation and drugs lead to altered states of awareness, proving that we are not locked into one and only one way of engaging with reality. The Buddha's first teachers were terrific at leading him to altered states of consciousness. The problem was that when the meditation session was over, the altered state swiftly came to an end, producing no lasting transformation or freedom. Realizing the difference between state-effects and trait-effects, temporary altered states and permanent liberation from all mental afflictions, the Buddha set off to seek a lasting, irreversible state of enlightenment. When we are in touch with our deepest aspiration, like Buddha himself, we are seeking more than a temporary altered state of awareness. We are seeking a profound and permanent shift in how we view and engage with reality.

Dharma practice transforms the patterns of thought that percolate through our minds day after day, producing progressively more stable results. Gradually, these shifts manifest in more beneficial ways of responding to adversity, pain, loss, frustration, and disappointment. Gradually, adversity doesn't dominate us. We discover more inner strength, more inner ballast, to make our way through all times, good and bad. To achieve the lasting trait-effects we are after entails no less than the irreversible transformation of our minds, and for this, twenty minutes a day isn't likely to be enough. What's needed is commitment to a full range of spiritual practices throughout the entire day, not just temporary state-effects that occur during formal meditation practice.

There is a famous story about a Dharma practitioner who prided himself on his diligent efforts applied to devotional practices, study, and meditation. While his teacher, Dromtönpa, the principal disciple of Atisha, acknowledged the value of these practices, he counseled him that it is "even better to practice Dharma." When asked by his perplexed student, "What is Dharma?" Dromtönpa replied, "Give up all attachment to this life, and let your mind *become* Dharma." Giving up attachment to this life means giving up attachment to the eight mundane concerns, no longer placing priorities upon externals such as money, possessions, honor, respect, and transient pleasures. The more we free ourselves of attachment to these external resources, the freer we are to discover our own inner resources of genuine happiness. When we outgrow the dualistic sense that *we* are practicing something special called *Dharma*, when our lives and our spiritual practice merge, then our minds truly *become* Dharma.

Do not engage in malicious sarcasm.

Malicious sarcasm hurts. The Tibetan image for sarcasm is throwing a rock wrapped in wool. The person on the receiving end of sarcasm may at first think a friendly little fluff ball is coming his way, only to discover that it was really a rock in disguise. Malicious sarcasm might seem clever and humorous to some, but its intention is to inflict pain. Of course, if you never indulge in sarcasm, this is an easy pledge to keep.

Of the 253 monastic precepts I took as a Buddhist monk, I had to pay careful attention to many but others I didn't worry much about breaking. Of the eighteen primary bodhisattva precepts, one I don't worry much about is, "do not destroy towns and villages with psychic powers." I keep that precept effortlessly! But not engaging in malicious sarcasm may require a lot of attention and is especially difficult for clever people with a quick tongue. When the mind is virtuous, the tongue can be trusted. But when the mind is afflicted, the tongue can do a lot of damage in a short time. Sarcasm, even malicious sarcasm, is often deemed acceptable in our society when it is thought to be warranted or true. But the Buddhist position is that many truths don't need mentioning, certainly not with contempt or disdain.

Do not wait in ambush.

This is a common Tibetan idiom with deep meaning. Tibetan Buddhist medicine describes the differences in temperament among people as being related to their individual humoral constitutions, of which there are three: wind, bile, and phlegm. "Waiting in ambush" is a behavior typical of people with a "phlegmatic" constitution. "Windy" people tend to speak quickly, be hyperactive, fun-loving, and sociable. Annoy a windy person and he will probably snap at you right away, and then forget about it. "Bilious" people tend to be sharp-witted and sharp-tempered. Insult a person with a bilious temperament and he, too, may react quickly and vehemently. "Phlegmatic" people tend to be forbearing and can endure pain and grief that would cause other types of people to cave in. They may take insult after insult without any overt reaction, but they are especially prone to "waiting in ambush," quietly plotting their moment of revenge. This pledge is couched in the idiom of Tibet, where waiting in ambush was a very finely honed skill.

Do not load the burden of a *dzo* on an ox.

A *dzo* is a cross between a yak and an ox, and it is considerably stronger than an ox. The meaning here is don't shift the burden of any task or responsibility onto the shoulders of those who can't bear it.

Do not flatter your way to the top.

Flattery looks nice. It appears to be showing respect or appreciation and looks like a virtue. But flattery is devious. Under the veneer of appreciation, flattery's intention is to manipulate. Keeping this pledge, like all the others, is most effectively done if we ponder its significance in our own lives. Comb deeply through your memory to see if this is a type of behavior to which you are prone. If on occasion you use flattery to get what you want, you have something to practice.

Avoid pretense.

Pretense stems from an inner motivation that is at variance with outer conduct. Avoiding pretense is a difficult precept to keep. Monks, lamas, and spiritual teachers have to be very careful about pretense because people who seriously engage in spiritual practice are tempted to think of themselves as exceptional people who are a cut above the crowd. Gyatrul Rinpoche likens the tendency of pretense to a cat covering its poop with sand. We do something that is completely at variance with our ideals, and then we hastily cover it up, leaving the world with the impression, "Not me!"

Do not bring a god down to the level of a demon.

While engaging in this Mind-Training, we are emulating the awareness and conduct of the buddhas and bodhisattvas, likened here to "gods." But it is possible to reduce such practice to the "level of a demon" when it results in an exalted sense of self, "I am special," or "I am holy." The notions "my Dharma is pure," "my way is the only right way," or "I am a pure practitioner" all bring the god of Dharma down to level of the demon of egotism. The practices of the

Mind-Training are all designed as antidotes for the afflictions of our own minds. That is what it is all about.

Do not take advantage of another's misfortune.

There are certain types of pleasure that can be had at the expense of other people. When we see the prospect for some pleasure, we might try to get it before someone else does. Or we might cause suffering to someone else to get something good for ourselves. However, genuine happiness is found without resorting to this. Therefore, we are encouraged not to take advantage of another's misfortune in our own pursuit of happiness.

The pledges of the Sixth Point of this training are not morality for morality's sake. All these pledges are designed to shed light on specific behavioral tendencies that are pitfalls on the path of spiritual awakening.

The Seventh Point:
The Precepts of the Mind-Training

Synthesize all meditative practices in one.

"One" refers to the Seven-Point Mind-Training. Whatever happens, use the Mind-Training to transform your experience into the two bodhichittas, the heart of the practice. Just as it is possible to reduce the spiritual to the mundane by letting "the god fall to the level of a demon," it is possible to transform the mundane into spiritual practice. It is possible to turn grocery shopping, working, relaxing, and taking care of children into spiritual practice. Driving becomes spiritual practice by sending the wish to your fellow travelers, "May you all get to your destinations swiftly and safely." Instead of being irritated with traffic and wishing others, "Get out of my way," use imagination and transform the mundane into Dharma. It is possible.

Respond in one way to all bouts of dejection.

After practicing for a while you may feel you are not making much progress and wonder whether the problem is with the practice or yourself. Dejection may come from lack of confidence in the practice. You might find that your mind becomes heavy after practicing *tonglen* or you may feel unhappy. Or you may simply feel depressed by your exposure to a world that is so filled with delusion, aggression, selfishness, conflict, and misery.

This aphorism refers to discouragement. You may find that your mind, which was fairly scattered before you started meditating, now seems even more scattered. This is called "the first sign of progress." The first sign of progress is to see your true situation. When you become more aware of what has been going on all along, that is a good sign, a painful sign, but a good one. Discouragement, or "dejection," is a natural response to bringing our situation into finer focus. From the Buddhist viewpoint, we have had these mental afflictions for a long time, many lives. We have become accustomed to our afflictions and it takes effort just to recognize them. Furthermore, afflictions will not disappear overnight, or even, sometimes, over many years.

Recognizing this, the Mind-Training counsels, "Respond in one way." We are in the habit of becoming deeply dejected about many concerns that have no long-term significance—the person we love doesn't love us back, the great job collapsed, our money was stolen. So many causes for despair. We fall into despair right, left, and center. If you become discouraged about Dharma, at least the despair is about something that is deeply meaningful. Counteract dejection by practicing Dharma, practicing *tonglen*, and reaching out to others and offering them your happiness.

There are two tasks, at the beginning and at the end.

This aphorism is widely cited in the Tibetan Buddhist tradition. For every situation that has a start and finish, any situation with a sense of closure, at the beginning there is one task and at the end there is another task. The beginning task is setting the motivation. Why are you going to do what you are about to do? Going to school, setting up a business, changing jobs, moving, meditating, getting married—why? By attending to motivation and transforming it into bodhichitta, all otherwise mundane activities are transformed into something meaningful and beneficial.

In following this precept, the first thing in the morning, before getting out of bed, we establish our motivation for the rest of the day. What will make the day meaningful? What will give satisfaction when we reflect back at the end of the day? Think: If this were my last day on earth, how could I look back on the day with satisfaction? The ideal motivation, bodhichitta, is summarized in the prayer, "May my activities in this day lead me to a state of spiritual awakening so that I can be of greatest service to others." Let this motivation guide the day.

The second task is "at the end." Dedication of merit is the second task. When a task or a day has been completed, look back and see where there was something good. Then dedicate the merit for the benefit of all sentient beings. Merit is spiritual power, it has momentum and can be directed or dedicated wherever you want it. The default dedication of merit is usually toward mundane concerns, the acquisition of money or to gain respect. The other option is to plow merit right back into the field of Dharma for your spiritual maturation and the welfare of all sentient beings by dedicating merit "at the end."

Bear whichever of the two occurs.

The "two" are felicity and adversity. In both good times and bad, continue practicing Dharma, noting the relativity of each. It is so easy for the mind to shrink on either occasion: when things are going terrifically, we can become obsessed by how well we're doing; and when everything goes downhill, it can seem like the world's coming to an end. Whichever of the two occurs, keep your mind spacious, maintaining a sense of equanimity no matter what the circumstances. This is a sure sign of spiritual maturation.

Guard the two at the cost of your life.

The "two" are the two bodhichittas, relative and ultimate. The point here is that the two bodhichittas are more precious than life itself. Tibetans say that if you are living a virtuous life, then living long is a boon; but if you are living a non-virtuous life, then it's better to have a short life. There is nothing intrinsically good about having a long life, but in the Buddhist view, a human life with leisure and opportunity to engage in spiritual practice is more valuable than a wish-fulfilling gem. The two bodhichittas are what give value to life. Therefore, guard these two at the cost of your life.

Practice the three austerities.

The three austerities are (1) remembering, (2) averting, and (3) cutting off the flow.

1. Remembering refers to bearing in mind the remedies for mental afflictions when they arise. In the warfare analogy frequently found in Buddhist writings, the soldier venturing into battle is thoroughly familiar with his arsenal of weapons and knows how and when to use them. When your mind is besieged with afflictions, if you don't remember the specific or general countermeasures against them, you have no chance of using them in battle with mental afflictions. Memorizing the aphorisms of this Mind-Training is an effective way to maintain the inventory of your spiritual arsenal.

2. Averting is another warfare tactic. There are many people who are not pleasant and many calamities occur in the turbulence of daily life. There are bound to be occasions when mental affliction will be poised to engulf you, when a wave of righteous indignation or contempt is about to inundate your mind. With practice, you will begin to see this approaching. Don't just get swept away. Avert! When

you recognize oncoming distortions of your mind, direct your attention to them thinking, "I see you coming, anger, jealousy, attachment, and you're not going to capture me!" Recognize the affliction, recall the specific antidote, and avert by moving out of the path of the affliction.

3. Cutting off the flow of mental afflictions as soon as they arise is the third austerity. Cutting the flow requires keen vigilance. Just as reading a book on swimming won't keep you from drowning, a scholar who has stored away a warehouse of Buddhist knowledge won't be able to cut the flow of mental afflictions without practice. There are two general strategies for cutting the flow of mental afflictions. One strategy is to recognize an affliction arising, and then settle the mind in its natural state, observing the affliction without identifying with it. The strategy of settling the mind in its natural state is simple but difficult to accomplish and takes great vigilance. This strategy can be effective, though, because mental afflictions are parasitic and if observed without identification, they die for lack of nourishment. This is like cutting off the supply lines of the enemy—a very effective and nonviolent way of winning a war.

A second strategy to cut the flow before getting dragged into the vortex of afflictions is to apply a specific antidote, such as the cultivation of relative and ultimate bodhichitta. It is helpful to keep in mind that the defining characteristic of a mental affliction is something that disrupts the equilibrium of the mind. To discern experientially whether your mind has succumbed to a mental affliction, check the mind's balance and equilibrium. If it is disrupted, then it is under the influence of an affliction.

When you practice breath awareness, some degree of mental balance is likely to arise. There are also times when the mind is relatively balanced without meditating. With a relatively balanced and healthy state of mind, we work hard, get tired, and go to sleep. That is what a balanced mind does—work, fatigue, sleep, wake up, work, fatigue, sleep. There are occasions when the mind is balanced, serene, but then for some reason, we lose balance. How is it lost? There is nothing "out there" that directly or inevitably disturbs the equilibrium of the mind. What the "out there" does is catalyze mental afflictions, and the afflictions, the tendencies of the mind for anger, attachment and the rest, do the work. I remember when I was visiting the Red Fort in Delhi, I think it was, I asked whether this massive fortress with its mighty ramparts had ever been conquered. The reply was yes, each time by the enemy bribing someone *inside* the fort to open the gates so the hostile forces could enter freely. The principal traitors inside the fortress of our minds are self-grasping and self-centeredness, which allow the mind to be overwhelmed by external circumstances without a fight.

Suppose your feelings are hurt by an insult. The insult didn't directly cause your unhappiness. Rather, the insult triggered a sense of pride, you identified with your sense of pride, and that identification destroyed your mental equilibrium. Our habitual propensities for mental afflictions are triggered by outside circumstances, then the problem is compounded by grasping onto and identifying with our own afflictive responses.

All mental afflictions upset the equilibrium of the mind. Another characteristic all afflictions have in common is that they occur only when the mind is in a conceptual mode. That doesn't mean, of course, that when the mind is operating conceptually it is always under the influence of mental afflictions. Some conceptualizations, such as the meditative cultivation of loving-kindness or *tonglen*, counteract mental afflictions. Conceptualization itself is not a problem. Grasping is the problem. Non-conceptual modes of awareness, such as are cultivated in the development of meditative quiescence, do not support mental afflictions. Therefore, to cut the flow of mental affliction, one technique is to switch from the conceptual mode of awareness to a non-conceptual mode. This is not a cure but a respite. In the meantime we can develop a healthy sense of vengeance regarding afflictions: "This mind is not big enough for the two of us. So you'd better be out of mind before sundown. Now git!"

Acquire the three principal causes.

The three "principal causes" of a flourishing spiritual practice are (1) receiving guidance from a qualified spiritual mentor, (2) devoting yourself to all stages of practice in accordance with the guidance you have received, and (3) assembling the outer and inner conditions necessary for effective practice.

1. The first principal cause of spiritual maturation is receiving guidance from a qualified spiritual mentor who is not only knowledgeable and experienced, but teaches effectively and with a motivation of compassion. Like a good physician, a worthy mentor is a person who has both knowledge and experience. The analogy between one's relation with a spiritual mentor and with a physician is a close and important one. For years in Dharamsala, India, I assisted Dr. Yeshi Dhonden, who was then the Dalai Lama's personal physician. Dr. Dhonden treated all types of ailments, from colds to terminal cancer. His diagnoses, made on the basis of questioning, visual examination, urine analysis, and pulse diagnosis, were in many cases stunningly accurate.

Tibetan medicine is aimed not merely at eliminating symptoms but at curing afflictions from their source. After the diagnosis is made and treatment prescribed, the patient must report back on a regular basis and tell the doctor how the treatment has been going. When the patient reports in, the doctor will do another exam and often adjust medication.

Sometimes there is a phase in the healing process when some symptoms get worse, but if the patient can endure those symptoms, brought on by proper medical treatment, they pass. Of course it can also happen that one feels worse, or at least not better, after treatment because it was not the appropriate treatment in the first place. So close consultation with the physician is essential. The parallels between physician and spiritual teacher and between healing and spiritual maturation run deep.

If you are sick of being under the domination of mental afflictions, tired of suffering from attachment, hostility and resentment, jealousy and competitiveness, depression, and generally having a dysfunctional mind, Buddhism provides a welcome second opinion to the diagnosis that being subject to these afflictions is simply part of the human condition. The Buddhist hypothesis is that afflictions are ingrained by habit; they are not an intrinsic part of you. In other words, the mind can be healed. Irreversibly.

Primordial awareness, by its nature never distorted and never afflicted, is the fountainhead of compassion, wisdom, and power. Primordial awareness is your birthright and already lies within you. You don't need to become someone else to become a buddha; you just need to be who you already are, and *recognize who that really is.* When you seek out a Buddhist teacher in order to be healed, he or she will point out your buddha-nature and help you realize it. Superficially, we may initially seek Dharma as a respite from the turmoil of daily life, a respite that meditative quiescence can provide. This is like going to a doctor with a stuffy nose, expecting a quick fix. The doctor may tell us, though, "I'll treat your stuffy nose. By the way, you have cancer. Do you want treatment for that, too?" Our condition turns out to be a lot worse than we thought. Similarly, we might expect something modest from Dharma like a little mental vacation, but find out much more than we anticipated. The potential is quite extraordinary. Coming to a spiritual mentor is like going to a doctor with what seems to be a simple problem, but is actually a matrix of complex, deep problems for which there is a time-tested cure.

We are looking for help in alleviating our afflictions. A qualified spiritual mentor is familiar with a range of methods that are effective in treating a wide variety of people, not just people with his or her own personal constellation of afflictions. We entrust ourselves to a spiritual mentor just as we entrust ourselves to a doctor. However, just as the doctor or spiritual mentor is checking us over, we are likewise checking out the doctor.

The relationship between mentor and student can be a source of immense benefit or immense grief. There are criteria for determining if you are receiving benefit from a mentor. If you find joy in practice, find that virtue arises more easily and mental afflictions are gradually being attenuated, those are signs of real benefit. It is better to find a little-known spiritual mentor from whom you receive benefit rather than a renowned mentor from whom you do not receive much benefit.

The analogy between spiritual mentor and doctor also holds true regarding communication. Suppose a patient says to a doctor, "You are the best doctor in the world and I will do whatever you say." When the patient is asked a week later how the treatment is progressing and says, "It must be good because you are the greatest doctor in the world," that is not answering the question. This type of breakdown in communication happens often in mentor-student relationships.

Another type of communication breakdown happens when a mentor demands such blind faith on the part of his students that they are not allowed to question the type of teachings or practices he is dispensing. "The teachings I am granting you are absolutely pure, transmitted down from perfectly enlightened beings. So if you're not benefiting from them, the fault is yours alone! Don't blame me or the tradition I represent!" This is a situation in which all responsibility and knowledge are allegedly concentrated in one authoritarian person or tradition, and students are told to suspend their own powers of judgment and intelligence in deference to this authority. How at odds this is with the original stance of the Buddha and his relation with his immediate disciples! When you enter into a relationship with a spiritual mentor, healthy two-way communication is crucial. The stronger the relationship, the more important the dialogue. The Buddhist tradition of honest dialogue began with the Buddha himself, who taught through dialogue. Within Buddhism one has the freedom to say, "That doesn't make sense to me," or "This is not working for me." The tradition of open dialogue has made Buddhism adaptable and durable, and relevant in a wide variety of cultural settings.

I dwell on the importance of dialogue because there are two strong forces coming into collision as Buddhist Dharma is brought to the West. Tibet was a hierarchical society. Everything within Dharma was hierarchical with many ranks: incarnate lamas, abbots, monastic teachers, fully ordained monks and nuns, monastic novices, and so on. In this hierarchical system, one can easily get the impression from Tibetan Buddhist teachings that students are to regard their spiritual mentor with pure perception, seeing the teacher as a buddha. In the meantime, they may be encouraged to regard themselves as deluded sentient beings. This radical disparity can easily cause an unhealthy sense of dependence upon the all-knowing guru and an equally unhealthy sense of one's own depravity, lack of intelligence, and unworthiness. We in the modern West can go overboard with our egalitarian ideal, especially when this robs us of any real appreciation or reverence for those with greater qualities than ourselves. On the other hand, an excessively hierarchical attitude with regard to the Buddhist tradition can hamper the development of our own powers of observation and sound judgment. There is a way to turn the apparent adversity of this collision of cultural norms into an aid to spiritual practice: engage in honest and respectful dialogue with your spiritual mentor. Express your reservations openly and without disrespect, then listen to the response with an open mind. But as the old saying goes, "Not so open that your brains fall out."

How necessary is it to find a spiritual mentor to guide you? On the day that the Dalai Lama received word that he had been awarded the Nobel Peace Prize in 1989, I was interpreting for him during one of our Mind and Life conferences with a group of neuroscientists. That day he was interviewed by a correspondent from a Canadian television network, who asked him about the importance of having a guru. His reply was short and to the point, "Having a spiritual mentor may not be indispensable, but it can sure save you a lot of time!" Learning from someone who has mastered a skill or knowledge saves time if you want to master the same skill or knowledge. This is at least as true of spiritual practice as it is for music, art, technology, and science.

2. The second of the three principal causes is devoting oneself to all stages of practice in accordance with the guidance received from one's mentor. Regardless of the quality of our spiritual mentor or the amount of learning we have acquired, nothing will transform our lives unless we apply ourselves to sincere practice. As Shantideva reminds us, "How can someone who could be cured by medicine be restored to health if he strays from the physician's advice?"[76]

3. The third of the three principal causes that yield a fruitful spiritual practice is assembling both the inner and outer conditions necessary for practice. Three crucial inner conditions are the cultivation of faith, intelligence, and zeal. Three crucial outer conditions are having adequate food and clothing and the company of good spiritual friends. An old Buddhist aphorism states, "Half of spiritual practice is engaging with good spiritual friends."

Cultivate three things without letting them deteriorate.

The three things to be cultivated are faith and reverence for one's mentor, enthusiasm for training one's mind, and conscientiousness regarding one's pledges and precepts. The fundamental issue regarding the relation with a spiritual mentor is that on our own, despite the fact that each of us is endowed with a buddha-nature, we don't know how to realize our own potential without guidance. We seek out a mentor who can guide us along the path to enlightenment, and if we are to derive full benefit from his or her counsel, we must do so with faith and reverence. Cultivating these qualities is not for the sake of the mentor, it's for our own sake. Without them, the mere acquisition of information from a teacher is of little benefit. To ensure that our practice is effective, such trust needs to be combined with the other two factors: enthusiasm and conscientiousness. There is a formula for success.

Maintain three things inseparably.

The three things to maintain inseparably are bodily virtue, verbal virtue, and mental virtue. Bodily virtue entails physical activity, such as being of service to one's mentor, one's Dharma friends, and the surrounding community. Verbal virtue includes reciting verses of Dharma and any other beneficial use of one's speech. Mental virtue is principally cultivating the two bodhichittas.

Meditate constantly on the distinctive ones.

The "distinctive ones" referred to here are those who arise as your adversaries, like thorns in your side. Dharma practice can fall apart when tested by those who harm you and those whom you resent. Meditate constantly on these distinctive people; bring them to mind. These people provide a test. When your practice is going well, you might come to the conclusion that you are a holy person, maybe a bodhisattva. But it is meeting people who harm you for no apparent reason that really tests the strength of practice. Distinctive people are the ones who help us by showing us what we need to work on.

Do not depend on other factors.

For some practices, external conditions are important. For example, traditional treatises on meditative quiescence recommend finding a solitary place without barking dogs, with easy access to food, little exposure to people, and a good water supply. Good health is also important. For some practices, Tibetans may consult an astrologer to find the best time for retreat. But for the Mind-Training, you do not need any external support. You can live anywhere, your health can be good or poor. You can be dying. This practice is for all the seasons of a person's life.

Now practice what is important.

Practicing what is important means getting your priorities straight in terms of your spiritual practice. Sechil Buwa's commentary to this practice lists the following set of priorities, which are as pertinent now as they were when he wrote them down from the lineage of Atisha's oral explanation.

1. Spiritual practice over mundane pursuits. We are bound to be drawn into the eight mundane concerns on occasion, but this precept is to place a higher priority on spiritual practice.

2. *Practicing Dharma over talking about it.* The Tibetans say, "Let the Dharma be in your heart and not in your mouth."

3. *The cultivation of bodhichitta over other practices.* Those who have had long exposure to Tibetan Buddhism are introduced to a wide range of practices, many of them quite fascinating. But regardless of the allure of other practices, we are encouraged here to focus principally on bodhichitta, the heart of all the teachings.

4. *Your mentor's personal guidance over teachings of the scriptures and logic.* If you develop a relationship with a mentor, then rely on his or her knowledge and experience over more general teachings. For example, Tibetan meditation manuals often comment on the importance of living in total solitude so that one can practice meditation single-pointedly. This is a fine ideal, but whether it is one that each of us should follow here and now is best left to the personal counsel of our spiritual mentors.

5. *Inner practice over changing the place you live.* It is easy to let your environment be the scapegoat. Practice where you are. In short, in the world as a whole, people who hear the Dharma are rare. Among them, those who deeply ponder the Dharma are rare. Among them, those who sincerely practice the Dharma are rare. Among them, those who persevere in the practice are rare. It is for these reasons that spiritual maturation and awakening are rare.

Make no mistake.

Sechil Buwa lists six mistakes that can easily be committed in the course of this training.

1. *Mistaken forbearance: Not bearing the tribulations of Dharma, but only those of mundane concerns.* People are willing to go through great hardships to set up a new business, go to school, or raise a family. We may have great forbearance

in many endeavors. But then if our knees hurt, we don't meditate. Having little forbearance for the one thing that could actually overcome suffering, Dharma, is mistaken forbearance.

2. *Mistaken desires: Not desiring spiritual maturation but mundane goals.* This error, as common as it is, needs no explanation.

3. *Mistaken experience: Striving not for the experience of hearing Dharma, thinking about it, and meditating, but striving instead for various outer and inner mundane pleasures.* In the modern West when people speak of "living life to the fullest," they often are referring to an endless list of exciting mundane experiences. But no matter how many fascinating experiences we accumulate by traveling, meeting new people, becoming expert in various sports and hobbies, none of these experiences by itself alleviates our mental afflictions. Therefore seek above all the transformative experience of practicing Dharma.

4. *Mistaken compassion: Pitying Dharma practitioners who undergo hardships but feeling no compassion for those who dwell in suffering and the causes of suffering.* A story from Milarepa's life exemplifies this. Through dedication and perseverance over many years, he became a great yogi dwelling in the bliss of his own pristine awareness, but due to his austerities, his body became emaciated. One day when he was relaxing by the side of a path, a group of young women came strolling by, and, seeing his poor physical state, one of them exclaimed, "Oh, how miserable this mans looks! May I never be born in such a state!" With genuine compassion for them, with their misplaced pity, he replied, "Ladies, you don't need to worry yourselves on that account. You would not take birth as a person like myself even if you wished and prayed for it. It is praiseworthy to feel compassion, but an error to confuse compassion with self-conceit."[77]

5. *Mistaken priorities: For the affairs of this life instead of spiritual practice.*

6. *Mistaken satisfaction: Not taking satisfaction in the virtues of sentient beings and buddhas, but rejoicing in the misfortunes of your enemies and those whom you despise.* These final two points also need no explanation.

Do not be erratic.

This precept counters the tendency to practice sporadically, only when we feel all conducive conditions are present, which of course leads to an erratic practice. Psychologists and neuroscientists tell us that the brain can be voluntarily altered physiologically when consistent and sustained effort is made. The brain is malleable even as we enter middle age and beyond. The functioning of the brain can be altered, and, contrary to a long-standing assumption, new brain cells can be generated even at a very advanced age. Psychologically, even old and deeply ingrained habits can be overcome with sustained effort, and new, more wholesome habits can be formed. All this comes with continuity of practice.

I remember hearing about a meditator at a retreat center who drew the attention of his fellow practitioners by his great dedication. All his movements were slow and seemed filled with mindfulness. His practice seemed awesomely constant and others regarded him as a very serious yogi. After the retreat was over, one of his Dharma friends saw him at a party, where he seemed to have lost all composure and was wildly babbling on about one topic after another. When asked what had happened to his impressive discipline in practice, he replied, "My practice now is watching my mindfulness degenerate." This is a fine example of erratic practice.

Practice with total conviction.

We seek happiness and try to avoid unhappiness. The issue is how to succeed. If we are confident that we will find happiness by having more money or a better job, we will strive for that. Or we might think that to find satisfaction we need a better reputation, nicer surroundings, or a better set of friends, and that's where our efforts will be directed. If we are sure that these things will make us happy, we will strive for them with total conviction. On the other hand, if we believe that a lasting sense of fulfillment and well-being is impossible through the practice of Dharma, that conviction, too, will have a major impact on the way we lead our lives.

Practicing Dharma with total conviction means penetrating through the fallacy of the eight mundane concerns. Having enough money is fine and enjoying the respect of others is okay. But it is possible to be happy in miserable circumstances when no one is praising you at all, and similarly, even if you meet with great worldly success, there is no guarantee of happiness or satisfaction. Therefore, carefully draw conclusions by examining your experience and the experience of others. This is the first step toward "total conviction."

Dharma doesn't promise wealth, a great job, perfect health, or respect. The goal of Dharma is to fulfill your innate capacity for happiness. Total conviction arises by seeing through the seductions of the eight mundane concerns and seeing that Dharma holds the only real hope of genuine happiness.

Free yourself by means of investigation and analysis.

Through investigation we can discover which afflictions are strongest in our mind-streams and counteract them. Buddhist psychology has various classifications of mental afflictions. One common set of afflictions is known as the five poisons: delusion, anger, attachment, jealousy, and pride. If we observe carefully, most of us find that one of these five mental poisons tends to disrupt the equilibrium of our minds more than the others. Counteracting the most virulent poison brings the most benefit.

After identifying your most troubling affliction through careful investigation, see if you can distance yourself from the catalysts that trigger those tendencies. As practice matures and the mind becomes more balanced, there is greater freedom. With progress, you can go anywhere and do anything without aggravating your dominant affliction. Part of this freedom derives from the resolve to truly recognize an affliction as the "real enemy," rather than believing the cause of unhappiness is an outside agent. Human beings come and go, but mental afflictions remain as the true enemy and do more harm than any human being can.

Do not try to make an impression.

We all want respect, and those of us who have been practicing for a long time may try to gain the admiration of others by calling their attention to how many years we have been practicing, how many years we've spent in retreat, how many hours we meditate each day, or how long we meditate in each session. Or we might pride ourselves on our renowned teachers or on the scope of our service to humanity. The point of this precept has been made before, but it's worth repeating: showing off to others how advanced we are in spiritual practice is simply a way of reinforcing our commitment to the eight mundane concerns.

Dromtönpa, the principal disciple of Atisha, advised, "Do not place great hopes in people. Pray to the divine." What Dromtönpa means by "the divine" is all the buddhas, the quintessence of whom is none other than primordial awareness. Entering into a personal relationship with the divine by projecting it out as an image of the Buddha or a personal deity such as Tara is as legitimate in Buddhism as it is in other religious traditions. What we are engaging with in these images is the wisdom, compassion, and power they symbolize, and the source of all these is ultimately our own pristine awareness. Place your deepest hopes not in other people but in your own primordial awareness, and let your deepest aspiration be for spiritual awakening.

Do not be bound by distemper.

When someone else is abused, we are often not troubled, but when we ourselves are abused, self-centeredness tends to raise its head, and our response is far more passionate. The Mind-Training encourages us not to retaliate verbally or harbor resentment when we are abused or slandered, but rather counteract our own self-centeredness, the true cause of our distress in such situations. We don't have much control over anger arising in the first place, but once we notice anger, we have a choice. Even if everything else in our practice is perfect, if we choose to feed resentment, contempt, and self-righteousness, this unwinds the whole ball of yarn of our Mind-Training. Therefore, don't be bound by distemper or resentment. The most direct way to free yourself from anger is not to identify with it.

Don't be temperamental.

Flaring up at little adversities irritates others and damages our mental and physical health. Sometimes when we are exhausted, regardless of how much Dharma we know, reining in the stallions of irritation can be difficult. This is why developing meditative quiescence is so important. If we are able to find the delicate balance of mind that is vigilant without being tense, the nervous system can be calmed and refreshed.

Do not yearn for gratitude.

If you want acknowledgment for any good that you have done, you are missing the point. Do not expect others to reward you with their gratitude. Just release it. In the practice of *tonglen*, no gratitude is expected from the person we bring to mind. Not expecting anything back is part of the practice's transformative power. Practicing *tonglen* opens your heart and mind, opens your buddha-nature and therein lies happiness. No need for gratitude. The practice is its own reward.

Conclusion

The key to spiritual maturation is transforming all of life, adversity included, into spiritual practice. The Seven-Point Mind-Training, a synthesis of teaching and practices developed over hundreds of years during the flowering of Indian Buddhist civilization, is wonderfully effective for cultivating the two bodhichittas during the course of an active way of life. No method other than embracing all of life, adversity, suffering, and joy, will be effective when there are many obstacles to spiritual practice.

Dilgo Khyentse Rinpoche's final teaching to his Western students was the Seven-Point Mind-Training. He was a master of the profound teachings of Mahamudra and Dzogchen, yet of all the teachings he knew, this Mind-Training was what he most wanted to leave us with. In his own words,

> There exist many teachings, profound and vast, such as Mahamudra and Dzogchen. But our capacity is small, we are without perseverance and lack sufficient respect and devotion to be freed through teachings such as these. Nevertheless, if we practice this Mind Training, we will experience great benefits. It is an extraordinary instruction, the very essence of the Bodhisattva teachings, and has been praised again and again. Therefore let us practice it without distraction.[78]

This was the final testimony of Dilgo Khyentse Rinpoche.

The Seven-Point Mind-Training is a synthesis of three general types of practice—non-conceptual, devotional, and discursive—aimed at transforming the entirety of one's life, day by day, minute by minute, into practice to attain spiritual awakening. The non-conceptual cultivation of quiescence entails training attention, honing the mind into a fine tool. Devotional practice, the way of prayer, intuition, and opening one's heart to others, common to every religious path, is also an integral part of the Mind-Training, in the practices of cultivation of compassion and *tonglen*. Additionally, any of the lines of the Seven-Point Mind-Training can be the basis of discursive meditation. The following is an example of a 30-45 minute formal meditation based on the Mind-Training that can be done each morning and integrated into the rest of life, with all its felicity, adversity, and activity.

Meditation

1. Sit comfortably with your spine erect.

2. Traditionally, the first step in formal meditation is to take refuge in the three jewels, the Buddha, the Dharma, and the Sangha.

3. Next, set your motivation, specifically by aspiring to achieve perfect awakening for the benefit of all beings.

4. Take three deep, relaxing, cleansing breaths into the abdomen. Relax your face and eyes.

5. Practice breath awareness. Place your awareness in a perceptual mode by focusing on your breath, attending to the tactile sensations above the upper lip or at the nostrils, wherever you feel the in-breath. Cultivate mindfulness by attending experientially. Count twenty-one breaths.

6. While focusing on the breath, secondarily monitor the state of awareness right in the moment with introspection. Let awareness rest in the perceptual, purely experiential mode and be aware, without grasping, of any imagery and internal dialogue that arises in the space of awareness. Whenever you become aware that you have grasped onto a thought, emotion, or image, simply release the effort of grasping and relax more deeply. Come to rest in the gentle rhythm of the breath. Practicing introspection, sustain mindfulness without distraction throughout the entire course of twenty-one breaths.

7. Move to the more subtle practice of settling the mind in its natural state. Rest your gaze and attention in the space

in front of you, unfixed on any object or process. Whatever comes to mind, simply be present with it. Note it clearly, without grasping, without identifying with it. Let your awareness be a gracious host in the midst of the unruly guests of disturbing thoughts, memories, and emotions. Be aware non-interactively of whatever comes up, simply noting its nature and let it play itself out without intervention. Discover the stillness of your own awareness in the midst of the activity of your mind.

The practices of breath awareness and settling the mind in its natural state cultivate a sense of inner serenity and clarity, a calm stillness relative to the rest of our waking awareness. But this serenity deteriorates when we venture into active life. The most powerful protection for the balance of mind cultivated in formal meditation is cultivating loving-kindness.

8. The first step in the practice of the cultivation of loving-kindness is simply to attend to mental states opposite to loving-kindness and mental balance—hostility, aggression, anger, resentment, hatred, and contempt. Examine how these mental states affect the mind. Bring forth the aspiration, "May I be free of this poison." Reflect that self-righteousness is poison with a sugar coating. Bring forth the aspiration, "Regardless of whom I meet or the situations I encounter, may my mind be free of afflictions," and imagine it to be so. Imagine encountering situations in which the flames of anger and hatred would be easily ignited and retaining composure, equanimity, and freedom.

Think of other types of distress—arrogance, grasping, attachment, jealousy, sadness, grief, despair, and depression. Bring forth the yearning, "Regardless of the adversities that I encounter, may I be free of these afflictions." Imagine it to be so.

Bring to mind the afflictions of useless fear and anxiety. Then bring forth the yearning to be free of anxiety, free of useless fear and its origins. Imagine that in the midst of the uncertainties of life, relationships and circumstances, you are free of anxiety. Imagine being fearless.

Finally, bring forth the wish, "May I be well and happy in the midst of adversity and felicity, ill health and good health, poverty and prosperity, rejection and acceptance." Imagine a profound state of well-being right here and now.

9. Focus on your kinship with all sentient beings. Attend to the reality that all sentient beings wish to be free of suffering and to find genuine happiness. Expand the field of awareness to every person in your environment. Send forth the heartfelt wish, "May each person, and myself, be free of affliction, anxiety and fear." Imagine it to be so. Expand your awareness to include the surrounding community, all the thousands of people like yourself, wishing to find happiness and be free of troubles, sorrow and anxiety. Send out the wish that each be well and happy and imagine it to be so. Further expand your awareness in all directions to all sentient beings, north, south, east and west, excluding no one. Reach out with the field of loving-kindness to embrace each one. Wish that each one, like yourself, be well and happy, free of hostility and aggression. Imagine it to be so here and now.

10. Synthesize the above reflections in the practice of *tonglen*.

11. With eyes open and your gaze resting in the space in front of you, move your attention briefly to that which has been engaging in this meditation. Observe the observer.

12. Bring the meditation to a close. Dedicate the merit from your practice with the prayer:

> Wherever this precious, supreme spirit of awakening,
>   bodhichitta,
> Has not arisen, may it arise,

And where it has arisen, may it never decline,
But grow stronger and stronger.

The above meditation is an excellent start to the day. For the remaining hours of the day, practice all the points of the Seven-Point Mind-Training. May you swiftly accomplish your eternal longing to find genuine happiness.

The Aphorisms of the Seven-Point Mind-Training

composed by Chekawa on the basis of Atisha's oral tradition

The First Point: The Preliminaries

First, train in the preliminaries.

The Second Point: Cultivating Ultimate and Relative Bodhichitta

Once you have achieved stability, reveal the mystery.

Regard all events as if they were dreams.

Examine the unborn nature of awareness.

Even the remedy itself is free right where it is.

The essential nature of the path is resting in the universal ground.

Between sessions, be an illusory person.

Alternately practice giving and taking.

Mount them both upon your breath.

Three objects, three poisons, and three roots of virtue.

In everything you do, practice with words.

The Third Point: Transforming Adversity into an Aid to Spiritual Awakening

When the whole world is enslaved by vices, transform adversities into the path of spiritual awakening.

Blame everything on one culprit.

Reflect on the kindness of all those around you.

By meditating on delusive appearances as the four embodiments, emptiness becomes the best protection.

The best strategy is to have four practices.

Whatever you encounter, immediately apply it to meditation.

The Fourth Point: A Synthesis of Practice for One Life

To synthesize the essence of this practical guidance, apply yourself to the five powers.

The Mahayana teaching on transferring consciousness is precisely these five powers, so your conduct is crucial.

The Fifth Point: The Criterion of Proficiency in the Mind-Training

The whole of Dharma is synthesized in one aim.

Attend to the chief of two witnesses.

Constantly resort to a sense of good cheer.

The Sixth Point: The Pledges of the Mind-Training

Always abide by three principles.

Shift your priorities but stay as you are.

Do not speak of others' limitations.

Do not stand in judgment of others.

Abandon all hope of reward.

Avoid poisonous food.

Do not indulge in self-righteousness.

Do not engage in malicious sarcasm.

Do not wait in ambush.

Do not load the burden of a *dzo* on an ox.

Do not flatter your way to the top.

Avoid pretense.

Do not bring a god down to the level of a demon.

Do not take advantage of another's misfortune.

The Seventh Point: The Precepts of the Mind-Training

Synthesize all meditative practices in one.

Respond in one way to all bouts of dejection.

There are two tasks, at the beginning and at the end.

Bear whichever of the two occurs.

Guard the two at the cost of your life.

Practice the three austerities.

Acquire the three principal causes.

Cultivate three things without letting them deteriorate.

Maintain three things inseparably.

Meditate constantly on the distinctive ones.

Do not depend on other factors.

Now practice what is important.

Make no mistake.

Do not be erratic.

Practice with total conviction.

Free yourself by means of investigation and analysis.

Do not try to make an impression.

Do not be bound by distemper.

Don't be temperamental.

Do not yearn for gratitude.

Notes

1. Zara Houshmand, Robert B. Livingston, and B. Alan Wallace, eds. (1999), p. 127.
2. See Dr. Yeshi Dhonden (2000).
3. William James (1890/1950), p. 322.
4. See Buddhaghosa (1979) I: XII, 4.
5. Daniel Dennett (1991), pp. 21-22.
6. Sigmund Freud (1961), pp. 23-24.
7. An extensive explanation of the Buddhist principle of the conservation of consciousness is found in the chapter "A Contemplative View of the Mind" in B. Alan Wallace (1996).
8. See Bhikkhu Ñāṇamoli (1992), pp. 23-25.
9. For the edited proceedings from this conference, see Zara Houshmand, Robert B. Livingston, and B. Alan Wallace, eds. (1999).
10. Śāntideva (1997) I: 28.
11. Sigmund Freud (1961), p. 16.
12. See Ñāṇamoli (1992), pp. 10-29.
13. William James (1897/1979), p. 80.
14. See Peter Galison and David J. Stump, eds. (1996).
15. William Kingdon Clifford (1879) 2:183. Cited in William James (1897/1979), p. 18.
16. William James, "Faith and the Right to Believe," cited in John J. McDermott (1977), p. 736.
17. For a much more detailed explanation of the cultivation of meditative quiescence, see B. Alan Wallace (1998).
18. David Galin (1992), p. 152.
19. William James (1890/1950), p. 424.
20. Ibid., p. 420.
21. *Saṃyutta-Nikāya* v. 321. Cited in Buddhaghosa (1979) I: VIII, 145, p. 285.
22. For a traditional Tibetan Buddhist account of ways of developing meditative quiescence, see Gen Lamrimpa (1995).

23. For a classic presentation of this technique taught by the Indian Buddhist master Padmasambhava, see the section entitled "Quiescence" in Padmasambhava (1998).
24. René Descartes (1960) VI-62, p. 45.
25. Cited in John Bartlett (1980) p. 560, line 27, from Thoreau's *Walking*, 1862.
26. Cited in John Bartlett (1980) p. 637, line 16, from Muir's *Alaska Fragment*, 1890.
27. *Ratnameghasūtra*, cited in Śāntideva (1961), p. 68. This passage is found in the English translation of Śāntideva's work, Śāntideva. (1981), p. 121. A similar point is made by the Buddha in the opening verse of *The Dhammapada*: "All phenomena are preceded by the mind, issue forth from the mind, and consist of the mind." Nikunja Vihari Banerjee (1989) I: 1.
28. Cited in Werner Heisenberg (1971), p. 206. To compare this view with that of modern cognitive science, see B. Alan Wallace (1999a).
29. See, for example, Jack Kornfield (2000).
30. For a detailed explanation of this issue see the section entitled "Quiescence in Theravāda Buddhism" in B. Alan Wallace (1998).
31. Sigmund Freud (1961), p. 33.
32. Daniel J. Boorstin (1985), p. xv.
33. Bernard d'Espagnat (1999), p. 23.
34. Werner Heisenberg (1971), p. 63.
35. Niels Bohr (1961), p. 1.
36. Nick Herbert (1985), p. 248.
37. Padmasambhava (1998), p. 116.
38. Ibid., pp. 116-118.
39. Ibid., p. 119.
40. See Karma Chagmé (2000), pp. 81-87.
41. Śāntideva (1997) IV: 46.
42. Cited in Karma Chagmé (1998), p. 100.
43. Ibid., p. 107.
44. Ibid., p. 108.
45. Ibid., p. 109.
46. Śāntideva (1997) IX: 30-32.
47. Padmasambhava (1998), pp. 141-146.
48. Ibid., pp. 146-150.
49. For a detailed account of the meditative cultivation of these four immeasurables, see B. Alan Wallace (1999b).
50. Śāntideva (1997) III: 17.

51. Buddhaghosa (1979) I: IX.
52. Nikunja Vihari Banerjee (1989) Twin Verses: v., p. 121.
53. For a full account of this fascinating dialogue, see Daniel Goleman (1997), pp. 189-207.
54. *Saṃyutta-Nikaya* i. 75; *Udāna*. 47.
55. Śāntideva (1997) IV: 28.
56. See Palden Gyatso (1997).
57. *Aṅguttara Nikaya* V: 342.
58. Śāntideva (1997) VIII: 94.
59. Ibid., VIII: 91.
60. Dilgo Khyentse Rinpoche (1993), p. 36.
61. Śāntideva (1997) VIII: 104.
62. Cited in Walpola Rahula (1974), pp. 2-3.
63. Gyatrul Rinpoche (1993), pp. 20-21.
64. Śāntideva (1997) VI: 17-18.
65. Ibid., VIII: 134.
66. Ibid., IV: 34.
67. Ibid., VIII: 130.
68. Ibid., IV: 34.
69. Cited in Brian Easlea (1980), p. 4; Thomas Sprat (1667/1959), pp. 339-341.
70. See Terrence Horgan and James Woodward (1990), pp. 414, 418 n. 18.
71. Düdjom Lingpa (n.d.), p. 91. I am currently completing a translation of this entire work, which will be published in English under the title *The Vajra Essence: From the Primordial Wisdom Matrix of Pure Appearances, a Tantra on the Self-arisen Nature of Existence.*
72. Ibid., pp. 155-156.
73. Śāntideva (1997) VI: 14.
74. Ibid., VI: 10.
75. Ibid., I: 28.
76. Ibid., IV: 48.
77. See W.Y. Evans-Wentz (1976), p. 217.
78. Dilgo Khyentse Rinpoche (1993), p. 99.

Bibliography

Banerjee, Nikunja Vihari, trans. 1989. *The Dhammapada*. New Delhi: Munshiram Manoharlal Publishers.

Bartlett, John. 1980. *Familiar Quotations*. Boston: Little, Brown and Co.

Bohr, Niels. 1961. *Atomic Theory and the Description of Nature*. London: Cambridge University Press.

Boorstin, Daniel J. 1985. *The Discoverers: A History of Man's Search to Know His World and Himself*. New York: Vintage Books.

Buddhaghosa. 1979. *The Path of Purification*. Trans. Bhikkhu Ñāṇamoli. Kandy, Sri Lanka: Buddhist Publication Society.

Chagmé, Karma. 1998. *A Spacious Path to Freedom: Practical Instructions on the Union of Mahāmudrā and Atiyoga*. Gyatrul Rinpoche, commentary; B. Alan Wallace, trans. Ithaca, NY: Snow Lion Publications.

Chagmé, Karma. 2000. *Naked Awareness: Practical Instructions on the Union of Mahāmudrā and Dzogchen*. Gyatrul Rinpoche, commentary; B. Alan Wallace, trans. Ithaca, NY: Snow Lion Publications.

Clifford, William Kingdon. 1879. *Lectures and Essays*. Leslie Stephen and Frederick Pollack, eds. 2 vols. London: Macmillan and Co.

Dennett, Daniel C. 1991. *Consciousness Explained*. Boston: Little, Brown and Co.

Descartes, René. 1960. *Discourse on the Method*. Laurence J. Lafleur, trans. New York: Bobbs-Merrill Co.

Dilgo Khyentse Rinpoche. 1993. *Enlightened Courage: An Explanation of Atisha's Seven Point Mind Training*. Padmakara Translation Group, trans. Ithaca, NY: Snow Lion Publications.

Düdjom Lingpa. n.d. *Dag snang ye shes drva pa las gnas lugs rang byung rgyud rdo rje'i snying po.* Included in the Collected Works of H. H. Dudjom Rinpoche.

Easlea, Brian. 1980. *Witch-hunting, Magic and the New Philosophy: An Introduction to Debates of the Scientific Revolution 1450-1750.* New Jersey: Humanities Press.

Espagnat, Bernard d'. 1999. "Physics and Philosophy: Perspectives on Reality." In *Science and Spirit,* April/May 1999, p. 23.

Evans-Wentz, W. Y., ed. 1976. *Tibet's Great Yogi Milarepa: A Biography from the Tibetan.* New York: Oxford University Press.

Freud, Sigmund. 1961. *Civilization and Its Discontents.* James Strachey, trans. & ed. New York: W. W. Norton & Co.

Galin, David. 1992. "Theoretical Reflections on Awareness, Monitoring, and Self in Relation to Anosognosia." *Consciousness and Cognition* I (2), pp. 152-162.

Galison, Peter and David J. Stump, eds. 1996. *The Disunity of Science: Boundaries, Contexts, and Power.* Stanford, CA: Stanford University Press.

Goleman, Daniel, ed. 1997. *Healing Emotions: Conversations with the Dalai Lama on Mindfulness, Emotions, and Health.* Boston: Shambhala.

Gyatrul Rinpoche. 1993. *Ancient Wisdom: Nyingma Teachings on Dream Yoga, Meditation, and Transformation.* B. Alan Wallace & Sangye Khandro, trans. Ithaca, NY: Snow Lion Publications.

Heisenberg, Werner. 1971. *Physics and Beyond: Encounters and Conversations.* New York: Harper & Row.

Herbert, Nick. 1985. *Quantum Reality: Beyond the New Physics.* Garden City, NY: Anchor Press/Doubleday.

Horgan, Terrence and James Woodward. 1990. "Folk Psychology Is Here to Stay." In *Mind and Cognition: A Reader.* William G. Lycan, ed. Cambridge, MA: Basil Blackwell, pp. 399-420.

Houshmand, Zara, Robert B. Livingston, and B. Alan Wallace, eds. 1999. *Consciousness at the Crossroads: Conversations with the Dalai Lama on Brain Science and Buddhism.* Ithaca, NY: Snow Lion Publications.

James, William. 1890/1950. *The Principles of Psychology.* New York: Dover Publications.

James, William. 1897/1979. *The Will to Believe and Other Essays.* Cambridge: Harvard University Press.

Kornfield, Jack. 2000. "No Enlightenment Retirement." *Inquiring Mind*, Vol.16, No. 2 (Spring).

Lamrimpa, Gen. 1995. *Calming the Mind: Tibetan Buddhist Teachings on the Cultivation of Meditative Quiescence.* B. Alan Wallace, trans. Ithaca, NY: Snow Lion Publications.

McDermott, John J., ed. 1977. *The Writings of William James.* Chicago: University of Chicago Press.

Ñāṇamoli, Bhikkhu. 1992. *The Life of the Buddha According to the Pali Canon.* Kandy, Sri Lanka: Buddhist Publication Society.

Padmasambhava. 1998. *Natural Liberation: Padmasambhava's Teachings on the Six Bardos.* Gyatrul Rinpoche, commentary; B. Alan Wallace, trans. Boston: Wisdom Publications.

Palden Gyatso. 1997. *The Autobiography of a Tibetan Monk.* New York: Grove Press.

Rahula, Walpola. 1974. *What the Buddha Taught.* New York: Grove Press.

Śāntideva. 1961. *Śikṣāsamuccaya.* P. D. Vaidya, ed. Darbhanga: Mithila Institute.

Śāntideva. 1997. *A Guide to the Bodhisattva Way of Life.* Vesna A. Wallace and B. Alan Wallace, trans. Ithaca, NY: Snow Lion Publications.

Śāntideva. 1981. *Śikṣāsamuccaya.* Cecil Bendall and W. H. D. Rouse, trans. Delhi: Motilal Banarsidass.

Sprat, Thomas. 1667/1959. *The History of the Royal Society of London.* J. I. Cape and H. W. Jones, eds. London: Routledge.

Wallace, B. Alan. 1996. *Choosing Reality: A Buddhist View of Physics and the Mind.* Ithaca, NY: Snow Lion Publications.

———1998. *The Bridge of Quiescence: Experiencing Tibetan Buddhist Meditation.* Chicago: Open Court.

———1999a. "The Buddhist Tradition of *Śamatha*: Methods for Refining and Examining Consciousness." *Journal of Consciousness Studies* Vol. 6, nos. 2-3, pp. 175-187.

———1999b. *Boundless Heart: The Four Immeasurables.* Ithaca, NY: Snow Lion Publications.

———2000. *The Taboo of Subjectivity: Toward a New Science of Consciousness.* New York: Oxford University Press.

Yeshi Dhonden. 2000. *Healing from the Source: The Science and Lore of Tibetan Medicine.* B. Alan Wallace, trans. Ithaca, NY: Snow Lion Publications.

Commentaries in English on the Seven-Point Mind-Training

Advice from a Spiritual Friend. Geshe Rabten and Geshe Ngawang Dhargyey. Trans. Brian Beresford. Boston: Wisdom Publications, 1996.

Becoming a Child of the Buddhas: A Simple Clarification of the Root Verses of Seven Point Mind Training. Gomo Tulku. Boston: Wisdom Publications, 1998.

Enlightened Courage: An Explanation of Atisha's Seven Point Mind Training. Dilgo Khyentse Rinpoche. Ithaca, NY: Snow Lion Publications, 1993.

The Great Path of Awakening. Jamgon Kongtrul. Trans. Ken McLeod. Boston and London: Shambhala, 1987.

A Passage from Solitude: Training the Mind in a Life Embracing the World. B. Alan Wallace. Ithaca, NY: Snow Lion Publications, 1992.

Start Where You Are: A Guide to Compassionate Living. Pema Chödrön. Boston & London: Shambhala, 1994.

Training the Mind & Cultivating Loving-Kindness. Chogyam Trungpa. Boston & London: Shambhala, 1993.

Training the Mind in the Great Way. Gyalwa Gendun Druppa, the First Dalai Lama. Trans. Glenn H. Mullin. Ithaca, NY: Snow Lion Publications, 1993.

Transforming Problems into Happiness. Lama Zopa Rinpoche. Boston: Wisdom Publications, 1993.